THE JOYCE PARADOX

THE JOYCE
PARADOX

FORM AND FREEDOM IN HIS FICTION

BY

ARNOLD GOLDMAN

NORTHWESTERN UNIVERSITY PRESS

First published in the U.S.A., 1966
by Northwestern University Press
Evanston, Illinois 60201

Copyright Arnold Goldman 1966

Library of Congress Catalog Card No. 65-24632

Printed in Great Britain

CONTENTS

v

NOTE ON REFERENCES

References to Joyce's own writings are included as far as possible within the text and identified only by page number—and by short title where necessary. The editions referred to are:

The Critical Writings of James Joyce, eds. Ellsworth Mason and Richard Ellmann, London: Faber & Faber and New York: The Viking Press, 1959.

*Dubliners, London: Jonathan Cape, 1954 and New York: The Modern Library, 1954.

Exiles, A Play in Three Acts, London: Jonathan Cape, 1952.

Finnegans Wake, London: Faber & Faber and New York: The Viking Press, 1939, etc.

Letters of James Joyce, ed. Stuart Gilbert, London: Faber & Faber and New York: The Viking Press, 1957.

*A Portrait of the Artist as a Young Man, London: Jonathan Cape, 1956 and New York: The Modern Library, 1944.

*Stephen Hero, ed. Theodore Spencer, London: Jonathan Cape, 1956 and New Directions, 1955.

*Ulysses, London: The Bodley Head, 1960 and New York: The Modern Library, 1946.

In citing from the American edition of *Ulysses*, the pagination of the pre-1961 text has been retained, this being the basis of the Hanley *Word-Index*, Richard Ellmann's biography of Joyce and the other critical works here quoted.

* In page references separated by a stroke—as, (35/72)—the first number is the page of the British edition and the second, the American.

PREFACE

BY PURSUING A GROUP of cognate themes, I hope to relate if
not reconcile major critical approaches to the fiction of James
Joyce. That there are radically opposed positions available
is evident on even a perfunctory glance at past and current
criticism. The major issues, in the last analysis, are questions
of the mode of existence of 'symbols' in the fiction and of the
quality of Joyce's feeling, the extent of his human sympathies.
Attitudes to these, and to other matters, combine variously, in
ways I discuss.

Only through an understanding of the ways in which conflicting responses can be related does it seem to me possible
to make sense out of the criticism of Joyce to date; and only
in this manner can the varieties of critical opinion hope to
appear functions of Joyce's work itself.

Syntheses have a knack of being but old theses writ large,
as everyone who confronts the history of 'solutions' to the
continuing problems of philosophical debate knows. Even the
acknowledgement of radical and perpetual conflict provides no
easy answers. The terms of conflict must still be elaborated in
specific contexts, and language—let alone personal ineptitude—
has its ways of betraying the most careful of balancing acts.

In adducing analogues for my particular balancing, the
notions of Søren Kierkegaard come in for some emphasis. To
my knowledge there is no direct proof that Joyce read much
Kierkegaard, either in the original—though the Dano-
Norwegian he learned in order to read Ibsen would have
enabled him to—or in translation or criticism.* To be sure,

* See ahead, p. 65ff. Ibsen wrote in *riksmaal*, the cultivated Danish of the
Norwegian urban class of his time.

vii

there are a handful of allusions in *Finnegans Wake* to Kierke-gaard's name and to the titles of some of his works,* but only one of them implies any relation between Kierkegaard's world and Joyce's own: when, near the end of the *Wake*, HCE's cyclic 'rebirth' is being predicted, he—and by implication all mankind—is described as 'sorensplit and paddypatched' (596). The implications of this pun have been my pillars of cloud and fire.

I have, however, stopped short of discussing *Finnegans Wake*. Whether the *Wake* confronts at a different level problems like potentiality for human development or evades them altogether is moot. *Ulysses*, it seems to me, does obviously imply a radical, even self-conscious confrontation of the major problems raised by Joyce's earlier fiction. If Charles N. Feidelson is correct, the *Wake* does too, for he calls it 'a symbol of the tension between the infinity of symbolic aspiration and the conclusiveness which the objective work entails'.[1] Proper expansion of that would require as many pages again as I have written here.

I am under obligation to the following publishers for per-mission to quote from books whose copyright is in their possession: John Calder (Publishers) Ltd. (for Alain Robbe-Grillet's *Jealousy*), Jonathan Cape Ltd. (for *Dubliners*, *A Portrait of the Artist as a Young Man* and *Stephen Hero*), Chatto & Windus Ltd., Barnes & Noble, Inc. and S. L. Goldberg (*The Classical Temper: A Study of James Joyce's Ulysses*), The Clarendon Press, Oxford (for Werner Jaeger's *Aristotle*), Faber & Faber Ltd. (for Stanislaus Joyce's *My Brother's Keeper*), Indiana University Press and Chatto & Windus Ltd. (for Hugh Kenner's *Dublin's Joyce*), New Directions Publishers (for *Stephen Hero*), Penguin Books Ltd. (for J. A. K. Thomson's translation of Aristotle's *Ethics*), Prince-ton University Press (for Søren Kierkegaard's *Fear and Trembling* and *Philosophical Fragments*) and The Viking Press (for *Dubliners*, *A Portrait of the Artist as a Young Man* and Stanislaus Joyce's *My Brother's Keeper*).

For their assistance at various stages of this study I wish to

---

* Adaline Glasheen thinks Kierkegaard's *Either/Or* 'rather important' in *Finnegans Wake*, but she does not give her reasons (*A Second Census of Finnegans Wake* [Northwestern University Press, 1963], p. 140).

thank J. S. Atherton, Ann Congleton, Richard Ellmann, Dorothy Emmet, John V. Kelleher, Frank Kermode, Martin Price, Thomas K. Swing, J. Heywood Thomas, Bjorn Tysdahl, Judith Wilde and Dorothy Goldman, my wife.

A. G.

Manchester,
England, 1961–5

Here the impossible union
Of spheres of existence is actual
     —ELIOT: 'The Dry Salvages'

at the same instant predestinate and
free, creation's very self
     —YEATS: *The Trembling of the Veil*

I

THE EARLY STORIES IN
DUBLINERS

Our nature is one of movement; to be completely still is to be dead.

—Pascal

SOMETIME SHORTLY BEFORE AUGUST 13th, 1904—on on which date 'The Sisters', the first story in *Dubliners*, was printed in the *Irish Homestead*—Joyce sent a short note to Constantine Curran: 'I am writing a series of epicleti—ten— for a paper. I have written one. I call the series *Dubliners* to betray the soul of that hemiplegia or paralysis which many consider a city.'[1] The tone Mulliganesque—acknowledged, we might say, when Joyce began *Ulysses* with an *epiclesis*, Buck Mulligan's blasphemous invocation of the Holy Ghost to enter into and consecrate his shaving bowl—should alert us not to expect extraordinary precision from this sanguine outpouring. The analogy

epiclesis :mass : :*Dubliners* :Joyce's *æuvre*

seems more suggestive than useful. That Joyce should think of his fiction and his task in religious terms, and *vice versa*, is, however, characteristic.*

---

* It was at about this time that Joyce was saying to Stanislaus, on one of their 'interminable' peripaties 'across the city to the National Library', 'Don't you think ... there is a certain resemblance between the mystery of the Mass and what I am trying to do? I mean that I am trying in my poems to give people some

The Early Stories in 'Dubliners'

The stories are not only intended as *epicleti*, however, they are to be *betrayals* as well, exposures of 'the soul' of Dublin. Further, we are told something of this 'soul': it is half-paralysed 'or'—another quick transition—wholly paralysed. This the stories will, apparently, demonstrate—unless it is totally presupposed and in no need of proof. A glance at a second letter of Joyce's will prepare us to dip into *Dubliners* and see.

The ten stories grew to fifteen, and in the long agony of finding a publisher began. On May 5th, 1906, an exasperated Joyce wrote from Trieste to Grant Richards, 'My intention was to write a chapter of the moral history of my country and I chose Dublin for the scene because that city seemed to me the centre of paralysis.'[2] If the identification of Dublin and 'paralysis' seems off-hand in the note to Curran, here it is established with schoolmasterly fussiness. From beginning to end in the writing of *Dubliners*, however, the association of Dublin and paralysis persisted in Joyce's mind. It reappears in a passage in *Stephen Hero* to which I will be turning shortly.*

kind of intellectual pleasure or spiritual enjoyment by converting the bread of everyday life into something that has a permanent artistic life of its own. . . . The Mass on Good Friday seems to me a very great drama' (Stanislaus Joyce, *My Brother's Keeper, James Joyce's Early Years* [London and New York, 1958], pp. 103–4. See ahead, p. 133ff.).

* Joyce had used the word in concluding the sketch titled 'A Portrait of the Artist' written in early 1904—'amid the general paralysis of an insane society' (*Yale Review*, Vol. XLIX, No. 3 [Spring 1960], p. 366). In their prefatory note R. M. Kain and Robert E. Scholes comment on Joyce's uses of 'paralysis' (p. 358). The syphilitic note of 'g.p.i.'—which found its way into *Ulysses*, where Mulligan claims someone he met says Stephen has it (5/8)—is to be found elsewhere as well. In his diary, Stanislaus Joyce noted on or about August 13th, 1904, that James

Talks much of the syphilitic contagion in Europe, is at present writing a series of studies in it in Dublin, tracing practically everything to it. The drift of the talk seems to be that the contagion is congenital and incurable and responsible for all manias, and being so, that it is useless to try to avoid it. He even seems to invite you to delight in the manias and to humour each to the top of its bent. (*The Dublin Diary of Stanislaus Joyce*, ed. George Healey [London, 1962], p. 47.)

At one stage of composition, at any rate, Joyce was willing to phrase his intention allegorically. The incidents in the stories are to be referred back to the pre-existent condition for their cause, and that condition is held to be sufficient explanation for all particular events. Joyce had, it is said, read every word of Ben Jonson during his first Paris stay in 1903, and there is something of Jonson's *humours* in the contagious manias to be delighted in. (See Herbert Gorman, *James Joyce* [London, 1941], p. 94.)

2

The Early Stories in 'Dubliners'

Turning to *Dubliners*, we meet one of our terms on its first page, handled with much self-consciousness, or at least much elaborateness:

> There was no hope for him this time: it was the third stroke. Night after night I had passed the house (it was vacation time) and studied the lighted square of window: and night after night I had found it lighted in the same way, faintly and evenly. If he was dead, I thought, I would see the reflection of candles on the darkened blind for I knew that two candles must be set at the head of a corpse. He had often said to me: 'I am not long for this world,' and I had thought his words idle. Now I knew they were true. Every night as I gazed up at the window I said softly to myself the word paralysis. It had always sounded strangely in my ears, like the word gnomon in the Euclid and the word simony in the Catechism. But now it sounded to me like the name of some maleficent and sinful being. It filled me with fear, and yet I longed to be nearer to it and to look upon its deadly work. (7/7)

The young boy has no comprehension of the meaning of the 'word paralysis', but he concedes it a mysterious power. As a non-discursive focus of attention, it both repels and attracts, creates 'fear' and longing. The image of 'paralysis', detached almost from the afflicted and dying Reverend James Flynn, provides if not a tragic experience, the embryo of one according to the definition of Joyce's own young artist:

> —Pity is the feeling which arrests the mind in the presence of whatsoever is grave and constant in human sufferings and unites it with the human sufferer. Terror is the feeling which arrests the mind in the presence of whatsoever is grave and constant in human suffering and unites it with the secret cause.
>
> (*Portrait*, 209/239)[3]

Interestingly, when 'The Sisters' appeared in the *Irish Homestead* (under the *nom de plume* 'Stephen Daedalus'), its first paragraph, subsequently largely rewritten by Joyce, did not include any reference to 'the word paralysis'. That Father Flynn should need to have been paralysed may seem gratuitous in the context of the whole story. Marvin Magalaner, who calls Flynn's paralysis 'a literary expediency', thinks it a 'symbol' (of metaphorical paralysis in the Church, in Dublin, in Ireland).[4] If the word stands now on the first page of *Dubliners* primarily because a young writer was anxious that we take his meaning, we may well be considering the only concession that James Joyce ever made to the reading public. The position of the word invites attention, and, in the way of symbolical readings, has received it, but the 'expediency' ought more properly to restrain us from having too much depend on it. If the notion is pervasive, perhaps even structural, it should reappear in other contexts.

To examine each story in *Dubliners* for analogies to physical paralysis can take us some way into the stories.[5] Father Flynn's 'scruples' and his torpid life, his sisters' constricted round of duties seem analogous and not difficult to relate, loosely, to a notion of paralysis. Similarly, Eveline is powerless to leave Dublin and Bob Doran (in 'The Boarding House') succumbs to the pressures of convention and Mrs Mooney—with what disastrous result we see in *Ulysses*. Little Chandler ('A Little Cloud'), Farrington ('Counterparts'), Maria ('Clay'), Mr Duffy and Mrs Sinico ('A Painful Case'), to name only a few, lead severely restricted lives, unable or unwilling to break out of webs of containment which seem overpowering, whether they are self-created or imposed from outside. When Farrington returns to his child the blow dealt him at his office, we taste a sub-human form of repetition: of such incidents Blake built his dull round, the meaningless, endless cycle of mundane triviality.

We could probably probe further along these lines, always with our trope in mind, watching it radiate outwards. Or we might discriminate the particular nature of the paralysis in each instance, even without prejudicing our commitment to the ontological status of our thematic term. If, on the other hand, we could not also discover a polar term (in this case some radical notion of freedom of movement, say) and an opposing set of illustrative incidents—or an opposing interpretation of the same incidents—it would be proper to decide that our first term constituted an aesthetic presupposition and had the action of an unobstructed magnetic node. Paralysis, having nothing to oppose it, would reign supreme as a controlling trope, and there would be no definition of its limits. (Hence,

4

the tendency of symbolic readings to proliferate endlessly: they are not held in tension with any contrary limiting force.) Even more significant would be the *human* consequences—the consequences for the fictional characters as imagined persons: we might conclude metaphorically that the patients, like Rev. Flynn, had all 'died' before the stories began, that the fiction was autopsy, that Joyce's Dublin world was, as Henry Miller has claimed, 'The Universe of Death'.[6] More literally, radical tension and conflict in the relationships between characters or between character and environment cannot be posited (or discovered) in such a universe. It is finally indifferent whether the environments are thematic reflections of characters' personalities (symbolic expressionism) or whether the personalities themselves are only functions of the environment (determinism). Both of these versions of experience are controlled from outside, holistically, according to the rules of a thematic monism, and become finally indistinguishable.

Much of what follows will be an attempt to clarify and illustrate these last statements, first through the following parergon: that the focus of attention in a writer who prosecuted thoroughly such a thematic intent would be on his own methods of exposure.

Oliver Gogarty understood Joyce's notion of 'epiphany' as a key to such an intent in his one-time friend:

> Probably Father Darlington had taught him, as an aside in his Latin class—for Joyce knew no Greek—that 'Epiphany' meant 'a showing forth'. So he recorded under 'Epiphany' any showing forth of the mind *by which he considered one gave oneself away.*
>
> Which of us had endowed him with an 'Epiphany' and sent him to the lavatory to take it down?
>
> 'John,' I said, seeking an ally, 'he is codding the pair of us.'[7]
> [my italics]

Gogarty here illuminates, perhaps not intentionally unkindly, a connotation of 'epiphany' (to give oneself away) viewed as an artistic strategy. If it is the task of the writer to expose, one method of exposure is to have one's characters do the job for you. (The question of whether the artist *discovers* or *makes* epiphanies is not thereby prejudiced. Aside from biographical

5

considerations—how Joyce in fact went about his business—
these two may be different ways of talking about the same
thing.) The posthumously published *Epiphanies*[8] alone, though,
suggest the limitations of Gogarty's understanding, though
Joyce may himself have held such a view at some stage.

Joyce's only exposition of 'epiphany', in *Stephen Hero*,
demonstrates that he was not solely tied to the Gogartian
moral-satirical intention. The implication that an epiphany
is the revelation by the artist of a previously existent—though
hidden—state persists, however: it is either the accident or the
engineering of exposure. It does not concern the relationship
of character to event. The personality of the observing artist
(Stephen Daedalus) is not involved in the epiphanic scene
before him; except that he is in a position to see it, he is unnecessary:

> It was hard for him [Stephen] to compel his head to preserve
> the strict temperature of classicism. More than he had ever
> done before he longed for the season to lift and for spring—the
> misty Irish spring—to be over and gone. He was passing through
> Eccles' [sic] St one evening, one misty evening, with all these
> thoughts dancing the dance of unrest in his brain when a trivial
> incident set him composing some ardent verses which he en-
> titled a 'Vilanelle of the Temptress'. A young lady was standing
> on the steps of one of those brown brick houses which seem the
> very incarnation of Irish paralysis. A young gentleman was
> leaning on the rusty railing of the area. Stephen as he passed
> on his quest heard the following fragment of colloquy out of
> which he received an impression keen enough to afflict his
> sensitiveness very severely.
> The Young Lady—(drawling discreetly) . . . O, yes . . . I was
> . . . at the . . . cha . . . pel. . . .
> The Young Gentleman—(inaudibly) [sic] . . . I . . . (again
> inaudibly) . . . I . . .
> The Young Lady—(softly) . . . O . . . but you're . . . ve . . .
> ry . . . wick . . . ed. . . .
> This triviality made him think of collecting many such
> moments together in a book of epiphanies. By an epiphany
> he meant a sudden spiritual manifestation, whether in vulgarity
> of speech or of gesture or in a memorable phase of the mind
> itself. He believed that it was for the man of letters to record
> these epiphanies with extreme care, seeing that they themselves
> are the most delicate and evanescent of moments. He told

Cranly that the clock of the Ballast Office was capable of an epiphany. (215–16/210–11)

There is more on the subject, to the effect that 'epiphany' is the moment of Aquinian *claritas* and that '*Claritas* is *quidditas*' (218/213), all notions shrewdly revised before inclusion in *A Portrait of the Artist as a Young Man*, where 'epiphany' is noticeably absent.

The 'theory' of epiphany 'is not of much use to a dramatist', wrote Theodore Spencer, glossing too quickly, perhaps, over its links with the classical *anagnorisis*.[9] If, however, an epiphany constitutes the 'showing forth' of an already established condition—the exposure of *being*, rather than itself part of the process of *becoming*—that which is paralysed ('one of those brown brick houses which seem the very incarnation of Irish paralysis') forms a congenial subject-matter. It is *available*, as is 'the vulgarity of speech or of gesture'. The glib addition of 'or in a memorable phase of the mind itself' complicates the situation immeasurably, for it suggests the involvement of the recording mind as an essential agent, actively constituting the epiphany. What follows in *Stephen Hero*, identifying *claritas* ('radiance') as the 'moment which I call epiphany', when the soul of the aesthetic image (or, apparently, real event) 'leaps to us from the vestment of its appearance', allows for, without insisting on, the implications of this new dimension. 'The soul of the commonest object, the structure of which is so adjusted,* seems to us radiant. The object achieves its epiphany' (218/213). Through its association with the supposed Aquinian aesthetic, the notion of epiphany is here raised to a level from which Joyce possibly saw fit to demote it when he omitted the word from the aesthetic of the *Portrait*.[10]

Such terms are worth carrying along in lengthy discussion of Joyce, not because they turn out to be the controlling vision behind his fiction, but because he invariably turns them into the subject of later work. Though the term epiphany is not present in *Portrait*, it appears in *Ulysses*, as Stephen, a little older now, walks along the beach towards Dublin, thinking,

Remember your epiphanies on green oval leaves, deeply deep, copies to be sent if you died to all the great libraries of the world,

---

* Who makes the adjustment or what is adjusted? Does the 'structure' include the observer?

including Alexandria? Someone was to read them there after a few thousand years, a mahamanvantara. (50/41)

This is critical—and distanced enough to suggest it would be unfruitful to pursue the term further as an index of Joyce's own continuing method.[11] A mahamanvantara is the great cycle of eternity, the 'eternal return' of Mircea Éliade's study of 'the archaic ideology of ritual repetition', after which all things begin over again.* Joyce had used the expression, which probably came to him through the theosophists, in his broadside 'The Holy Office':

> Those souls that hate the strength that mine has
> Steeled in the school of old Aquinas. . . .
> Though they may labour to the grave
> My spirit shall they never have
> Nor make my soul with theirs as one
> Till the Mahamanvantara be done.†[12]

As the 'eternal return' would cancel out the soul-difference Joyce so values, it is the enemy of art. The trail of the epiphany despite its clouds of glory, returns us to the notion of a dull round. It maintains, as hitherto examined, intimate connections with the notion of paralysis.

II

Thus far it has been suggested that there is one tendency in 'epiphanic' perception (or composition) to gravitate towards the exposure of a static situation. (It is moot, in Joyce's texts,

---

* Mircea Éliade, *Cosmos and History, The Myth of the Eternal Return*, trans. Willard R. Trask (New York, 1959), p. 114. Stuart Gilbert quotes A. P. Sinnett's explanation in *Esoteric Buddhism*: 'Man has a manvantara and pralaya every four-and-twenty hours, his periods of waking and sleeping; vegetation follows the same rule from year to year as it subsides and revives with the seasons. The world too has its manvantaras and pralayas, when the tide-wave of humanity approaches its shore, runs through the evolution of its seven races, and ebbs away again, and such a manvantara has been treated by most exoteric religions as the whole cycle of eternity' (*James Joyce's Ulysses* [New York, 1956], p. 123).

† Clive Hart in *Structure and Motif in Finnegans Wake* (London, 1962), pp. 55–6, discusses Joyce's use of the Mahamanvantara in the *Wake*, where it forms an essential ingredient in the notion of cyclic form on which Hart considers the structure is grounded. Hart thinks that Joyce took his knowledge of eastern world-cycles from the theosophists, particularly Blavatsky's *Isis Unveiled* (1877).

whether aesthetic 'apprehension' occurs in an instant of time.) Epiphany, under this aegis, does not imply either the recognition or the creation of a reality in which the act of perception alters the perceiver, or is conditioned by his human individuality as distinct from his presumably shareable aesthetic sense. It is inflexible in its determination of the relationship between subject and object. The matter can be complicated when the character *in*, rather than the author *of* a fiction apparently lays claim to 'having' an epiphany, for the question enters at a more obvious level as to whether we are to allow ourselves to be bound by the character's own rules of epiphany in interpreting the nature of the bond between artist and artifact.

What is supposed to change is apparently not the 'character' of the observer—fictional person, artist or reader—but his understanding of what is observed: his apprehension *of* as distinct from his relationship *to* the object epiphanized. One sees—and think that the subject matter is characteristic—in some 'triviality' or 'vulgarity of speech or of gesture' what had existed *sub specie aeternitatis* before being seen. The long passage from *Stephen Hero* previously quoted continues with Stephen's description of *how* the Ballast Office clock becomes epiphanized: 'I will pass it time after time, allude to it, refer to it, catch a glimpse of it. It is only an item in the catalogue of Dublin's street furniture. Then all at once I see it and I know at once what it is: epiphany' (216/211).

While this particular strategy of approach has obvious alignments in earlier literary theories of *suggestion* and in the history of the pictorial arts, I would like to stress its similarity to the epistomological and ontological assumptions of certain of Freud's explanations of the methods of the psychoanalyst. Lecturing in 1915, Freud stated, with characteristic mock-self-depreciation,

> It is true that psychoanalysis cannot boast that it has never occupied itself with trifles. On the contrary, the material of its observations is usually those commonplace occurrences which have been cast aside as all too insignificant by other sciences, the refuse, so to speak, of the phenomenal world. . . . Is it not possible, under certain conditions and at certain times, for very important things to betray themselves in very slight indications?[13]

9

There is a direct line here from 'the psychopathology of everyday life'—the 'Freudian slip'—to the psychoanalyst's couch ('under certain conditions and at certain times'). Betrayal through only apparently trivial detail is a crucial point in the Freudian epistomology, and not only by way of verbal slips, mistakes, and lapses of memory.

Further, these betrayals through trivialities only reveal what was present but hidden in situations:

> Psycho-physiological factors such as excitement, absent-mindedness, distraction of attention, obviously provide very little in the way of explanation. They are mere phrases; they are screens ... They facilitate the slip ... [and] cannot provide the real explanation of them.[14]

In this, his most careful exposition of psychoanalysis, Freud begins with the analogy of mistakes and proceeds to the analogy of dreams (he is recapitulating the history of the development of psychoanalysis, a little ideally, as a pedagogical device). There likewise, 'the external and internal stimuli operating upon the sleeper are merely the occasion of the dream and afford us no insight into its true nature'.[15] For the psychoanalyst then, temporal events merely facilitate or are occasions of manifestations of pre-existent psychic 'conditions'; they do not alter these conditions. They only reveal them as they already are. It is easy to see from this how any real crises of personality would tend to be pushed back in time: the infantile familial complex is, on this account, a buffer against dissipating entirely any notion that events have more than a demonstrative status.

An ideal literature constructed according to a corollary aesthetic would tend to find congenial the exposure of psychic conditions. That is, exposure would function as a *modus operandi*: the reader, in turning the pages, would come to know more and more about the characters, to erect provisional concepts of the 'true state' of being of the characters and test these against the following incidents. The end of this approach —and it does not finally signify whether one speaks in terms of the reader, the writer or the meaning of the work—is to arrive at an understanding of what characters *are*. Like Stephen, one would circle around and around until one perceived the

quidditas. While this attitude ought to be difficult enough to
maintain in tracing the career of an individual over any length
of time in any minuteness, it is done all the time by literary
critics of symbolist persuasion. Their attitude is bolstered by
the implicit Freudianism in which significant change through
events would hardly be looked for in anyone over, say, four
years of age. Since novels persist in being, in good part, about
adults—or at least not about infants—the terminus of this
approach to fiction would be to understand fictional adults as
analogies of early stages of psychosexual development. To the
extent that these early stages are felt to be more significant than
the adult manifestations of personality, analogy shades into
allegory.

As is evident from *Moses and Monotheism* (1939), Freud finally
came to read the whole history of culture by such a light. The
history of religious movements is governed by an iron law of
compensation which merely recapitulates ontogenesis. It is
significant that culture so understood is presumed to be a
cyclic process: the religion of Ikhnaton is rejected by the next
generation of Egyptians, revived by Moses, rejected by the
Jews during the Exodus, revived by the Prophets, rejected
by Christianity. Freud himself, as the newest avatar of the
Primal Father, must expect to be rejected by his 'sons' (Jung,
Rank *et al.*).[16] Our analogy to the procedure involved in the
epiphany likewise brought us to the eternal return, which may
help to illuminate the morphology of the exposure (or betrayal)
of pre-existent conditions through trivial detail.*

The anecdote which Stephen Dedalus tells of 'Two Dublin
vestals . . . [who] want to see the views of Dublin from the top
of Nelson's pillar' in *Ulysses*, preceded as it is by the single
word 'Dubliners' (183/143), might be called in to justify the
reading of the stories in *Dubliners* as a series of literary epiphanies. The anecdote itself is enigmatic and might well be

* That the vehicle of *exposure* should be an alogical 'symbol'—an image, for
example, part of a narrative context, whose significance lies in its pointing to
another, suprasyntactical context ('displacement')—points to a further *rapprochement* between psychoanalysis and literary interpretation, as has been suggested by
Graham Hough in *Image and Experience* (London, 1960), Ch. III (esp. pp. 122–8).
Hough maintains that modern criticism owes its success in discriminating 'the
shifting boundaries of the symbol' (p. 124) to Freud's influence—his 'researches
on symbolism and on the dream mechanism—"distortion", "projection",
"condensation" and "displacement" ' (p. 123).

an epiphany gone bad, or still imperfectly formulated. It tells us something about Stephen. But while Stephen's predilection for the epiphanic mode may tell us this, Stephen did not write *Dubliners*, and epiphany is only a single element to be related to others in Joyce's own work. I return to an earlier question: whether there is anything in the stories which might serve as a counter-principle in tension with the syndrome of 'paralysis'.

Hugh Kenner, whose short view is that Joyce's whole terrain is a blasted wasteland of paralysed being, will not allow, for example, that the very young boy in 'The Sisters' is anything but a prisoner in the procession. For Kenner, the boy 'is' young Stephen Dedalus (another damned soul) and will 'most probably be a cheerful habitual inhabitant of the boot-heel world' which the other characters occupy.[17] This denominated judgement is intended to fix the character of the boy once for all and to see in a particular moment of time what he has been, is and cannot help but become. For Kenner, then, there would be no counter-principle.

Kenner's phrase 'boot-heel world' derives, however, from a passage in Joyce's text which does not entirely support the weight of authority he expects it to have. One of Father Flynn's sisters, the boy and his aunt enter the bedroom where the deceased is laid out:

> I went in on tiptoe. The room through the lace end of the blind was suffused with dusky golden light amid which the candles looked like pale thin flames. He had been coffined. Nannie gave the lead and we three knelt down at the foot of the bed. I pretended to pray but I could not gather my thoughts because the old woman's mutterings distracted me. I noticed how clumsily her skirt was hooked at the back and how the heels of her cloth boots were trodden down all to one side. The fancy came to me that the old priest was smiling as he lay there in his coffin. (13/13–4)

This passage does not seem necessarily to imply cosmic damnation, or even certain indication that the character is not in a state of grace, what Kenner considers a telling failure of nerve to contemplate the 'mystery'.

Using a vocabulary—and therefore finally an ontological supposition—closer to the narrator's own, we might say that

the boy's wandering of attention implies a dissatisfaction with
and lack of ease in the scene of which he is a part, a desire to
dissociate himself from it and from the feeling he thinks
required of him, perhaps a flicker of sensibility, for the precision
of his observation is underlined ('I noticed how'). As the
transcendental significance of this would vary greatly depending
on one's particular standpoint—damnation, or on another
hand, right behaviour—it seems difficult to insist on any
particular one. Nor can any wider context be called in to
determine this larger significance: it can only suggest the
possibility of one. Of this, more later. Here it is enough to
suggest that close inspection of the basis for determinate
judgement has loosened rather than tightened our grip on the
blanket application of a particular theoretical approach to
the text. To dethrone the approach does not, however, impair
its thematic relevance. Kennerian 'fixity' and the potential
freedom of dissociation may share the passage.

In 'The Sisters' it is the relationship between Rev. Flynn
and his sisters that forms the centre for the notion of paralysis,
under the aspect of society or of Joyce's social *donnée*. This
relationship is a paradigm for Stephen's claim in the *Portrait*
that there are three 'nets flung' at the soul of an Irishman 'to
hold it back from flight' (207/238). While these are first named
as 'nationality, language, religion', they are later replaced by
the more dangerous (as Stephen thinks) triad: 'I will not serve
that in which I no longer believe, whether it call itself my
home, my fatherland or my church' (251/291). These three
elements are conjoined in a single situation in 'The Sisters'.
They form a nexus of pressures under which Flynn, given his
particular sensibility, became immobilized, 'scrupulous'. He
retreated into insentience. The failed priest is the first of Joyce's
trial self-projections in *Dubliners*—what he might have become
had he remained in Dublin. (The method was being used
contemporaneously in short stories by Henry James, most
notably perhaps in 'The Jolly Corner'.)

An impoverished Irish family like the Flynns—'all born
down in Irishtown' (16/17)—would nevertheless have sunk all
its meagre resources into the education of a son who claimed a
call to the priesthood, even to the deprivation of other children,

13

In such a situation, the uneducated daughters would probably have been precluded from making a 'good' marriage (they would have no dowry) and would more likely not marry at all. In return for an education gained at the expense of other members of his family, the priest would be expected to take on, in later years, the support of any unmarried sisters. Often they would become his housekeepers. Though celibate, he would be held by Irish society to a strict accounting in the way of familial obligation.

Consequent upon Flynn's having been relieved of parish duties—that his mind seems to have given way we learn in the story's last words—this expected pattern of responsibility had been reversed. His support had devolved upon his sisters: 'God knows we done all we could, as poor as we are' (14/16). They seem to have been forced into running a 'drapery'. Their conversation with the boy's aunt reveals a current of ill-focused and hardly acknowledged animus against their dead brother as well as a clear strain of the feeling that they have been obscurely cheated in life. Eliza tells a good deal more about James than she originally intends. In this last crisis of all, her *censor* is weakened, but she would be upset to be told that her feelings are ambiguous. There is something of a similar animus in the way one of Joyce's sisters spoke of 'Jim' in the 1950 British Broadcasting Company 'Portrait of James Joyce', and of the parents who would have done 'anything' for Jim in the days when they hoped he was going to become a priest. Anything for Jim, nothing for them. As an emblem of social immobility, Joyce could hardly have found a better implication of Church, state and family in a single situation to set at the head of his published fiction.

But the young boy who sometime later narrates the story has no part in this, except as it represents one possibility for him:

My uncle explained to old Cotter.

'The youngster and he were great friends. The old chap taught him a great deal mind you: and they say he had a great wish for him.' (8/9)

Yet oddly enough, the boy does sense the priest's death as a release for himself, and we learn that Flynn's 'teaching' had been more in the way of a confusion, an inculcation of his own scruples than an enlightenment for the boy:

I walked away slowly along the sunny side of the street, reading all the theatrical advertisements in the shop-windows as I went. I found it strange that neither I nor the day seemed in a mourning mood and I felt even annoyed at discovering in myself a sensation of freedom as if I had been freed from something by his death. . . . he had explained to me the meaning of . . . the different vestments worn by the priest. Sometimes he had amused himself by putting difficult questions to me, asking me what one should do in certain circumstances or whether such and such sins were mortal or venial or only imperfections. His questions showed me how complex and mysterious were certain institutions of the Church which I had always regarded as the simplest acts. The duties of the priest towards the Eucharist and towards the secrecy of the confessional seemed so grave to me that I wondered how anybody had ever found in himself the courage to undertake them. . . . Often when I thought of this I could make no answer or only a very foolish and halting one upon which he used to smile and nod his head twice or thrice. (11–12/11–12)

This smile had come to the boy the previous night, in a dream he is at this juncture trying to recall:

the grey face still followed me. It murmured; and I understood that it desired to confess something. I felt my soul receding into some pleasant and vicious region; and there again I found it waiting for me. It began to confess to me in a murmuring voice and I wondered why it smiled continually and why the lips were so moist with spittle. But then I remembered that it had died of paralysis and I felt that I too was smiling feebly as if to absolve the simoniac of his sin. (9/10)

It is not until the moment when the boy's attention wanders from his prayers to Nannie's clumsily hooked skirt and her 'trodden down' cloth boots that this sinister smile is dissipated:

The fancy came to me that the old priest was smiling as he lay there in his coffin.
But no. When we rose and went up to the head of the bed I saw that he was not smiling. (13/14)

The boy, like Eliza later, tells us more about his relationship to the priest than he himself understands about it. He also shows us his first steps, barely self-comprehending, beyond the priest's influence. He even still seems to believe he feels as he did. His progress, while ambiguous, displays the first tentative glimmerings of dissociation. It seems one of those 'small gradual readjustments' in which Edmund Wilson saw Joyce's major focus of attention.[18] It is a readjustment by means of a dream of a dead parent-figure rejected: the icon which will reappear, in a more complicated context, in *Ulysses*.

There is nothing in 'The Sisters' which insists on the permanency or impermanency of this adjustment: at thirteen one can hardly be trapped or freed for life—unless, of course, the incidents at hand are supposed to be 'symbolic' of an assumed condition. In 'The Sisters' there seems nothing which could prove this latter, though evidences of symbolical *correspondance*—as Flynn's physical paralysis—might be counted for it. Similarly, no particular determinate moral judgement seems implied in the boy's involuntary withdrawal from the priest's sphere of influence, unless one believes the opposite of Hugh Kenner's symbolist reading, namely that Joyce's is 'the gospel of individualism'.[19] The rhythm of constraint and freedom need not necessarily be tied to either moral position, despite the difficulty of talking without implying one or the other. This short story lays down the relationships and dynamic of opposed forces, and while it does not disallow transcendental interpretation, it does not force it. The problem becomes necessarily more complex as a protagonist's course is traced over a longer period of time.

III

When the young boy protagonist of the second and third short stories in *Dubliners*, 'An Encounter' and 'Araby', meets with frustration it begins to look as though the shades of the prison-house are closing about him. This is to assume that the first-person narrator of the first three stories is the same person. In any case, the narrative alters to third-person in the fourth story, 'Eveline', and never reverts, so at least one issue looming on the horizon cannot be referred to further incidents: is the boy going to be a 'failure'? whose fault would it be, his own or circumstance's? is the possibility of 'freedom' suggested in 'The Sisters' rendered illusory by the action of 'An Encounter' and 'Araby'?

Here are readings based in good part upon symbolist interpretations of these stories:

> The theme of the two modes of priesthood runs from 'The Sisters' through 'An Encounter' to 'Araby', at which point, with the passing of childhood, the scrupulous and imaginative mode loses its resilience *for good*.[20] [my italics]

> The only explication of 'An Encounter'—that of Marvin Magalaner in *Joyce: The Man, the Work, the Reputation*—treats the excursion of two truant schoolboys as an attempt to escape from the paralysis of Dublin life by visiting the Pigeonhouse Fort, which is interpreted as a religious and paternal symbol. 'The Pigeonhouse, then, is *identified in Joyce's mind* with the "father" of Christ and with fathers in general' (77). The pervert whom the boys encounter after they have abandoned their attempt to reach their destination *is*, according to this interpretation, both a perverted God and a perverted father. . . .

> For a long time I did not understand why a visit to the Pigeonhouse should be the climax of a day spent in seeing foreign ships; I then learned that *in the late eighteenth and early nineteenth century* the Pigeonhouse was the Irish terminus of the Irish-English packet service. . . .

> Thus, much of the pathetic futility of the boys' attempt to escape lies in the fact that they try a path that had been closed before they were born.[21] [my italics]

In the last comment, the writer comes to take his own metaphor ('escape') *literally*. Yet the confidence that Joyce belonged to a certain school of symbolist thought—in which narrative plot, for example, is only 'symbolic' of some other 'real' level—can produce such interpretation *ad infinitum*. Why else, for instance, is the vessel whose 'legend' the boy fails to 'decipher' 'Norwegian' (23/25)? Does this mean that the 'attempt to escape' being made here is wholly frustrated or merely premature, since knowledge of 'Norwegian' will later, when James Joyce encounters Ibsen, lead to a *true* escape?

In the case of 'An Encounter' and 'Araby', the 'theme' of escape or of a search for freedom needs little illustration. It is there, even if our understanding of what it *means* is clouded:

> The adventures related in the literature of the Wild West were remote from my nature but, at least, they opened doors of escape. . . .

17

I began to hunger again for wild sensations, for the escape
which those chronicles of disorder alone seemed to offer me.
The mimic warfare of the evening became at last as wearisome
to me as the routine of school in the morning because I wanted
real adventures to happen to myself. But real adventures, I
reflected, do not happen to people who remain at home: they
must be sought abroad. . . . (18–20/21–2)

   School and home seemed to recede from us and their in-
fluences upon us seemed to wane.   (22/25)

What I want to note here is the image which opposes itself to
the linear movement of escape. It is twice-repeated. The man
who accosts the boys when they have, with 'jaded thoughts'
(24/26), abandoned the 'project of visiting the Pigeon House'
(23/26),

   gave me the impression that he was repeating something which
   he had learned by heart or that, magnetized by some words
   of his own speech, his mind was slowly circling round and
   round in the same orbit. . . . He repeated his phrases over and
   over again. . . . (26/29)

   He began to speak on the subject of chastizing boys. His
   mind, as if magnetized again by his speech, seemed to circle
   slowly round and round its new centre.   (27/30)

The image of circular fixity and repetition has been glanced
at earlier; it will demand attention when we arrive at *Portrait
of the Artist* and *Ulysses*. Generally appearing in a context of
futility, it will attract some strange and prominent bedfellows.

IV

The structure of 'Eveline' is a progressive alternation of themes.
The attractions of escape from Dublin oscillate with the forces
conspiring to keep Eveline there. It is a simple pattern: will
the energy of the shop-girl—'Her head was leaned against the
window curtains . . . She was tired' (37/42)—be sufficient to
enable her to 'go away like the others, to leave her home'
(37/43), 'run away with a fellow' (38/43), 'to go away with him
by the night-boat to be his wife and to live with him in Buenos
Ayres where he had a home waiting for her' (39/45)? Realism
tugs against romance, in motive and style simultaneously:
the 'fellow' is 'awfully fond of music and sang a little' (40/45),

18

but when Eveline 'heard a melancholy air of Italy', her father had said, 'Damned Italians! coming over here!' (41/47).

At first the rhythm of oscillation is leisurely and the formulation of alternatives vague, undemonstrative and tangential to the specific items of greatest emotive call on Eveline. Attractive memories of the neighbourhood in her childhood, when 'father was not so bad' (37/42), a ruminating glance around the room at 'those familiar objects from which she had never dreamed of being divided' (38/43) are followed by a repellent aspect of the Dublin scene for her, a reminiscence of the shop where she works. Thus detaching her emotions she proceeds to a thought of 'her new home, in a distant unknown country' (38/44), but a memory of the family life since her mother's death—'now that she was about to leave it she did not find it a wholly undesirable life' (39/45)—recalls her to the sense of obligation to stay.

As the shortest of the stories in *Dubliners* proceeds, the pace of the alternations—on the one side, home and family responsibilities; on the other, Frank, escape and freedom—increases, and the individual images become more sharply detailed. Against Frank's 'tales of distant countries' are set her father's commands 'forbid[ding] her to have anything to say to him' (40/46). The attractive side of 'Dublin' is illustrated by a vivid memory of a family 'picnic to the Hill of Howth' (41/46). Then follows a memory of the focal experience of the forces of restriction, Eveline's 'promise to her mother, her promise to keep the home together as long as she could', made on the 'last night of her mother's illness' (41/47). Here, given her dreams, is the occasion of remorse, what will in Stephen Dedalus be the 'Agenbite'. It is the most vivid expression for the object of one cluster of feelings in Eveline; it is immediately followed by its polar opposite: 'She stood up in a sudden impulse of terror. Escape! She must escape! . . . she wanted to live. Why should she be unhappy? She had a right to happiness. Frank . . . would save her' (41–2/47).

These oscillations form a *resonance*, of the kind that tears suspension bridges apart. Similar resonances comprise the structural basis of numerous works.[22] In Arthur Miller's drama *Death of a Salesman*, episodes of alternating family happiness and unhappiness culminate in the dinner Willy

19

Loman's sons give him. This proudest moment ends in desertion and the hallucination/flashback of the scene in which his son Biff had discovered a prostitute in his father's hotel room. Out of this incident the whole plot has grown; to it, it obsessively returns. A dream-fantasy/nightmare resonating alternation likewise informs the structure of Hemingway's *A Farewell to Arms*, where the apparent success of the hero's 'romantic' desires is always followed by the occurrence of a feared nightmare of equal magnitude (the wound, the retreat from Caporetto): as the happy events increase in magnitude of importance, so do the disasters, the escape to Switzerland and the death of Catherine in childbirth being the last of each. Hemingway's use of resonance is, however, linear, while Joyce's and Miller's, mixing memory and desire, weave backwards and forwards in time, culminating in the simultaneous linear plot crisis and the uncovering of the 'traumatic' past experience, after which whatever is left of the plot—if anything—is *predictable*.

The growing tension of 'Eveline' can be partly accounted for by the greater pressure Dublin 'reality' amasses as the story proceeds over the necessarily vaguer pressure of Eveline's desires. This is true linguistically as well as psychologically. That is, the reality is determinate, it has occurred, it has the vernacular on its side; the desire is indeterminate, in the future, couched in the terms of romance and adolescent longing. The longer the story goes on, the more does the language bully the girl. The linguistic situation here produced is a function of the existential situation: it recurs, more importantly, in *Portrait of the Artist*.

Now the stage is set for the last scene, which will, apparently, demonstrate the result of Eveline's reminiscences. 'At the North Wall', Eveline is in 'a maze of distress'. A riot of conflicting feelings and images possesses her mind. At the last instant she pulls back, and her refusal or inability to leave is described initially by the metaphor of fear of drowning:

> All the seas of the world tumbled about her heart. He was drawing her into them: he would drown her. She gripped with both hands at the iron railing.
> 'Come!'
> No! No! No! It was impossible. Her hands clutched the iron in frenzy. Amid the seas she sent a cry of anguish!
> 'Eveline! Evvy!'

20

He rushed beyond the barrier and called to her to follow. He was shouted at to go on but he still called to her. She set her white face to him, passive, like a helpless animal. Her eyes gave him no sign of love or farewell or recognition.   (42–3/47)

The boldly sketched symbolism of fear of water as an inability to face the 'sea' of life has been familiarized by Jung. It returns in different, more expanded and articulated versions throughout Joyce as the artist's necessary 'choice of flux rather than any already created order'.[23] A death by drowning similar to the one Eveline foresees for herself if she boards ship is to be found in *Ulysses*, where Stephen's sister Dilly, as Marvin Magalaner has noted,[24] is a version of Eveline. Only in the novel, the positions are apparently reversed: Eveline, fearing that Frank and the unknown would be a drowning, prefers to stay in Dublin; Dublin itself, on the other hand, is drowning Dilly—and Stephen too, as he thinks:

> She is drowning. Agenbite. Save her. Agenbite. All against us. She will drown me with her, eyes and hair. Lank coils of seaweed hair around me, my heart, my soul. Salt green death.
>
> (313/240)

Whether it was ever possible for Eveline to have escaped seems hardly worth asking. It is answered, negatively, if we elevate a notion like 'paralysis' to any ontological status. Does Eveline end in Dublin *because* she was paralysed? Why not say Dublin is 'the centre of paralysis' because such things happen as happened to Eveline? This simple distinction becomes increasingly difficult to maintain as the action of a character complicates, partly under the inherent pressure of a longer form of fiction, partly because of certain artistic strategies we will be analysing. In a more complicated situation, given a more complex character like Stephen Dedalus, the 'flight' from Dublin which ends *Portrait of the Artist*, the return which precedes *Ulysses*, cannot be said so confidently to 'mean' what Eveline's unwilling decision seems to mean for her: that we have witnessed the crucial event of a life, that she has had and missed her one chance for self-assertion. If therefore, we 'interpret' the concrete actions of *Portrait* or *Ulysses* by reference to a supposed *causal* condition, like 'paralysis', we risk going (very strictly speaking) outside the text. We posit, as the enabling act of criticism, an *allegorical* intent in Joyce.

II

A PORTRAIT OF THE
ARTIST AS A YOUNG MAN:
DISENGAGEMENT

You must leave Fathers & Mothers & Houses & Lands if they stand
in the way of Art.

—Blake

ONE BURDEN OF THIS CHAPTER is to suggest why critical
preoccupation with 'symbolist' elements in Joyce's fiction—
recognizable in the use of terms like verbal motif, *correspondance*,
the universe of verbal discourse, image-pattern, theme- or
key-word—renders a less favourable portrait of the character of
Stephen Dedalus than in their absence. One aim is hopefully
synthetic—to demonstrate the equal necessity of major
'opposed' views in Joyce criticism. Not that their opposition
is less than complete: it is, on many levels. But the holding of
irreconcilable, mutually exclusive views circumscribes the
only areas of 'total meaning' which can properly delimit, in
different ways, Joyce's *Portrait of the Artist* and *Ulysses*.

That the presentation of character and action in the *Portrait*
or *Ulysses* should be finally paradoxical—what Kierkegaard
called the 'absolute paradox'[1]—should not be particularly
troublesome as a concept, however difficult its articulation may
prove. Criticism is acclimatized to the notion in respect of
metaphor, where 'tensions' established in the presence of

discrete meanings attachable to one and the same image have been long held a poetic virtue. 'Paradox' has been less rigorously applied, however, to the interpretation of fiction,[2] where it has met vigorous opposition from the insistence that an author is obliged to have a particular moral vision which the action of his story somehow demonstrates (mere authorial assertion of values being insufficient).

But an author's refusal to commit himself to a particular quasi-ethical interpretation of his created action, while it may appear 'immoral' at one level, may lead us on to another as the *ground* of his commitment. This is not to dissipate the 'immorality' at the first, but to recognize it as part of a wider meaning: Kierkegaard's Abraham (in *Fear and Trembling*) is 'ethically' immoral for offering to sacrifice Isaac, but equally (possibly) 'religious' in another sphere. To assert that such contradictions make nonsense of moral vision assumes that an author must judge—or put himself on record as attempting a judgement—of the ultimate meaning of his creation, and further, make it appear that the action of his story offers a moral comment on the characters involved. The outline of a defence can be found in Chapter Seven of the earliest lengthy study of poetic paradox, Empson's *Seven Types of Ambiguity*:

> A contradiction of this kind may be meaningless, but it can never be a blank; it has at least stated the subject which is under discussion, and has given a sort of intensity to it such as one finds in a grid-iron pattern in architecture because it gives prominence neither to the horizontals nor to the verticals, and in a check pattern because neither colour is the ground on which the other is placed; it is at once an indecision and a structure, like the symbol of the Cross.*

Extending our attention from Empson's spatial metaphors of pattern to existential antinomies such as the relationships between individuals and their experience, freedom and neces-

---

* William Empson, *Seven Types of Ambiguity* (New York, 1955), p. 128; 'when the two meanings of the word, the two values of the ambiguity, are the two opposite meanings defined by the context' (p. 217). Cf. also, 'Opposites, again, are an important element in the Freudian analysis of dreams' (p. 218); 'I have been searching the sources of the Nile less to explain English verse than to cast upon the reader something of the awe and horror which were felt by Dante arriving finally at the most centrique part of earth, of Satan, and of hell . . . the secret places of the Muse' (pp. 221–2).

sity, possibility and actuality, some further systematization of paradox can be attempted.

I hope to prove that a 'symbolist' reading of Joyce's *Portrait of the Artist* will be essentially different from a 'realistic' reading. It will be a further task to describe their relationship and to show that this relationship is by way of a description of the novel's meaning.

In writing of 'symbolism' I shall be making use of a distinction from Graham Hough's *A Preface to the Faerie Queene*. Hough distinguishes 'symbolism' from definitions such as Coleridge's in *The Statesman's Manual* (1816), according to which a symbol must 'partake of the reality which it renders intelligible'.[3] Hough calls this, and similar notions of symbolism, 'incarnation', and he reserves the term 'symbolism' for the basis of a more historical phenomenon in art:

> symbolism [is] like incarnation a form in which theme ['the moral or metaphysical "abstract" element'] and image ['the "concrete" characters, actions or objects'] have equal weight, but opposed to incarnation because the relation between the two elements is different. In symbolism there is none of the harmonious wholeness of incarnational literature ['in which any "abstract" content is completely absorbed in character and action and completely expressed by them']. Theme and image are equally present, they assert their unity, but the unity is never achieved, or if it is, it is only a unity of tension. The archetype for incarnational literature is the union of soul and body in the human person, but symbolism resists this human and accessible integrity. It seeks for the union of theme and image not through the representation of living, acting and suffering human beings, but through words as talismans, *alchemie du verbe* . . . [one version of which is characterized by] a realm of stratagems and devices, *dérèglement de tous les sens*, things seen as the equivalent of concepts, fragments that mysteriously contain wholes. . . .[4]

The problems of symbolism and 'realism' in Joyce can be clarified if Hough's distinction is borne in mind. They can be too easily dissipated by allowing the attempt to discover the nature of Joyce's symbols to shelter under the banner of 'incarnation'. A more vitalizing notion of their nature does not neutralize distinctions of genre, mode or strategy, but rather

24

sharpens them in order to perceive the limiting conditions they impose upon the fictions they inhabit. In the case of symbolism, this will require seeing it not at its nearest approach to realism, 'incarnation', but from its further side, where 'images tend to acquire magical properties. They engage in mysterious correspondences and enter into occult relations with vision'; or where 'the image shrinks and becomes stereotyped, and theme expands. We think of emblems . . .'.[5] It is to a critique of this dimension of a *Portrait of the Artist*—or to determine the status of such a dimension—that we turn first.

I

The option of tracking constellations of images and verbal recurrences, in fiction as well as poetry, is for us 'live'. That the unthinking pursuance of 'symbolist' critical method has led to a degree of reaction is not occasion to dismiss it as merely an illegitimate extension of either a particular historical phase of art or a critical fashion in the explication of poetry. That Joyce's attention in the construction of *Ulysses* was in great part given over to the discovery of correspondences and systematic schematizations is alone attested by his letters to Frank Budgen or his worksheets, lately studied by A. Walton Litz in *The Art of James Joyce*.[6] Let us examine the view of a critic who asserts a full symbolic claim for the *Portrait*.

Hugh Kenner understands the first two pages of *A Portrait of the Artist* as a symbolic overture of motifs awaiting later development. This means for him that they 'enact the entire action in microcosm':

> Once upon a time and a very good time it was there was a moocow coming down along the road and this moocow that was down along the road met a nicens little boy named baby tuckoo. . . .
> His father told him that story: his father looked at him through a glass: he had a hairy face. . . . (7/1)

> But *as we can see from the vantage-point of Finnegans Wake*, the whole book is about the encounter of a baby tuckoo with the moocow: the Gripes with the Mookse. The father with the hairy face is the first Mookse-avatar, the Freudian infantile analogue of God the Father.[7] [my italics]

25

Similarly, after this exchange in the novel—a near-transcript of the sixth 'Epiphany' in the University of Buffalo manuscript—

—O, Stephen will apologize.

Dante said:

—O, if not, the eagles will come and pull out his eyes.—

> Pull out his eyes,
> Apologize,
> Apologize,
> Pull out his eyes, [etc.]   (8/2)

Kenner comments, '[Stephen's] own grown-up failure to apologize will blend with gathering blindness'.[8]

In this last comment, the usage 'blend with' allows Kenner to skirt precise specification of the relationship between Stephen's physical short-sightedness and his moral behaviour. If pressed, Kenner might claim he did not intend to suggest that the failure to apologize was the *cause* of physical blindness, nor that the blindness was the reward of failure. He merely means that the notions are 'symbols', 'blended' together in a mixture. It may well be that no moral judgements ought to be passed upon the actions of characters in symbolist fiction—as they ought not in a 'determinist' world—the environments and events which meet these characters being merely *expressions* of their inner selves. (This is to transfer to a character what is often said of the symbolist author: 'If Baudelaire, for instance, calls up the image of a woman with black hair or green eyes, these are not so much personal characteristics [of the woman] as a definition of his own kind of sensibility'.[9]) Yet it is undeniable that Kenner does *judge* Stephen Dedalus—adversely—and that he implies the judgement is Joyce's own.

On a symbolist reading, events from Stephen's earliest years can be conflated with others some twenty years away in time and either held to 'contain' the other. If the notion of individual character is given any status in a symbolist fiction, the *rapprochement* between symbolism and determinism becomes evident. The casualty, in both symbolist and determinist fiction, is time. T. S. Eliot set the problem out in the opening lines of 'Burnt Norton':

> Time present and time past
> Are both perhaps present in time future,
> And time future contained in time past.
> If all time is eternally present
> All time is unredeemable.[10]

Sartre, in his essay 'François Mauriac and Freedom' (1939), has made a complex association of fictional determinism—under which he includes authorial pretence to absolute judgement in the sphere of morality—and atemporality:

> The time has come to say that the novelist is not God. . . .
> The introduction of absolute truth or of God's standpoint constitutes a twofold error of technique. To begin with, it presupposes a purely contemplative narrator, withdrawn from the action. . . And besides, the absolute is non-temporal. If you pitch the narrative in the absolute, the string of duration snaps, and the novel disappears before your eyes. All that remains is a dull truth, *sub specie aeternitatis.**

The loss of 'the string of duration' is equally true of symbolism as of determinism.

Though any one of a number of instances may be taken to symbolize the whole, Freudian approach to personality stands as an invisible guarantor that the earliest is the crucial incident. It would, however, be more proper to say that all individual 'emblems' are only particular examples of an underlying hypostatized substance, an unchanging core predisposed to respond along certain lines. Temporal events, when not just arbitrary symbols devised by the artist to reveal to us the character's inner state, may be considered as displaying facets of this hypothetical entity, for our fuller understanding of it. The earliest of these events, if not the *cause* of the latter, may be considered their *definition*, as the infantile Oedipal situation may be held to define, if not to cause, the more complex, sublimated adult situation. (Kenner's easy allusion to 'the Freudian infantile analogue' is here relevant.)

It may be seen that this understanding of the symbolic relationship between character and event restricts severely

---

* Jean-Paul Sartre, *Literary and Philosophical Essays*, trans. Annette Michelson (London, 1955), pp. 14–15. Cf. Joyce's complaint (of 1903) that Ibsen's women in *Catilina* 'are absolute types, and the end of such a play cannot but savour of dogma—a most proper thing in a priest but a most improper in a poet' (*Critical Writings*, p. 100).

what can be meant by both 'development' and freedom. In a symbolist work the writer may develop his fictional character by displaying in 'time' various facets of the character's inherent personality—though any tendency to intensify (or pack) individual incidents will suggest that all are present at any one moment. This we have before described as epiphanic. But there is no question of the character himself developing as a human being. The terms of the relationship between the individual and experience are shrunk by the pure symbolist approach to one side of a metaphysical antinomy. Insistence on the total absence of symbolist intent—that, in our instance the first pages of Joyce's *Portrait* are devoid of any denominative judgement on the character—is to determine the matter solely in favour of the other horn of the dilemma. As a determinism of the interior is implicated in the former, so a determinism of the exterior circumstances appears involved in the latter.

Symbolist hypostatization, then, not only tends to limit the possible significances of 'development', but in permitting a conveniently limited range of interpretation based on a fixed notion of character it can radically short-circuit our normal processes of judgement. In the case of the *Portrait's* 'apologize' tableau, the symbolist interpretation very nearly identifies all failures to apologize, conform or submit as ethically equivalent. The refusal to apologize for an unspecified childish misdemeanor is taken as a 'symbol' of the whole position of the artist: 'Dante' (so-called innocently enough by Stephen that Joyce may intimate she 'symbolizes' the Church and all authority) requires of the artist submission for a Promethean daring to *see too much*.[11] Such analysis contains no criterion of reasonableness (why should Dante Alighieri represent either religious *authority* or *unjust* religious authority?), but a symbolist work need not be thus reasonable.

In interpreting all events from a conveniently fixed point, it may be assumed that Stephen Dedalus *is*, constantly, 'the artist', his every childish motion an un-artistic response and that the novel is a portrait of the infant, child, youth and young man as an artist.

Now the artist-figure in a symbolist work—or, to preserve the critical figure, a work so interpreted—can hardly add any new tricks to a basic repertory, nor discard any. On this interpretation no radical transvaluation of values or 'new' response to a supposed objective reality could be allowed for.[12] Symbolist literary analysis predisposes one to expect a fictional character who spins his universe out of his own entrails, whose reported experience—in the autonomy of the individual work, his *whole* experience—demonstrates the entirety of his possibilities, perhaps in every individual event. Symbolist aesthetic presuppositions tend to exact from fictional characters, in other words, corollary inclinations. The more a work seems to satisfy these presuppositions, the more does a character seem what Jean Piaget calls an 'assimilative' personality.

In a categorization sometimes reminiscent of the Hedgehog and the Fox, Piaget defines the dimensions of the adaptions by which organisms reach equilibrium in their environments as 'assimilation' and 'accommodation'. Assimilation 'describe[s] the action of the organism on surrounding objects' and accommodation the converse, the environment's action on the organism ('it being understood that the individual never suffers the impact of surrounding stimuli as such, but they simply modify the assimilatory cycle by accommodating him to themselves').[13] Elsewhere Piaget extends his classification to psychological types, whereby certain people are more accommodative or assimilative than others.[14] The assimilative personality converts all external reality into its pre-existent mode of perception. Thus Piaget refines the tendency of Freudian epistomology analysed in Chapter I into one element in a dynamic of personality types.*

* 'Of course, Miss Tray. But we know, don't we, that many an atom-bomb is merely a Mrs. Finch? Think of her as a piece of film, wedged deep in the unconscious. We cannot eject her, so we place behind her the powerful light of guilty evasiveness, which projects her upon the screen of the outer world, distorted into the likeness of a bomb. Thus we rid ourselves of an internal mother, by transforming her into an external explosive.'
'Then the atom bomb does not exist?'
'Some of my colleagues say that it doesn't: they lump it in with all the other internal problems, like road-accidents, industrial injuries, cancer, death, and so on. Personally, I'm a middle-of-the-road sort of man: I believe that machinery, and motor-cars in particular, are intrinsically dangerous. I even claim that they have the power of moving quite often in a direction opposite to the one demanded by their victim's neurosis. But be good enough not to repeat my remark in the presence of any of my colleagues: any rehabilitation of the external world injures them far more than could the heaviest motor-lorry' (Nigel Dennis, *Cards of Identity* [Harmondsworth, 1960], p. 65).

If there is a tendency to assume that 'all time is eternally present' in a novel, and if the *end* product is certified an 'artist', it may be assumed that he must always be on the road to artistic success or failure. The 'artistic response' to experience seems always present to Hugh Kenner. As in the implications of the Freudian statements discussed in the first chapter, conditions and particular events only serve to display a basic prior complex in various poses. They may 'bring out' or 'call forth' certain responses in a character—albeit in a particularly limited meaning of these terms. They seem, however, to have little real part in the creation of these responses. The relationship between individual and environment is governed on *a priori* assumptions by a symbolist aesthetic: it is unchanging. These assumptions are the reverse of the coin of naturalistic ones, which also posit a constant relationship, but not qualitatively different from them. In both, the character and his 'universe' are in a determinate and unalterable relationship.

If this accounts for the artist-protagonist's always being seen in a constant path towards artistic success or failure, it is considerably easier to hold that Stephen Dedalus 'is'—or 'is becoming' (as time is finally irrelevant in symbolist analysis, where such distinctions are 'blended')—a failure than to maintain, as a few zealous admirers have, that his progress displays an unbroken series of successes.

Let us take, as an example, Stephen's first successful attempt to compose a poem:

> Before him lay a new pen, a new bottle of ink and a new emerald exercise. From force of habit he had written at the top of the first page the initial letters of the jesuit motto: A.M.D.G. On the first line of the page appeared the title of the verses he was trying to write: To E—— C——. He knew it was right to begin so for he had seen similar titles in the collected poems of Lord Byron. When he had written this title and drawn an ornamental line underneath he fell into a day dream and began to draw diagrams on the cover of the book. He saw himself [*etc.*]. . . .
>
> Now it seemed as if he would fail again but, by dint of brooding on the incident, he thought himself into confidence. During this process all those elements which he deemed common and insignificant fell out of the scene. There remained no trace

of the tram itself nor of the tram-men nor of the horses: nor
did he and she appear vividly. The verse told only of the night
and the balmy breeze and the maiden lustre of the moon. . . .
[T]he letters L.D.S. were written at the foot of the page and,
having hidden the book, he went into his mother's bedroom
and gazed at his face for a long time in the mirror of her dressing
table. (72–3/77–8)

Though one critic sees Stephen's method as an occasion for
high praise and claims it was Joyce's own process as he revised
Stephen Hero into the *Portrait*,[15] it is rather a jejune idealizing
and romanticization which accounts for the absence of 'common
and insignificant' elements, specification of the scene. Joyce's
own language here, through its use of negatives, includes those
very elements Stephen left out: the tram, the tram-men, the
horses.

Joyce is bearing down on Stephen here, in the description
of the elaborate self-consciousness of the fledgling effort (new
pen, new ink, new paper), the automatic jesuit superscription,
the inability to concentrate, the narcissism. The poem is blatant
wish-fulfilment: 'the kiss . . . withheld by one, was given by
both' (73/78). If one looks no further than the immediate
context as one focuses on Stephen's artistic moments, assumes
that each incident is a microcosmic reproduction of the whole
novel, and inclines to be rather solemn about children, one's
notion of Stephen will be darkly coloured.

Alternately, attention to a wider context—that is, away from
the 'symbolism' towards the individuality of the moment—
can suggest another limiting pole. Stephen is at this point
very young; having left Clongowes, he has not yet entered
Belvedere. His poem is written after a 'long spell of leisure and
liberty' (73/78) during which he has been at a loose end.
Immediately following the poem episode, there is a family
scene whose milieu resembles very closely that in 'The Sisters'.
It opens with Stephen's sullen response to his father: 'he knew
that his father would make him dip his bread in the gravy'
(ibid.). Stephen's unformulated reluctance to admit the claims
of poverty is similar to the young boy's attitude in the *Dubliners*
story. In the *Portrait* this scene ends with a harsh and ironic
picture of the way the adult world can betray a child: Father
Conmee, it seems, has told Simon Dedalus about Stephen's

earlier protest at having been pandied: '*Father Dolan and I and all of us we all had a hearty laugh together over it. Ha! Ha! Ha!*' (74/80). Simon's relation of this in front of Stephen may be unintentionally crass or intentionally mean; in either case the effect is the same and the psychological—and structural—crest reached with the protest here finds its trough.

Comparison with 'The Sisters' suggests that the protagonists may be in comparable stages, their eventual lines of travel comparatively unfixed, their attitudes towards their environment only beginning to crystallize. Given what we know of Stephen's experience of the world at the moment he wrote his poem—e.g. that Conmee had taken seriously his appeal against Father Dolan—the *naïveté* there displayed would seem to be less significant than if it had occurred *after* the revelation of Conmee's particular kind of 'diplomacy'. The conditions which make the composition of 'To E—— C——' relatively harmless in its meaning for Stephen at the time alter with time. Repetition, which on a symbolic view would make no difference, would make the most significant point when it is seen that Stephen will be a free and developing character to the extent that he can leave this poem, as it were, behind him. To the degree we think that he might, he remains charged with potential, not a determined failure or success. This can be decided, not by inspection of the local verbal context, but only by inference from the action which follows. This may help us to preserve a certain respect for the limitedness of the individual incident, its inability to encompass a denominated judgement of the whole action.

Nevertheless, the *Portrait* carries its protagonist further than does 'The Sisters', and one gravitates, even on an insistently unsymbolic reading, towards an expectation that the line of development will become more clear. When a novel's course does not appear to *give in* in this way, critics often balk:

[*Sons and Lovers*] has two themes: the crippling effects of a mother's love on the emotional development of her son; and the 'split' between kinds of love, physical and spiritual, which the son develops, the kinds represented by two young women, Clara and Miriam. The two themes should, of course, work together, the second being, actually, the result of the first:

32

this 'split' is the 'crippling'. So one would expect to see the novel developed, and so Lawrence, in his famous letter to Edward Garnett, where he says that Paul is left at the end with the 'drift towards death', apparently thought he had developed it. Yet in the last few sentences of the novel, Paul rejects his desire for extinction and turns toward 'the faintly humming, glowing town', to life—as nothing in his previous history persuades us that he could unfalteringly do.[16]

Mark Schorer expects the last event in *Sons and Lovers* to suggest a definitive direction for Paul Morel and that the previous course of the novel should support the feasibility of that end. That *Sons and Lovers* should support neither a definitive 'drift towards death' nor an unfaltering turn to life—the hyperbole is symptomatic of the similarity of expectation—does not enter into Schorer's view. Yet that Lawrence himself desired a thoroughly problematic presentation of his themes seems denied by the certainties of his language. That Paul *might or might not* survive the 'crippling' does not seem to be a suspension which Lawrence was much interested in sustaining, and thus he invites criticisms like Schorer's with some justice. The canons of what constitutes 'suspension' will come into discussion later; here I am interested in pointing what an approach similar to Schorer's decides about the *Portrait*.

Accounts of Stephen Dedalus which assume that his end (success or failure) must be visualizable in his beginnings do not permit of any thoroughgoing *dramatic* interpretation of the novel. If Joyce is supposed to take a position about the outcome of Stephen's relationship with his environment, then must not each incident selected be a stage showing us the rightness of the outcome? At this point the artist-figure begins to assume his God-like attributes.

The analogy between the work of art and created nature has a long and pre-Flaubertian history. Torquato Tasso, writing of the unity of the 'heroic' poem, claimed for it the variety of the creation itself. Though he includes a comparison between the artist and God—'I assert that the sublime poet (called divine for no other reason than that he models himself in his works on the supreme artificer and arrives at sharing thus his divinity)'[17]—Tasso's main focus is the nature of the incidents to be comprehended by a heroic poem. Subsequently, with

Romantic thrusts towards process and personality, creation as *natura naturans* and the creator have become the more well-lighted portions of the analogy. For present purposes, it is a single feature of this last which is of import. The artist/God analogy is often explored in the light of the extent of an author's 'control' over his material and this is held to have direct relation to the degree of 'freedom' which individual fictional characters may have.

As a metaphoric statement of a tension of conflict appercept-able within a work of art, the positing of auctorial 'interference' has its utility. The necessity of enforcing his thesis, we say, has made the author modify his characters; or, contrariwise, remaining faithful to the probabilities of action, the author has had to qualify the meaning he had intended. Such statements are descriptive either of a hypothetical genesis of the whole work as we have it or of alteration in the work as it progresses.* To say that the metaphor is really unnecessary, as what is being described takes place *within* the work, would, however, be an undue limitation inasmuch as the internal tension may be said to be symbolic of the relationship between author and work. If, given the analogy of the artist to God, a number of relations are potentially present—at least as many as there are theological statements of the relationship of God to creation—further matters suggest themselves.

The question of the 'freedom' of characters in fiction is not necessarily settled by appeal to a particular author's awareness of the analogy of his craft to the processes of the deity—which may vary greatly with his theological position. In Joyce's case the matter is complicated by the fact that it is a character, and not the author, who points the analogy to 'the god of creation'. But if Stephen Dedalus is correct in holding that the artist is the God of his creation, then his statement is valid for all authors, and thereby not especially valid for Joyce. Further, analysis of what Stephen intends by the comparison is no necessary key to the nature of the relationship as establishable in Joyce's fiction. Following Stephen out might

* 'Interference' may even describe a work thematically: in Muriel Spark's *The Comforters* (1957) a character attempts to resist the narrator at his task. The narrator, who is not a character in the action, but a standard 'omniscient' author, takes his revenge.

well lead to Hugh Kenner's conclusions, but whether one will wish to apply them beyond Stephen to the novel is another matter.

In denying, or ignoring the possibility of Stephen's 'freedom', his potential for contrary lines of development, we inflict on ourselves a one-sided picture, a deterministic burden. It can lead to taking Stephen up on particular issues before he reaches the age of reason because they seem 'symbolic' of what happens later, according to an interpretation of what happens later. Since y happened and means b, x (which appeared to be able to mean a or b or c, etc.) must also have meant b and only b, and

> What might have been is an abstraction
> Remaining a perpetual possibility
> Only in a world of speculation—[18]

that is, not in *this* world. The reality of the 'world of specula-tion' becomes suspect. This is one of the things which perplexes Stephen most in *Ulysses*:

> Had Pyrrhus not fallen by a beldam's hand in Argos or Julius Caesar not been knifed to death. They are not to be thought away. Time has branded them and fettered they are lodged in the room of the infinite possibilities they have ousted. But can those have been possible seeing that they never were? Or was that only possible which came to pass?[19]   (30/26)

The 'symbolist' critical position is correlative with an affirma-tive answer. Let us take an example from the *Portrait*.

As a baby, Stephen muddles a song into '*O, the green wothe botheth*' (7/1). At his desk in Clongowes he decides, 'But you could not have a green rose. But perhaps somewhere you could' (12/8). 'Improving the work of nature is his obvious ambition', writes Hugh Kenner, quoting this passage as evidence.[20] At what age does Kenner mean green rose-making is Stephen's 'obvious ambition'? At nine, as here? The fact is that Kenner is not concerned with Stephen's age at all. He has 'spatialized' the novel and for him only that is the meaning of any given situation which later comes, as he thinks, to pass. This is equivalent to eliminating *time* from the novel and *possibility* from the life of the character. By positing Stephen's 'obvious ambition', Kenner finds it 'latent' in his childish reflections; moreover, he voices no other possibility of meaning in them.

35

Kenner reads Stephen's day-dreaming as a parable of art and the (ineffectual) artist. Further attention to the particular temporal context can produce more about the green rose. Stephen's train of associations begins with the two opposing teams for sums, called 'Lancaster' and 'York'. Having been pushed into the cesspool the previous day by the school bully Wells, Stephen is coming down with a fever, and just as he shrank from playing rugby, he doesn't really want to 'race' for the answers to the sums. The classroom War of the Roses is for him an unwanted combat. The only thing which pleases him in his discomfort is to think about the colour of the prize card, which is pink, the reconciliation of red and white: 'pink roses were beautiful to think of' (12/8). After tea, the colours in his geography remind him of the day when Mrs Riordan 'ripped the green velvet back off the brush that was for Parnell'. Red was for Michael Davitt. 'He wondered which was right, to be for the green or for the maroon . . . . He wondered if they were arguing at home about that. That was called politics. There were two sides in it . . .' (17/13). Stephen may be mistaken in setting the colours at odds, but the significance is not lessened thereby.* Green and red—like red and white— symbolize for him another opposition of the sort he has been trying to avoid. The place where you could have a green rose blossom would reconcile his family. The events of the Christmas dinner that year soon prove that Stephen's apprehension has valid grounds.

It seems possible to domesticate this train of associations within the mind of young Stephen and to refuse the notion of any trans-personal system of correspondences in the 'world' of the novel. This does keep alive the integrity of the fictional character—as distinct from any function as a passive receptor of verbal motifs—and promote the possibility of mental creativity by him. Evaluation of this creativity still remains double-edged: Stephen's reverie can reflect an instinctive revulsion from the conflicts of life, partly excusable in the particular case by the onset of a genuine illness; or it may embody an embryonic version of a genuine creative mental

* Davitt's part in the Committee Room 15 deposition of Parnell is probably unknown to him, and at any rate 'Dante' Riordan deserted Parnell at the bishops', not the party's call (*Ulysses*, 611/481).

36

talent, if only at a barely conscious and unreflective level; or, the possibility of both.

None of this potential range of meaning is available, however, if the 'symbolism' is taken to be over Stephen's head, as it were. If the reds and greens exist as a pattern in the Joyce-universe only,[21] Stephen's integrity as a dramatic creation is shattered, and the process by which the 'symbols' are manipulated cannot be attributed to him—which is to say it affords us no insight into the nature of his character as a developing entity in time.

II

A few episodes from Joyce's *Portrait* have already been considered with a view to eliciting analogies to *freedom* and *fixity* and to suggesting what the *presupposition* of each does to our understanding of fictional characters. What is now required is an examination of the extent to which they are the subjects of the novel itself; otherwise, interesting as they may be in themselves, the notions would have no special relevance to Joyce's work. By this it will become evident that the *fixed* reading I have loosely typed as symbolist is the very one Stephen himself would apply were he a critic of the novel in which he is a character. Without taking the matter further, S. L. Goldberg has asserted as much: 'Indeed, to view Joyce's own art through the theory in the *Portrait* would lead to just that kind of formalistic analysis and evasion of judgement it has received from some of its commentators.'[22] This will suggest finally an implicit conflict between Stephen's view of art and the barely glimpsed vision of the life he wishes to lead: 'I will try to express myself in some mode of life or art as freely as I can and wholly as I can' (251/291). To see this conflict growing, unsuspected by Stephen himself in the *Portrait*, we must attempt to relate Stephen's ideas (of art and life) and his (fictitious) life.

Stephen's aesthetic 'conversation' with Lynch falls into two main parts, which Stephen connects verbally by reference to two 'senses' of the word *beauty*, a 'wider' (that is, *literary*) sense and a 'marketplace' sense (218/250). His discussion of the literary sense subdivides into his remarks on pity and terror and on the requirements for beauty. Exposition of the 'market place' sense concerns the relation of the art object—which Stephen calls the 'esthetic image'—to audience and author. His key terms are 'arrest', 'stasis' and 'indifference'.

Pity and fear, Stephen says, both 'arrest the mind' (209/239):

—The tragic emotion, in fact, is a face looking two ways, towards terror and towards pity, both of which are phases of it. You see I use the word *arrest*. I mean that the tragic emotion is static. Or rather the dramatic emotion is. The feelings excited by improper art are kinetic, desire or loathing. Desire urges us to possess, to go to something; loathing urges us to abandon, to go from something. The arts which excite them, pornographical or didactic, are therefore improper arts. The esthetic emotion (I used the general term) is therefore static. The mind is arrested and raised above desire and loathing. (209/240)

On this account, both pity and terror are 'static' responses. Each arrests its 'kinetic' opposite, desire or loathing (see 209/239: 'Pity is the feeling which arrests the mind [etc.]. . . . Terror is the feeling which arrests the mind [etc.]. . . .'). True tragic art arrests not by presenting or inducing a tensional balance of desire and loathing, not through the co-presence of pity and terror pulling in opposite directions, but by including two logically independent arresting actions. Stephen's use of 'stasis' as the opposite to didactic and pornographic (erotic) involves respect for aesthetic autonomy, but in attempting to eliminate 'kinetic' response he exposes a weak side. Sir Kenneth Clark, who begins his study of 'the nude' by defining its difference from 'the naked' as a matter of form, nevertheless allots to a 'kinetic' response a valid role in aesthetic apprehension:

'If the nude', says Professor Alexander, 'is so treated that it raises in the spectator ideas or desires appropriate to the material subject, it is false art, and bad morals.' This high-minded theory is contrary to experience. In the mixture of memories and sensations aroused by the nudes of Rubens or Renoir are many which are 'appropriate to the material subject'. And since these words of a famous philosopher are often quoted, it is necessary to labour the obvious and say that no nude, however abstract, should fail to arouse in the spectator some vestige of erotic feeling, even although it be only the faintest shadow–and if it does not do so, it is bad art and false morals.[23]

One need not assume that Lynch has Clark's awareness of the significance of the position, but his immediate response to Stephen crudely makes the same point:

— You say that art must not excite desire—said Lynch—
I told you that one day I wrote my name in pencil on the
backside of the Venus of Praxiteles in the Museum. Was that
not desire?—
—I speak of normal natures—said Stephen—You also
told me that when you were a boy in that charming carmelite
school you ate pieces of dried cowdung.— (209/240)

After this supercilious interlude, Stephen calls Lynch's response 'simply a reflex action of the nerves':

Beauty expressed by the artist cannot awaken in us an emotion
which is kinetic or a sensation which is purely physical. It
awakens, or ought to awaken, or induces, or ought to induce,
an esthetic stasis, an ideal pity or an ideal terror, a stasis called
forth, prolonged and at last dissolved by what I call the rhythm
of beauty. (210/241)

Focusing on the effect of the work of art upon the mind of the beholder, Stephen implies that the proper effect of true art is a continuous—if not instantaneous—state of mind, 'the luminous silent stasis of esthetic pleasure' (217/250). This follows naturally on the elevation of both pity and terror to the status of independent arresting forces. Recalling Clark's 'mixture of memories and sensations' as he regards Rubens and Renoir, we might say that Stephen's view is 'contrary to experience'. Still, he thinks it true to his own experience. He does not state directly that 'stasis' is a structural property *in* a work of art, but by defining it as the end result of the mind's process of apprehension, he suggests that the experience of art is a recreation of the process of creation in the mind of the artist.

Stephen is at pains to eliminate from the apprehension of art all consideration of temporal extension. Lest the description of 'stasis' as 'called forth, prolonged and at last dissolved' be taken to represent any notion of movement in the work, his

D

definition of 'the rhythm of beauty' immediately spatializes the concept:

> —Rhythm—said Stephen—is the first formal esthetic relation of part to part in any esthetic whole or of an esthetic whole to its part or parts or of any part to the esthetic whole of which it is a part.— (210/241)

Stephen will generally bolster a shaky argument with quasi-scholastic or quasi-legalistic formulae (like 'awakens . . . awaken . . . induces . . . induce'). His *termini* are more important to him than the bridges he builds to span them. Here, directly considering for the first time the properties of art—as distinct from the processes of creator or beholder—he once again eliminates suggestions of temporal development and flux. He sees experience as valuable only in atemporal terms, apprehended instantaneously in congeries of discrete events. He projects the conditions of experience as hostile to his values, which, despite his dismissal of the notion of an 'esthetic image' which 'outshine[s] its proper conditions' (217/250), lends an idealizing cast to his argument:

> —We are right—he said—. . .to try slowly and humbly and constantly to express, to press out again, from the gross earth or what it brings forth, from sound and shape and colour which are the prison gates of our soul, an image of the beauty we have come to understand—that is art.—
>
> They had reached the canal bridge and, turning from their course, went on by the trees. A crude grey light, mirrored in the sluggish water, and a smell of wet branches over their heads seemed to war against the course of Stephen's thought.
> (211/242)

To Stephen at this stage, the 'proper conditions' of 'esthetic images' of Dublin are crudity and sluggishness, from which he is turning away.*

Having drawn 'rhythm' into line with the atemporal implications of 'arrest' and 'stasis', Stephen's Aristotelian revision is complete. As with the 'epiphany', it is suggested that atemporality is a property of the work itself, mainly by defining

* See, 'the change of fortune which was reshaping the world about him into a vision of squalor and insincerity' (69/73), and 'The spectacle of the world which his intelligence presented to him with every sordid and deceptive detail' (*Stephen Hero*, 45/40).

the proper response to art as unaffected by 'kinetic' claims. This is similarly the major thrust of Stephen's interpretation of Aquinas, to which he passes next.

First he manœuvres a paraphrase of Aquinas, *'pulchra sunt quae visa placent'*, towards the favoured stasis:

> —He uses the word *visa*, said Stephen, to cover esthetic apprehensions of all kinds, whether through sight or hearing or through any other avenue of apprehension. This word, though it is vague, is clear enough to keep away good and evil, which excite desire and loathing. It means certainly a stasis and not a kinesis. (212/243)

One wonders, of course, if 'any other avenue of apprehension' might not include Lynch's (or Clark's) reaction. More importantly, 'it' in the last line refers to *'visa'*. Stasis becomes a faculty of apprehension, not a property of the beautiful. It is the way one looks at art which 'keeps away good and evil', not that some art keeps them away and some does not. A definition which moves from the operational ('keeps away') to the essential ('means') is suspect. For Stephen to end with stasis seems to be more important than the strict logic of the argument, as in the cavalier sweep of the following lines: 'How about the true? It produces also a stasis of the mind' (212/243).

Stephen's second 'Aquinian' point, in which the three requisites for beauty are viewed as stages in the mind's perception of the work of art, rather than as qualities inhering in the object, moves to a similar conclusion:

> The instant wherein that supreme quality of beauty, the clear radiance of the esthetic image, is apprehended luminously by the mind which has been arrested by its wholeness and fascinated by its harmony is the luminous silent stasis of esthetic pleasure, a spiritual state very like to that cardiac condition which the Italian physiologist Luigi Galvani . . . called the enchantment of the heart. (217/250)

Even as an aesthetician he considers himself something of an artist, and he thinks that his discourse has the power to produce the very state which it undertakes to prove exists:

> Stephen paused and, though his companion did not speak, felt that his words had called up around them a thought-enchanted silence. (218/250)

Stephen's aesthetic, in its direction, does hold fast to the subject's etymological meaning as a science of feeling. The kind of feeling he posits as 'esthetic' does characterize his own understanding of his emotions to this point in the novel. So far, the young man is an artist by his own definition.*

Finally, if *stasis* is the fitting response in the beholder, *indifference* is the corresponding state in the creator of art. As the former means for Stephen an absence of conflicting pulls, not their tension, so the other tends towards an uncaring, rather than an equally caring (disinterested) attitude:

> The personality of the artist . . . finally refines itself out of existence, impersonalises itself, so to speak. . . . The artist, like the God of the creation, remains within or behind or beyond or above his handiwork, invisible, refined out of existence, indifferent, paring his fingernails. (219/252)

The parting shot is a throwaway, a bit of conscious irony at his own expense, directed at the implications of his own abstractions. An ambiguity hovers as well over the word 'refined', which can suggest moral etiolation as well as alchemical purification. As Stephen knows, it was 'Lady' Boyle at Clongowes who was 'always at his nails, paring them' (44/44).†

In *Ulysses* Joyce has Stephen offer a theory of the relation of an author to his work which is in some ways the converse of the one he offers in the *Portrait*.[24] There, the author is held to be *unable* to retire 'within or behind or beyond or above' his work. Shakespeare must perforce appear in each of his characters; like Shem in *Finnegans Wake* (192) he is bound to the cross of his own cruelfiction. Our knowledge that Joyce had alternative formulations helps support the suggestion that the myth of impersonality has its primary significance in its relation to Stephen's own character. In fact, it has just been illustrated rather baldly:

> —This hypothesis, Stephen began.
> A long dray laden with old iron came round the corner of sir Patrick Dun's hospital covering the end of Stephen's speech with the harsh roar of jangled and rattling metal. Lynch closed

---

* Stephen's subsequent composition of a villanelle is described predominantly in sexual (kinetic) terms, which reflects either on the aesthetic theory (which is tacitly abandoned) or the process (which deserts the theory).

† In *Ulysses*, Bloom regards his in order to avoid noticing Boylan (115/91).

his ears and gave out oath after oath till the dray had passed. Then he turned on his heel rudely. Stephen turned also and waited for a few moments till his companion's illhumour had had its vent.

    —This hypothesis, Stephen repeated. . . .   (213/245)

This response, or lack of it, instances one term in a growing process of disengagement which Stephen has been undergoing.

The rhythm of the *Portrait*, like 'Eveline' in *Dubliners*, approximates a pattern of *resonance*. It alternates, with increasing scope, episodes of engagement and disengagement, ordering and disordering. Stephen engages himself with various 'orders' only to disengage himself from them. Hugh Kenner has pointed this out, though with his usual pejorativeness:

> Each chapter closes with a synthesis of triumph which the next destroys. The triumph of the appeal to Father Conmee from lower authority, of the appeal to the harlots of Dublin, of the appeal to the Church from sin, of the appeal to art from the priesthood (the bird-girl instead of the Virgin) is always the same triumph raised to a more comprehensive level.[25]

S. L. Goldberg comments that Stephen 'has to balance a necessary engagement with the outer world and a necessary separation from it',[26] and as Kenner details the engagements, so we may point the 'necessary separation'. As Stephen's perceptions of the *differences* between things widens, it is paralleled by a progressive *indifference*, a detachment of the individual who reacts and suffers from the mind which observes.

III

There is considerable reference to Stephen's growing indifference in the *Portrait*. In human terms, the instances most often reflect forms of self-protection against a hostile environment. They extend over a wide period of time and the analogy between the artist and the indifferent God with which Stephen completes his 'esthetics' is their culmination (or quasi-theological justification). The novel in this respect moves towards an explicit statement of its implicit concerns.

The first hint of detachment is a single short reference. Unjustly pandied at Clongowes,

> Stephen knelt down quickly pressing his beaten hands to his
> sides. To think of them beaten and swollen with pain all in a
> moment made him feel so sorry for them as if they were not
> his own but someone else's that he felt sorry for. (52/55)

The merest suggestion of a distancing is present here. Stephen's
response should be contrasted with the self-pitying reverie of
his own death as he lay in the infirmary earlier—'He might
die. . . . Wells would be sorry' (24/22).

Verging on adolescence in Dublin, Stephen

> was angry with himself for being young and the prey of restless
> foolish impulses, angry also with the change of fortune which
> was reshaping the world about him into a vision of squalor and
> insincerity. Yet his anger lent nothing to the vision. He
> chronicled with patience what he saw, detaching himself from
> it and testing its mortifying flavour in secret. (69/73)

As 'chronicled' hints, this detachment is synchronized—whether
as cause or result—to the growth and expression of his artistic
nature. The relation between experience and perception
stated here is interesting. Instead of Stephen's 'kinetic' response
(his anger) diminishing the value of his perception by introduc-
ing an element of bias, it leaves it unaffected ('lent nothing').
There follow some pages of his 'chronicled' observations, his
aunt's kitchen (69/73-4), 'the narrow breakfast room' (69-70/
74-5), 'a children's party at Harold's Cross' (70-1/75-6),
related almost inconsequentially, in the manner of the *Epiphanies.**

When Stephen is in this mood, however, the detachment
seems to hinder action. On the tram with Emma, 'he stood
listlessly in his place, seemingly a tranquil watcher of the scene
before him' (71/76).

It is through this narrow wedge that the image of the artist
as a renouncer of personal experience enters the novel, in
tacit conflict with Stephen's desire for such experience.† Here,

* 'Each of the three passages beginning with ["He was sitting"] forms an
"epiphany" ' (J. S. Atherton in his edition of *A Portrait of the Artist as a Young Man*
[London, 1964], p. 59).

† See Cyril Connolly's description, apropos of Thomas Mann, of the artist-
type 'content to remain an observer of life and of one's own life, often deprived of
the experiences which render more rounded and full those of other human beings'
(*The Condemned Playground* [London, 1945], pp. 63-4, and see Frank Kermode,
Romantic Image [London, 1957], Ch. I and *passim*).

Stephen's unpremeditated, almost undesired, indifferent response to Emma's flirting becomes the apparent precondition for his first poem, already discussed. As the artist, in such a situation, becomes more self-conscious of what appears a necessary response in him if he is to turn his experience into art, his problem acquires complexity.

Later, remembering the night he had been attacked by Belvedere classmates, Stephen

> wondered why he bore no malice now to those who had tormented him. He had not forgotten a whit of their cowardice and cruelty but the memory of it called forth no anger from him. All the descriptions of fierce love and hatred which he had met in books had seemed to him therefore unreal. Even that night as he stumbled homewards along Jones's Road he had felt that some power was divesting him of that sudden woven anger as easily as a fruit is divested of its soft ripe peel. (84/91–2)*

The objects of Stephen's detachment broaden to include his parents and their contemporaries. In a Cork barroom, embarrassedly watching his father drink with cronies, he thinks,

> An abyss of fortune or of temperament sundered him from them. His mind seemed older than theirs: it shone coldly on their strifes and happiness and regrets like a moon upon a younger earth. No life or youth stirred in him as it had stirred in them. . . . Nothing stirred within his soul but a cold and cruel and loveless lust. . . . (98/107–8)

As the point of view holds the narrator to the present instant, we can have no comment on the permanence of this mood. How basic it is is for us to decide, and to the extent that we think it is, Stephen is deprived of essential freedom. But the mode of the narrative leaves it equally moot whether Stephen's later panting desire for a wide experience of life means, on the other hand, that he has passed beyond stages of indifference and coldness directed towards that which he feels hostile to him.

In the present context, Stephen's indifference is brought into contact with the notion of cyclic movement ('vast inhuman cycles of activity'). The connection is soon made even more

---

* See also 89/96, 'A power, skin to that which had often made anger or resentment fall from him, brought his steps to rest'.

explicit as Stephen, with a month's initiation into Dublin brothels, sits at his schoolroom desk:

> The equation on the page of his scribbler began to spread out a widening tail, eyed and starred like a peacock's; and, when the eyes and stars of its indices had been eliminated, began slowly to fold itself together again. The indices appearing and disappearing were eyes opening and closing; the eyes opening and closing were stars being born and being quenched. The vast cycle of starry life bore his weary mind outward to its verge and inward to its centre, a distant music accompanying him outward and inward. What music? The music came nearer and he recalled the words, the words of Shelley's fragment upon the moon wandering companionless, pale for weariness. The stars began to crumble and a cloud of fine star-dust fell through space.
>
> The dull light fell more faintly upon the page whereon another equation began to unfold itself slowly and to spread abroad its widening tail. It was his own soul going forth to experience, unfolding itself sin by sin, spreading abroad the balefire of its burning stars and folding back upon itself, fading slowly, quenching its own lights and fires. They were quenched: and the cold darkness filled chaos.
>
> A cold lucid indifference reigned in his soul. At his first violent sin he had felt a wave of vitality pass out of him and had feared to find his body or his soul maimed by the excess. Instead the vital wave had carried him on its bosom out of himself and back again when it receded: and no part of body or soul had been maimed, but a dark peace had been established between them. The chaos in which his ardour extinguished itself was a cold indifferent knowledge of himself.
>
> (106–7/116–17)

The 'soul going forth to experience' also 'fold[s] back upon itself, fading slowly, quenching its own lights and fires'. The form of movement embodied in the various metaphors is a diastolic-systolic cycle.* This too has its antecedents in the novel: the 'roar like a train at night' made by closing and opening the flaps of the ears in the Clongowes refectory (13/9), later explicitly connected with the rhythm of school life— term, vacation, term, vacation, etc. (17/13); the reading down

* A 'Kinetic' cycle essentially dissimilar to 'that cardiac condition which the Italian physiologist Luigi Galvani ... called the enchantment of the heart' (217/250).

and then up of the geography flyleaf inscription (Stephen Dedalus/Class of Elements/Clongowes Wood College/etc.) (15–16/11–12);* the celebration of Stephen's protest to Conmee among a shower of thrown caps by a circle of boys who 'closed round [Stephen] in a ring' and then 'broke away in all directions', leaving him 'alone . . . happy and free' (59–60/63–4).

The movements implied in Stephen's meditation on the scribbler suggest his developing formulation of his relation to his experience. It appears as a process of alternate entrance into and immediate disengagement from experience, paralleled psychologically in the movements of desire and indifference, attraction and repulsion, longing and fear. Stephen's attention moves in and out, centripetally and centrifugally, in towards himself and out towards the universe.†

The alternations increase in force and significance—the pattern of resonance—as the novel proceeds. Rejection of the Church and acceptance of the artist's calling comprise the final major oscillation in the novel's structure—though the contrary modes are by then so implanted as to hover about the remainder in implication, as has been seen in the case of the 'esthetics' and as will be discussed apropos of Stephen's diary. The structural utility of an increase in force in each episode accounts for two alterations which Kevin Sullivan has noted Joyce made when refashioning the events of his own life into the novel: that 'Joyce's refusal of a vocation is quite distinct from his later rejection of Catholicism'—in the *Portrait* they are conflated—and that 'Joyce thought longer and more seriously about becoming a Jesuit' than does Stephen, whose rejection of the order is immediately consequent upon his 'temptation'.[27]

By not carrying the different possibilities of a career in the

* 'Cette double tendance, centrifuge et centripète' (Harry Levin, 'James Joyce et l'Idée de Littérature Mondiale', *Contexts of Criticism* [Cambridge, Mass., 1957], pp. 273–4).

† Carl Jung's reflections on the systolic-diastolic cycle are apposite to Stephen's case: 'In extraversion and introversion it is clearly a matter of two antithetical, natural attitudes or trends, which Goethe once referred to as diastole and systole. They ought, in their harmonious alternation, to give life a rhythm, but it seems to require a high degree of art to achieve such a rhythm. Either one must do it quite unconsciously, so that the natural law is not disturbed by any conscious act, or one must be conscious in a much higher sense, to be capable of willing and carrying out the antithetical movements' (*Two Essays on Analytical Psychology*, trans. R. F. C. Hull [New York, 1956], p. 69).

47

Church and a calling in Art along together, Joyce relinquishes the opportunity to present Stephen's choice as between alternatives equally distinct. The *meaning* of the priesthood to Stephen is concrete enough—'He longed for the minor sacred offices, to be vested with the tunicle of the subdeacon at high mass' (162/184)—for however much he romanticizes the 'voice bidding him approach, offering him secret knowledge and secret power' (162/185), he knows the very feel of the life— 'The trembling odour of the long corridors of Clongowes came back to him and he heard the discreet murmour of the burning gas flames' (164/186). What he is rejecting this *for* cannot be so precisely rendered. It is 'some instinct' which turns him against acceptance, but the burden of detail is on what is being rejected —'the raw reddish glow . . . on the shaven gills of the priests' (164/187). The narrative moves on negative wheels: 'He would never swing the thurible before the tabernacle as priest' (165/188).

The irony of the situation, and Stephen recognizes it, is that the disengagement precedes any definite engagement. The alternative to the Order is 'disorder':

> He smiled to think that it was this disorder, the misrule and confusion of his father's house and the stagnation of vegetable life, which was to win the day in his soul.   (165/188)

The point is brought home a moment later:

> He pushed open the latchless door of the porch and passed through the naked hallway into the kitchen. A group of his brothers and sisters was sitting round the table. Tea was nearly over and only the last of the second watered tea remained in the bottom of the small glass jars and jampots which did service for teacups. Discarded crusts and lumps of sugared bread, turned brown by the tea which had been poured over them, lay scattered on the table. Little wells of tea lay here and there on the board and a knife with a broken ivory handle was stuck through the pith of a ravaged turnover.   (165–6/189)

The 'remorse' which Stephen feels at the sight of this is the emotion by which Ireland—home, fatherland and Church— attempts to keep her own. It is clear to Stephen that if he would go into orders he could rescue his family from this squalor. It was for that, he has been told, he has been educated: 'All that had been denied them had been freely given to him, the eldest' (167/189). It is the 'net' of 'The Sisters' once again.

Towards the end of this chapter Stephen is vouchsafed the vision of the wading girl, who appears as if in reply to his ecstatic choice of vocation:

> This was the call of life to his soul not the dull gross voice of the world of duties and despair, not the inhuman voice that had called him to the pale service of the altar. An instant of wild flight had delivered him. . . .
> His soul had arisen from the grave of boyhood, spurning her graveclothes. Yes! Yes! Yes! He would create proudly out of the freedom and power of his soul, as the great artificer whose name he bore, a living thing, new and soaring and beautiful, impalpable, imperishable. (174/197)

But if 'no word [broke] the holy silence of his ecstasy' (176/200) in her presence, one has but to turn the page to realize that there is still an area of life to which Stephen is attached, as artist and man:

> He drained his third cup of watery tea to the dregs and set to chewing the crusts of fried bread that were scattered near him, staring into the dark pool of the jar. . . . The box of pawn tickets at his elbow had just been rifled. . . .
> —Is your lazy bitch of a brother gone out yet? (177–8/202–3)

That Stephen's latterly presented 'engagement' is merely a flourish imperfectly grafted upon a basically cold and retiring nature is at the root of much uneasiness over Stephen, even among his admirers. To his detractors, the engagement is a 'set-up':

> the exalted instant, emerging at the end of the book, of freedom, of vocation, of Stephen's destiny, winging his way above the waters at the side of the hawk-like man: the instant of promise on which the crushing ironies of *Ulysses* are to fall.[28]

Richard Ellmann goes half the distance here with Hugh Kenner, agreeing that the flight at the *Portrait*'s end is based on an illusory notion, but claiming that the fallen state pictured in *Ulysses* contains a saving grace:

> Flying for Stephen turns out to be paradoxically a lapse from humanity, a failure; while falling is a recognition of life's

49

saving lowliness, a success. . . . Through flying beyond life we learn only our own presumption; through falling into life, even into low life, we educate ourselves into community with others.[29]

Rarely does a critic hold out against seeing the ending as un-ironical. Eugene Waith, writing against the views of Kenner and Caroline Gordon, claims they emphasize 'the theme of the fall while neglecting the theme of creativity'.[30] Waith attempts to relate the two so that 'the fall is assimilated into the preparations for the flight. . . . The flight of Daedalus is not only an escape but a widening of consciousness, an investigation of the unknown'.[31] That what we comprehend under the 'themes' of flight and fall may enter into other relationships Waith does not consider. It is, however, equally likely that fall and flight both increase in scope as the novel proceeds and yet can be regarded as undermining each other.

III

A PORTRAIT OF THE
ARTIST AS A YOUNG MAN:
DRAMA

It was revealed to me that those things are good which yet are
corrupted which neither if they were supremely good nor unless they
were good could be corrupted.
—Stephen Dedalus remembering
St Augustine, *Ulysses* (180/140)

'WELCOME, O LIFE! I go to encounter for the millionth time
the reality of experience' (257/299), Stephen's diary exuber-
antly asserts. The entry echoes an earlier description of Stephen
at Belvedere: 'In vague sacrificial or sacramental acts alone his
will seemed drawn to go forth to encounter reality' (162/184).
Is the verbal echo evidence that Stephen is held fixedly by his
past, the timeless Image of the Aesthete? The qualifications in
the Belvedere passage invite ironical evaluation of Stephen,
especially the adjective 'vague', the alternative 'or', the exclusive 'alone', and the passivity of 'drawn'. The diary, however
definite in its assertion, is itself 'vague' in that it is unencumbered
by such qualifications. If we think that Stephen's character has
altered, we do so by imputation: the kind of life which he is
unconditionally welcoming is not specified.

Let us examine the effect which Joyce's inclusion of condition-
ing factors at this juncture would have had. If they permitted

51

us to view Stephen's final gesture ironically, as the earlier qualifications lead us to view the acolyte's sacerdotalism, the balance of the story would be tilted once for all towards fixity of character in Stephen. Such a 'fixed' finale would add immeasurably to the impetus of reading fixity back into the earlier portions of the novel. By altering his point of view in the last pages of the novel to the direct record of Stephen's diary, Joyce contrives to let up on Stephen at the very end, to *suspend* his irony. On the other hand, the very absence of qualification which follows on the shift from indirect discourse withholds any final approbation from Stephen. If Joyce had qualified favourably the 'life' Stephen welcomes, writing approvingly of the values of, let us say, St Germain-des-Prés, the significance of Dublin as an Enemy of Promise would be lessened by just so much. Dublin would no longer be both a symbol of all constraining and inimical environment and simultaneously the artist's necessary subject, that with which he must come to terms. 'Provincial life' is less of a symbol of environmental frustration in *Middlemarch* by virtue of the discovery of a constituency for Will Ladislaw. Given such a constituency, Middlemarch itself shrinks to a sociological phenomenon which the sensitive must, but can escape. Alternatively, if Joyce had 'conditioned' Stephen's flight from Dublin with a letter from Lady Gregory and a send-off by Yeats, and treated them ironically (as was his wont), we might come more strongly to doubt the value, even the existence of Stephen's 'promise'.*

Joyce made Stephen in many ways less accomplished, less rounded, less cheerful, altogether less appealing than he himself had been.† To have made Stephen stronger would have been to endow him with an inherent and invincible power to stand out against Church, state and family. Stephen's victory would have been merely muscle-flexing, as Christ's in *Paradise Regained* is often claimed to be. To have made him weaker would have been tantamount to an assertion that a hostile environment can ruin a bad poet (or a bad poet gets the environment he deserves), again to the detriment of a dramatic

* After writing the pages in *Ulysses* in which Stephen remembers his Paris trip, Joyce said to Budgen, 'I haven't let this young man off very lightly, have I?' (Frank Budgen, *James Joyce and the Making of Ulysses* [Bloomington, Indiana, 1960], p. 51).

† Compare the 'Sunny Jim' of Ellmann's *James Joyce*, Chs. V-VII (1898–1902).

conflict. The dramatic problem Joyce set himself—in this view —was to poise Stephen, at each point of the way, on an edge between success and failure; to weaken him to the precise point at which he may be taken in by the nets, in order to define how *little* in the way of natural endowment is necessary to retain the possibility of flying by them and how *much* it is possible to have and still be capable of failing. Only this postulates a 'dramatic' mode of action for the novel.

I

The suspension of potentiality and possibility I am calling dramatic—and which Sartre calls 'freedom'—may be located in a wider context than the technique of plotting the book's ending. In the *Portrait* Joyce extended the point of view attributed by Percy Lubbock to Henry James:

> let the book [*The Ambassadors*] stand as the type of the novel in which a mind is dramatized—reflecting the life to which it is exposed, but itself performing its own peculiar and private life. . . . The author does not tell the story of Strether's mind; he makes it tell itself, he dramatizes it.
>
> Thus it is that the novelist pushes his responsibility further and further away from himself. The fiction that he devises is ultimately his; but it looks poor and thin if he openly claims it as his, or at any rate it becomes more substantial as soon as he fathers it upon another.[1]

Lubbock's assumption of the language of James's prefaces is never entirely happy, and there are more explanations for 'dramatization' than the desire to cloak poverty and thinness in substantiality. Dramatization of this sort permits an additional dimension of awareness in James, an opportunity to represent Strether's responses without committing himself to editorial interpretation: *here* is the way Strether sees things, but it is only the way *Strether* sees them.

Lubbock does seem to assume that the words James uses to paraphrase Strether's responses are the words Strether either did use to himself or would have used. The formula 'he was later to think' does show that James was interested in not allowing analysis to go beyond the bounds of what was probable to his character. *Le style indirect libre*, however, logically permits

53

a range of attributions running from (1) the presentation in indirect discourse of what the character said in so many words to himself (or to others) to, (2) what he might have said had he thought to say it, to (3) the kind of thing he might have said, to (4) the *author's* definition in his *own* words of the character's thought or mood.* The fact is, it is extremely difficult to locate precisely any remark on a scale which stretches from Stephen's formulation to Joyce's.

James's dramatization of the mind of Lambert Strether undergoes little alteration in texture in the course of *The Ambassadors*, whatever claims we may make for Strether's widening moral and/or aesthetic vision. Joyce, following his protagonist over a larger span of time, alters his dramatization to imitate Stephen's age. Because of the shifts in narrative style, even the ordinary suppositions we make by attention to the artist's tone become suspect, for Joyce cannot be held wholly 'responsible' for the *tone* of a descriptive passage, while Stephen may not be responsible for the *words* in which it is rendered. The episode which relates Stephen's encounter with the girl wading in a rivulet by the shore presents a clear instance of the problems involved here:

> He felt above him the vast indifferent dome and the calm processes of the heavenly bodies: and the earth beneath him, the earth that had borne him, had taken him to her breast.
>
> He closed his eyes in the languor of sleep. His eyelids trembled as if they felt the vast cyclic movement of the earth and her watchers, trembled as if they felt the strange light of some new world. His soul was swooning into some new world, fantastic, dim, uncertain as under sea, traversed by cloudy shapes and beings. A world, a glimmer, or a flower? Glimmering and trembling, trembling and unfolding, a breaking light, an opening flower, it spread in endless succession to itself, breaking in full crimson and unfolding and fading to palest

* Sartre's comments on 'the ambiguity of the "third person"', are relevant, though his distinction between the character regarded as *subject* and as *object* is so uncalibrated as to be only a rough linguistic tool (Sartre, p. 11ff.). On Joyce's use of *le style indirect libre* see Harry Levin, pp. 136 and 162. 'I do not suppose that Joyce means us to think of Bloom as actually formulating these words in his mind: it is the author's way of conveying in words a vision which on the part of Bloom must have been a good deal less distinct, or at least a good deal less literary, than this . . . we are not, I take it, to suppose that Joyce's hero necessarily frames all these sentences to himself' (Edmund Wilson, *Axel's Castle* [London, 1961], pp. 182, 183).

rose, leaf by leaf and wave of light by wave of light, flooding all the heavens with its soft flushes, every flush deeper than other. (176–7/200–1)

Kenner is certain this is part of a condemnation of Stephen's Pateresque romanticizing.[2] But the style which approximates a close paraphrase of the character's point of view has in Joyce's hands a tendency to pull simultaneously in opposing directions, towards the notation of limitation in Stephen's outlook (and towards parody), and, since the author seems at the moment caught up in his character's version of experience (at least is unwilling to risk another directly), towards raising a sympathetic response. Joyce's technique, like James's in *The Portrait of a Lady*, seems both to support the version of reality present to his major figure and to criticize it, to place it as *only* a version.

As Richard Poirier has written, 'James's tone . . . is above all self-confident. By the moderation of voice in the narrated style . . . James constrains us to habits of response and understanding that make us sympathetic observers of Isabel's career and partisans of the values to which she subscribes'.[3] Further,

> We are to admire Isabel's eager responsiveness . . . while feeling compassionate about the fact that the responses themselves are a function of her innocence. . . . In the effort of James's style to bring about this mixture of reactions, we can observe his desire to keep us from solidifying our attitudes about too un-inclusive a manifestation of character.[4]

James 'places' Isabel, in Poirier's view, by assuming the ironic and knowing 'comic tone' of the Gardencourt society in handling her while he simultaneously puts the most damaging interpretations of her behaviour in the mouths of the most unsympathetic comedy figures. What the ironic social tone achieved for James, the imitative or 'parodic' style did for Joyce: it brings us finally to value the protagonist's effort and simultaneously to hold in judgement the actual products in which particular efforts culminate. James achieved his complexity of vision through the assumption of the voice of a *social milieu*, partly of his own contriving, but social none the less; lacking this *milieu*, Joyce contrived to achieve a like complexity *stylistically*, employing a range of literary 'styles' as a principle of order and of suspension.

Further exposition of Poirier's account of James's *Portrait* can reflect more light on Joyce's. He sees James's novel in terms of a conflict between 'free' and 'fixed' characters, between 'those characters who "express" themselves . . . and those who "represent" something and whose expression is, therefore, theatrical and conventionalized to the point of self-parody'.[5] The conflict is, moreover, mirrored in James's own style, at once ironic and sympathetic. Isabel Archer, who carries James's own values, strives to become—and James strives to see her as—a 'free' character in a *milieu* dominated by 'fixed' characters like Henrietta Stackpole, Mrs Touchett, the Countess Gemeni and most importantly Madame Merle and Gilbert Osmund, all of whose capacities for full human response are submerged in the *rôles* they must play. Since it is precisely her responsiveness and development which James is attempting to keep alive, no one episode can be allowed to epitomise Isabel.[6] It is such a caution I have been exercising in the case of Stephen Dedalus, but logically it is requisite that we further hold even the possibility of epitomization—or absolute typing—in suspension. The view of Hugh Kenner and most symbolist critics is that each episode in Joyce's *Portrait* is an epitome: Stephen-at-nine performs actions which are a perfect reflection of Stephen-as-a-whole. It is, as in James, a question of Stephen's freedom to develop responsively. If he is developing, episodes are not emblems; if he is not, they are.

Poirier concludes that James might have written an even greater novel if he had only developed 'the implication that there can be no such thing as the "freedom" which Isabel wants and which Ralph and James want for her'. Though critical emphasis on this implication would be unfair to 'the experience which the novel offers as a whole', its elaboration by James would have meant that each and every one of Isabel's responses made in the name of the desired 'freedom' could be viewed simultaneously as 'the rationalization of an attempt to escape from . . . the "common passions" ', a rationalization, that is, of 'sexual fear'.[7] Such an Isabel would be poised *between* freedom and fixity, each a possible interpretation. The node of James's attention, to extend Poirier's speculation, would have altered: it would now consider freedom and fixity as permanent and mutually exclusive possibilities, contrary modes of apperception which intersect in the dramatic action.

II

Wyndham Lewis applied to 'the mind of James Joyce' rather than to the mind of Stephen Dedalus the tendency he saw in the *Portrait* towards an elevation of 'timelessness'. He quotes,

Stephanos Dedalos! Bous Stephanoumenos! Bous Stephane-foros!
Their banter was not new to him. . . . Now, as never before, his strange name seemed to him a prophecy. So timeless seemed the grey warm air, so fluid and impersonal his own mood, that all ages were as one to him. $(173/196)^8$

Lewis's use of the concept of time is notoriously confused, and has even, in its application to Joyce, confused his biographer Geoffrey Wagner. Wagner points out Stephen's tendencies towards the static reading of literature, but concludes that it is 'almost inexplicable' that Lewis should have considered Joyce 'the enemy'.[9] Much of the difficulty lies in Lewis's association of *time* with the internal mental life of characters and *space* with the external description of action. His sympathies in *Time and Western Man* are against the former and for the latter: 'I am for the physical world.'[10] Moreover, he does recognize Stephen's tendency—which he calls Joyce's—to shy away from 'the physical world' and turn towards his own mind, a tendency acknowledged in the *Portrait* in a passage which just precedes the one Lewis quotes:

Did he then love the rhythmic rise and fall of words better than their associations of legend and colour? Or was it that, being as weak of sight as he was shy of mind, he drew less pleasure from the reflection of the glowing sensible world through the prism of a language manycoloured and richly storied than from the contemplation of an inner world of individual emotions mirrored perfectly in a lucid supple periodic prose.
 $(171/193-4)$

'Reflection' versus 'contemplation' is a version of naturalism versus symbolism, a problem broached by Joyce as early as the paper on Mangan which he delivered as a university student.[11] The passage later appeared—with significant alterations—in *Stephen Hero:*

The artist, he imagined, standing in the position of mediator between the world of his experience and the world of his

57

dreams. . . . Such a theory might easily have led its deviser
to the acceptance of spiritual anarchy in literature had he not
at the same time insisted on the classical style. . . . [Classicism]
is a temper of security and satisfaction and patience. The
romantic temper . . . is an insecure, unsatisfied, impatient
temper which sees no fit abode here for its ideals and chooses
therefore to behold them under insensible figures. . . . The
classical temper on the other hand, ever mindful of limitations,
chooses rather to bend upon these present things and so to work
upon them and fashion them that the quick intelligence may go
beyond them to their meaning which is still unuttered.

(82–3/77–8)

Stephen favours the classical temper, but is himself faced with
an environment where 'to bend upon these present things'
would result in a naturalism antipathetic to the imaginative
values he cherishes.

What Stephen discovers around him, in both *Stephen Hero*
and the *Portrait*, is an environment hostile to his values, con-
centration on the externals of which (in both space and time)—
as Wyndham Lewis would seem to require—would leave scant
room for the development of those values. Thus, while Stephen
desires experience, he finds himself defeated by experience and
forced to turn in on himself, on his own emotions and ideals,
to preserve his moral and imaginative integrity. For all his
dislike of the 'internals' and the presented consciousness of
characters, Lewis realized the necessity:

There is nothing for it today, if you have an appetite for the
beautiful, but *to create new beauty*. You can no longer nourish
yourself upon the Past; its stock is exhausted, the Past is nowhere
a reality. The only place where it is a reality is in *time*, not
certainly in space. So the mental world of time offers a solution.
More and more it is used as a compensating principle.[12]

Lewis's problem and Stephen's are identical, only they turn
in opposite directions. (I am speaking of the Stephen of the
Portrait, who does not have 'the classical temper' passage.)
Lewis opts for concrete presentation; Stephen hypostasizes a
theory of apprehension which empties the universe of temporal
extension, and he applies his theory both to art and to his
response to the life about him. At the same time, Stephen, like
Lewis, desires the best of both worlds: Lewis wants to concen-

58

trate on 'the physical world' but wants beauty as well, Stephen has the beauty of his aesthetic stases, the 'rhythmic rise and fall of words', but he wants 'experience' of the concrete world as well. The problem is not solved by Stephen in the *Portrait*; it develops. By the end of the novel he has cut himself off from all the *conditions* the representation of which in art would be 'plot'. He is left with no context by which to express imaginative value. He is becoming an artist without a symbol of active, present value.*

Such a progress is no 'sport' in the history of ideas since the Romantic rebellion. It is perhaps an adumbration of the arch-romantic problem, one which all writers have been faced with since the dissolution of the neo-classical hegemony. In neo-classical eras, the deed is taken as fully expressive of the intent. In art, writers have confidence that the event symbolizes fully the value inherent in the character. As a movement, romanticism signals the breakdown of this confidence. The problem of presenting a plot which could be faithful to historical reality and simultaneously exhibit the triumph of value seems to be impossible to writers considering a worsening social situation. Literature moves in two directions, towards naturalism, Pound's 'cult of ugliness', and towards romantic symbolism, Pound's 'cult of beauty'. Nothing exists, in Yeats's words, 'to hold in a single thought reality and justice'.[13] (For Yeats this was the function of his 'gyres', which we incline to see as being more 'just' than 'real', more symbolic than naturalistic.)

Byron's public and artistic careers present parallel cases of this predicament, and perhaps mark its inception in the English scene. He attempted to find in real life some situation for himself where he might realize the inner potential of which he believed himself possessed, and which he came to feel was offered no field of action in England.† Those he sought out,

* Stephen's dilemma is reflected (rather sanguinely) in Ezra Pound's 1913 portrait of 'The Serious Artist': 'the cult of ugliness' is the naturalistic novel, 'diagnosis' of moribund society; 'the cult of beauty', expressed by 'sun, air and the sea and the rain and the lake bathing', is imagist poetry, which presents its material statically, avoiding a temporal dimension in its determination to present beauty (*Literary Essays of Ezra Pound*, ed. T. S. Eliot [London, 1960], p. 45).

† His response to the news of Napoleon's defeat at Waterloo shows Byron's full realization that his political career in England was finished. See *Life, Letters, and Journals of George Ticknor*, ed. George S. Hilliard (Boston, 1876), I, 52.

in Italy and Greece, were to become a proving ground for his potentiality. An 'objective correlative' was precisely what he felt himself to lack, both in life and in art. What artistic 'solution' he made came by the symbolization of the very problem with which he was beset, and one can trace in 'Childe Harold' and *Manfred* an exiled search for a context—a space—susceptible of the implication of imaginative values. These works are *about* attempts and failures to discover such contexts, and therefore allow of a limited perfection unavailable in his personal life. The lack of a so-called objective correlative for his emotion is not a derogation of these works, but precisely their subject. Joyce's portrait of an artist whose favourite poet is Byron* describes the genesis of a situation which by its end faces this major romantic paradox. Literature seems both obligated to and inhibited from fidelity to both the world and to values, to 'reality and justice'.

In this respect, the symbolist movement and Pound's Imagism appear continuous with Romanticism, 'a second flood of the same tide', as Edmund Wilson put it.[14] Value can be preserved by a shrinking of the temporal extension of symbolic action to the presentation of instantaneous 'symbolic' images, where *plot* (duration of time) leads only to naturalism. Pound's manifesto proclaiming the desirability of 'absolute' poetic notation, one image for one emotion, is effectuated only by eliminating the temporal element, coming to view experience, that is, much as Stephen Dedalus does, in terms of moments of *static* apprehension. Artistic achievement under these conditions bifurcates towards the 'deadness' (Henry Miller)[15] of the naturalistic novel or the 'deadness' (Lewis)[16] of the 'timeless' *symboliste* apprehension of reality. There is thus only a single apparent artistic synthesis, a dramatic presentation of the process by which the dilemma comes to pass. For Mark Schorer,

> What has happened to Stephen is, of course, a progressive alienation from the life around him as he progressed in his initiation into it, and by the end of the novel, the alienation is complete. . . . In essence, Stephen's alienation is a denial of the human environment; it is a loss; and the austere discourse of the final section, abstract and almost wholly without sensuous

---

* 'Byron was a heretic and immoral, too.
  —I don't care what he was, cried Stephen hotly' (83/90).

detail or strong rhythm, tells us of that loss. It is a loss so great that the texture of the notation-like prose here suggests that the end is really all an illusion, that when Stephen tells us and himself that he is going forth to forge in the smithy of his soul the uncreated conscience of his race, we are to infer from the very quality of the icy, abstract void he now inhabits, the inplausibility of his aim.[17]

Schorer proceeds from 'suggests' to 'implausibility', gradually sliding into the presentation of Stephen as finally fixed by the novel's last page—for him the diary 'reverts ... to the romantic prose of Stephen's adolescence' and displays 'excessive relaxation'.[18]

Some of the diary entries are, as Schorer notes, romantic, but not all are 'lyrical'. The diary is Stephen's attempt to convert his experience into art, or at least to capture it as prospective material. It becomes for Stephen what Charles Feidelson, writing of Thoreau's, has called 'an autonomous series of visionary events'.[19] Its order is 'fortuitous',[20] but in depending as it does on present event, the diary represents a forward thrust.* Most romantic and 'lyrical' when it concerns the past or the future, it is more spare when notation of the present. This alternation is counterpointed by an oscillation between feelings of freedom and fixity.

Imagining Cranly as 'the precursor' (252/293), he fixes his idea of himself as the Christ. That night, however, he feels free:

> *March 21, night.* Free. Soul free and fancy free. Let the dead bury the dead. Ay. And let the dead marry the dead. (252/293)

The next day he is betrayed into an instinctive reaction which shows him less 'free' than he had assumed:

> *March* 22. In company with Lynch followed a sizeable hospital nurse. Lynch's idea. Dislike it. Two lean hungry greyhounds walking after a heifer. (252/293)

Still, the humorous self-criticism detaches him somewhat.

On April 5th, it is 'O life!', but a day later he is worrying if Emma 'remembers the past' (255/296). Stephen's hope lies

---

* Richard Ellmann considers the diary 'Joyce's first interior monologue' (*James Joyce* [New York, 1959] p. 368) and notes its similarity to Stephen's thought in the first chapters of *Ulysses*.

not in the past, but in the present, and in the present only because of the promise of the future: 'The past is consumed in the present and the present is living only because it brings forth the future' (ibid.). This provokes Stephen's gloss on Yeats's 'Michael Robartes Remembers Forgotten Beauty': Stephen, unlike Robartes, 'desire[s] to press in [his] arms the loveliness which has *not yet come* into the world' (255/297, my italics).[21] Still, the nature of this future, when the claims of the romantic temper ('loveliness') and the classical temper ('the world') will be equally acknowledged, must remain for him indeterminate. The diary carries forward the novel's radical ambiguity.

As dramatic postulation would have Stephen neither hopelessly weak nor pre-eminently strong, so what is here required is as sweeping a personal separation as is possible without assuring the destruction of the value Stephen intends to protect. The action of the novel must occur at just that point at which Stephen's 'indifference' becomes so great that his protective posture endangers his gift: he may separate himself from so much that what is left to protect is inconsequential. Dramatically, the novel arrives at a point where Stephen is forced to hazard everything: 'I do not fear to be alone or to be spurned for another or to leave whatever I have to leave. And I am not afraid to make a mistake, even a great mistake, a lifelong mistake, and perhaps as long as eternity too' (251/292). Stephen's successively broadening disengagement from the life around him is required by the widening circles of force to whose claims on him he becomes awakened, 'my home, my fatherland . . . my church' (251/291). In their last interview, Cranly states the claims of all these, and of 'a mother's love' (246/285). His reaction in the *Portrait* leaves him at the point where it has endangered his gift most drastically, while leaving him the possibility of success; on the other hand, he may have arrived at just the point where he may lose, for 'eternity'. The ambiguity would need to be sustained if drama and human potentiality are to be preserved.

III

Joyce's early essay on Ibsen makes a similar point about both *An Enemy of the People* and *The Master Builder*:

How easy it would have been to have written *An Enemy of the People* on a speciously loftier level—to have replaced the *bourgeois* by the legitimate hero! Critics might then have extolled as grand what they have so often condemned as banal.

A lesser artist would have cast a spiritual glamour over the tragedy of Bygmester Solness.[22]

These remarks imply Joyce's early understanding of a radical form of ambiguity as the core of the 'drama' in Ibsen, that what appears to be 'life' to some characters—as Rubek and Irene in *When We Dead Awaken*, the subject of Joyce's essay—is delusion and death to others, or from another point of view. In the paradoxical treatment of subject, these opposed points of view are not reconciled, nor is one chosen in preference to another; but the full extent of their opposition is exposed.

Some would deny that Ibsen always resisted casting 'a spiritual glamour' over his heroes. G. Wilson Knight feels that 'everything possible is done' in *The Master Builder* and *When We Dead Awaken* 'to show their heroes' death as an extension of living'.[23] In this view Ibsen's romantic, 'spiritualistic'[24] leanings triumph over his more analytic and realistic appraisal of human nature. Joyce, here and in a passage from *Stephen Hero*, apparently felt the absence of such bias in Ibsen, and indeed that the conquering of the conflict between romanticism and realism was Ibsen's great achievement:

> [Stephen] had all but decided to consider the two worlds [of 'sordid' external reality and 'the monster' interior world of romantic idealism and passion] as aliens one to another—however disguised or expressed the most utter of pessimisms—when he encountered through the medium of hardly procured translations the spirit of Henrik Ibsen. He understood that spirit instantaneously. (45/40)

However much Stephen thinks that Ibsen had solved the conflict between romance and reality, Ibsen's own career shows his struggle with the same conflict. What is more, whenever this question has been canvassed in respect of Ibsen, it is the example of Søren Kierkegaard which has provided the terms of definition. In the chapter of his *Life of Ibsen* titled 'The Divided Mind' Halvdan Koht has written,

Even deeper and more bitter is the self-judgement in the longer poem, *On the Fells*, which he wrote . . . toward the close of the year 1859. Here he is in the midst of the crisis, divided between two basic tendencies of his mind, in the conflict between the aesthetic and the ethical view of life. As he himself formulated the contrast, we find the question most clearly and fully expressed in the life philosophy of Søren Kierkegaard, and it is undoubtedly from Kierkegaard that Ibsen has learned to raise the question in this form. This does not mean, however, that it is to Ibsen a mere philosophical theory. On the contrary, it goes down to the deepest depths of his soul, raising a conflict which year after year filled his inner life until the victory was finally won by the stronger element in him, the ethical demand. And still the question recurred in his old age, whether the aesthetic had not after all conquered the ethical.[25]

What the 'basic tendencies' here called 'aesthetic' and 'ethical' refer to will require some exposition of Kierkegaard, whose reputation was being kept alive in the English-speaking world only as footnotes to Ibsen. That they have a relationship to 'romantic' and 'classical', or idealistic and realistic approaches to life is, however, obvious. Koht examined the problem as it appeared to Ibsen in 1859:

> The poem, *On the Fells*, is an exposition of aestheticism as a power that captivates and makes itself master of the mind. Aestheticism is a philosophic view which makes of life a drama, a subject matter for art, while the artist himself remains outside as a mere spectator, or—like the 'Seducer' in Kierkegaard's *Either-Or*—gives impetus to intellectual and emotional conflict, always, be it noted, in others, so that he can himself enjoy the drama fully. The aesthetic view thus robs romanticism of all manly vigour, makes it what the Danish philosopher, Sibbern, describes as 'hollow-eyed'—a way of thinking by which everything is seen as in a mirror and reaches the mind only by reflection.[26]

Brand (1865)—Ibsen's first work after his self-imposed exile from Norway—seemed from the start to hew so close to Kierkegaard's thought that it was often held that its hero was modelled on the philosopher.[27] The 'hardly procured translations' of Ibsen which Stephen read would have included C. H. Hereford's translation of *Brand* (1894), whose introduction quoted from 'Kierkegjaard's' *Either/Or* a passage 'strikingly recall[ing]' Brand and commented, 'This and similar parallels to Brand's thinking led the Danish critics to assume as a matter of course that Brand was intended as a portrait of him: and the idea was widely accepted in Germany'.* Georg Brandes wrote that 'Almost every cardinal idea in this poem is to be found in Kierkegaard'.†

On August 1st, 1899, shortly before the then seventeen-year-old Joyce 'wrote the editor of *The Fortnightly Review*, W. L. Courtney, to ask brashly if he would like a general article on Ibsen's work',[28] the *Fortnightly* published an article titled 'New Lights on Ibsen's "Brand" ', by M. A. Stobart. This article presented the first extensive exposition of the relation between Ibsen's play and Kierkegaard's philosophy to be written in English. (It is perhaps the first exposition of Kierkegaard in English.) Mrs Stobart appears quite conversant with Kierkegaard's *œuvre*, and illustrates it from the Danish texts, covering such major Kierkegaardian topics as the difficulty of the religious struggle, its conflict with mere ethics, the aesthetic, ethical and religious stages of life and their mutual exclusivity (the 'either/or').‡

* *Brand: A Dramatic Poem in Five Acts by Henrik Ibsen*, trans. C. H. Hereford (London: William Heinemann, 1894), p. liii.

† Brandes three 'impressions' of Ibsen were translated into English in 1899: 'To Danes it could not but seem as if Ibsen had had Kierkegaard in mind [when he conceived Brand]. . . . But this misapprehension arose from our having no acquaintance with Ibsen's Norwegian models. From what the poet himself once gave me to understand, I conclude that some such Norwegian dissenting pastor as Lammers had more lot and part in the production of the character of Brand than any directly Danish influence. It must not be forgotten, however, that it was Kierkegaard's agitation that gave the stimulus to Lammers's course of action' (*Henrik Ibsen; Bjornstjerne Bjornson*, trans. Jessie Muir and Mary Morison, revised with an Introduction by William Archer [London, 1899], pp. 70–1). See also Henrik Jaeger, *The Life of Henrik Ibsen*, trans. Clara Bell, with the verse done into English from the Norwegian by Edmund Gosse (London: William Heinemann, 1890), pp. 155–6: 'Danish critics, among them Brandes, followed by the majority of German critics who have written on Ibsen within the last few years, have connected Brand with Søren Aabye Kierkegaard.'

‡ *The Fortnightly Review*, n.s. 66 (August 1st, 1899), pp. 227–39. There is every reason to believe that Joyce was an avid reader of the journal which published, among much else, Yeats, George Moore, 'Fiona Macleod' and others of the Celtic Revival, Arthur Symons (including the essays later to become *The Symbolist Movement in Literature*), essays on Wagner and continental philosophers and dramatists.

Mabel Annie (Boulton) Stobart (1862–1954) wrote under the name Mrs St Clair Stobart. After the death of St Clair Stobart she married John Stobart Greenhalgh. There is a notice of her in *Who Was Who*, 1951–1960. She died December 7th, 1954.

Stobart's article on Kierkegaard and Ibsen hoped to win readers to a study of Kierkegaard,

> a philosopher whose writings, outside the British Isles, already hold a high place in the esteem of the literary world. It would be not uninteresting to discuss the reasons for the neglect with which Kierkegaard has hitherto been treated by English readers, but this article will have attained a twofold object should it—in addition to the possible fulfillment of its primary motive [to illustrate *Brand* from Kierkegaard]—be the means of inducing any to turn in curiosity to a writer whose works may be with truth—as Dr Georg Brandes is agreed—be described as unparalleled in Danish literature for force, strength, and purity of ideal.[29]

In coming shortly to a 'Kierkegaardian analysis' of Joyce's *Portrait* and *Ulysses*, I will refer to the particular notions Joyce would have met in Stobart's essay, but whether Joyce did 'turn in curiosity' to Kierkegaard himself remains unknown.

There is only one tantalizing remark in *Stephen Hero* dangled before us. When Stephen 'encountered . . . the spirit of Henrik Ibsen', he began 'to study Danish instead of preparing his course for the examination and this fact was magnified into a report that he was a competent Danish scholar' (46/41). This Danish study is begun, apparently, in Stephen's second year at university (1899–1900), but near the end of his fourth and last year (1901–2), in a conversation with Lynch which has no counterpart in the *Portrait*, Stephen says, 'I was walking along the Canal with my Danish grammar (because I am going to study it properly now. I'll tell you why later on)' (239/233). We never learn why Stephen has resumed the study of Danish, long after being made free of Ibsen, as the *Stephen Hero* manuscript breaks off half a page later (p. 902 of the manuscript), before the conversation with Lynch has returned to Stephen's promise.* In the January 1st, 1902, issue of the *Fortnightly*, Mrs

---

* This is Chapter XXVI. Joyce could not have written much more of *Stephen Hero*. Ellmann says Joyce 'bogged down after Chapter XXV' (op. cit., p. 231), in the spring of 1906. He did not work on the manuscript during his abortive stay in Rome (July 31st, 1906– March 7th, 1907), wrote 'The Dead' in Trieste into the autumn of 1907 and began revising *Stephen Hero* immediately after he finished the short story (ibid., p. 274).

While in Rome Joyce spent badly needed money on Danish lessons from a man named Pedersen (ibid., p. 244) and wrote on February 11th, 'I have a new

Stobart published a second article on Kierkegaard, 'The "Either/Or" of Søren Kirkegaard',[30] which elaborates the paradox of the mutual exclusiveness of the aesthetic and ethical existences (with a tendency to sympathize more with the aesthetic) and touches on two other themes—again, both in respect of *Brand*—which will need development in the context of Joyce's work: (1) 'Kirkegaard [said], in words that Ibsen has vitalized in dramatic concepts, "the great thing in life is not to be this or that, but to be one's self; and everyone who *chooses* can be this" '; and (2) the relation of the hero to his mother is a symbol of the past and of the pressure of heredity: 'the Aesthetic Brand, who makes it his work of life to "blot out his mother's debt of sin".'[31]

Ibsen's *Brand* is well qualified to be the work which united the two worlds for Stephen. It appears to have produced an equal (if equally temporary) 'sense of jubilation' in Ibsen himself, whose reputation was made overnight—like Byron's with 'Childe Harold'—by it:

> while writing *Brand*, he had felt as if he were taking part in strife and action, and there had been a sense of jubilation within him. Writing this drama gave an outlet to the thoughts that tormented his soul.[32]

In reviewing *When We Dead Awaken*, Joyce makes incidental reference to 'the will-glorification of *Brand*', and it is interesting that this phrase hews so close to Stobart's exposition of the Kierkegaardian basis of Brand's character—more eccentric on the matter of 'Will-evolution' than elsewhere—as possibly to constitute an allusion for readers of *The Fortnightly Review*.[33]

While *Brand* (1866) is the focus, both in the years after it was published in Denmark, Germany and England and now, for the relation of Ibsen and Kierkegaard,[34] earlier and later Ibsen plays have been seen in Kierkegaardian terms. *Love's Comedy* (1862) has been related to Kierkegaard's paradoxical view of marriage.[35] Early in 1900, *The Fortnightly Review* published 'A Scene from Ibsen's "Love's Comedy" ', translated, with commentary, by Hereford. The whole was published later in the year. To upstage his friends, 'When they evinced an

hat and boots and vests and socks and a Danish book and Georgie has a new coat and hat and I gave a dinner. Now when you get this you will have to send me 10 crowns' (ibid., p. 249). 'You' was Stanislaus.

interest in Ibsen's thought, [Joyce] responded by discoursing instead on the technique, especially of lesser known plays like *Love's Comedy*.[36]

Just as some, like Stobart, have seen a Kierkegaardian *Brand* as wholly paradoxical—unethical from one point of view, spiritual* from another—and others have emphasized one or the other aspect, a similar group of opinions clusters around Ibsen's next work, *Peer Gynt* (1867):

> it would not be very far beside the mark to see in Peer Gynt the tragic consequences of not being a Kierkegaardian. Peer Gynt is obviously one whom Kierkegaard would think a base creature for remaining unmoved in the 'aesthetic *stadium* [or stage], carefully 'going round about' when an opportunity presents itself to qualify for the 'ethical *stadium*'. . . .
>
> The kernel of the thought implied in *Peer Gynt* is not only a Kierkegaardian notion, but even phrased in the language of Kierkegaard. Over and over again, the Danish moralist insisted on the vital importance for every man to 'be himself' ('væresig selv').[37]

Richard Ellmann has recorded his puzzlement over Joyce's notion, when in the autumn of 1907 he was revolving the idea of the book which was to become *Ulysses* in his mind, of a Dublin *Peer Gynt*:

> On November 10 [1907] Stanislaus noted in his diary: 'Jim told me that he is going to expand his story "Ulysses" into a short book and make a Dublin "Peer Gynt" of it. I think that some suggestion of mine put him in the way of making it important. As it happens in one day, I suggested he should make a comedy of it, but he won't. It should be good. . . . ' In what sense *Ulysses* was to be a *Peer Gynt* is not altogether clear, except that the hero was to sample all aspects of Dublin life. How he could be at once the clear-eyed Ulysses and the self-deceived Peer Gynt is also unexplained.[38]

* While Stobart understood the nature of categorical paradox, there seems to be a suggestion in the article that Brand represents an aesthetic/ethical conflict rather than an ethical/religious one, and that Brand asserts the superiority of the aesthetic. Arne Garborg thought this too, and wrote, '*Brand* is ideally what Kierkegaard wanted the man of his day to be in reality. Herein lies the way of escape. The absolute ethical demand is translated into aestheticism; thereby its sting is broken.' This is bad Kierkegaard, but seems to have had some credence.[39]

Joyce, in 1903, thought *Peer Gynt* the 'masterpiece' of Ibsen's 'romantic' period, 'recognizing its own limitations and pushing lawlessness to its extreme limit'. He has just caught up, in his review of *Catilina*, the distinction between the classical and romantic tempers broached in the essay on Mangan and which found its way into *Stephen Hero*, and he uses it to distinguish 'between Ibsen's earlier manner and his later manner, between romantic work and classical work'.[40] *Peer Gynt* ends the romantic period, perhaps by facing its character with the Kierkegaardian 'absolute paradox' of stages. Joyce's notion of a Dublin *Peer Gynt* followed closely on his beginning to rewrite *Stephen Hero* 'in five chapters—long chapters',[41] and the Peer Gynt of the novel may apply to Stephen as well as to 'Hunter' (later Bloom), both of whom may be defined in terms of the Kierkegaardian crisis-states.

IV

Analysis in Kierkegaardian terms, to describe the protagonist's state of mind (and 'being'), his basic difficulty and attempts at its solution, and a certain paradox of presentation which comprises the literary mode of expression, illuminates the case of Stephen Dedalus. Kierkegaard's formulation of the 'aesthetical' character forms a close analogy to Stephen's psychological situation. Stephen, in the *Portrait*, runs the course of Kierkegaard's aesthetic mode. The aesthete attempts to turn all his experience to artistic account, finally, that is, to make of his life a work of art. For treating his experience as aesthetic experiment, he is upbraided by the representative of the ethical life, Kierkegaard's Judge William ('B'), who simultaneously points out the static and 'epiphanic' nature of the apprehension entailed:

> since it is likely that in real life you will find very little that is beautiful if you strictly apply the requirements of art, you give another meaning to the beautiful. The beautiful about which you talk is the individually beautiful. You view every particular man as a tiny factor or moment of the whole, you view him precisely in his characteristic peculiarity, and thus even the accidental, the insignificant, acquires significance, and life has the impress of beauty. So that you regard every particular man as a moment.

. . . If there is to be any question of teleology *there must be a movement.* . . . What you call beautiful manifestly lacks movement. . . . you require movement, history, and with this you have passed beyond the spheres of nature and of art and are in the sphere of freedom and of ethics.[42]

Thus, in the 'ethical' view, aesthetics and freedom are mutually exclusive. Freedom requires choice, and 'A' has a basic indifference to alternatives. For him, all things are equally thinkable and none preferable, nor does he feel the possibility of change: his soul 'has lost its potentiality. If I were to wish to anything, I should not wish for wealth and power, but for the passionate sense of the potential, for the eye which, ever young and ardent, sees the possible'.[43]

This artist-type's most abiding passion is an antagonism towards the 'ethical', burgher class who have jobs, marry and get on. But as 'B' maintains, 'A's' own life seems to play itself out since it does not contain within itself any principle of continuity and expansion. The discreteness of his existence is admitted by 'A' in a grammatical parable:

My life is absolutely meaningless. When I consider the different periods into which it falls, it seems like the word *Schnur* in the dictionary, which means in the first place a string, in the second, a daughter-in-law. The only thing lacking is that the word *Schnur* should mean in the third place a camel, in the fourth, a dust-brush.[44]

A's own epitome of the aesthetic character is Mozart's Don Juan, who 'constantly finishes, and constantly begins again from the beginning, for his life is the sum of repellent moments which have no coherence. . . .'[45] The ambivalent relation between his life and his art is clear from another diary entry:

My grief is my castle, which like an eagle's nest, is built high up on the mountain peaks among the clouds. Nothing can storm it. From it I fly down into reality to seize my prey; but I do not remain down there, I bring it home with me, and this prey is a picture I weave into the tapestries of my palace. There I live as one dead. . . .[46]

This type of personality, unlike the 'ethical' with which it is contrasted, is confessedly 'static': 'Time stands still', the Kierkegaardian aesthete writes of himself in his aphoristic diary, 'and I with it'.[47] 'A's' diary makes clear his lack of a feeling of continuity and change:

> The result of my life is simply nothing, a mood, a single colour. My result is like the painting of the artist who was to paint a picture of the Israelites crossing the Red Sea. To this end, he painted the whole wall red, explaining that the Israelites had already crossed over, and that the Egyptians were drowned.[48]

Kierkegaard's aesthetic type and Stephen Dedalus have a similar dynamic of personality, and a tendency to view their own experience in similar lights. They characterize this experience by notions of repetition and endless cyclic movement in which *they see* no possibility of development. (See, for example, the 'endless reverberation' and 'recurrent note of weariness and pain' [*Portrait*, 168/190].) Simultaneously their view of beauty commits them to a formulation which lifts it *out of time*. Yet they are not willing to relax their grip totally on the world of experience as the subject-matter of their art. Nevertheless, both cut themselves off progressively from the ordinary life of the community, leaving them as their 'subject' only the process of severance or the adumbration of their feelings in isolation, and they waver between formal aesthetic presentation and 'excessive lyrical relaxation', to use Mark Schorer's words.*

Volume I of *Either/Or* is devoted to the aesthetic view; Volume II is the ethical 'review' of the first volume and is prefaced with a quotation from Chateaubriand: '*Les grandes passions sont solitaires, et les transporter au désert, c'est les rendre à leur empire.*' Just so by the end of the *Portrait* has Stephen been cut off, and though it may have been necessary for him to do so, the position entails certain limitations. Any further progression lies beyond the pages of the novel. For Stephen in the *Portrait* has not yet been confronted with the ethical alternative—that is what happens in *Ulysses*:

> it becomes clear to us, if not to Stephen Dedalus, not simply that his first conception [of the task before him] is inadequate

---

* See, in *Either/Or*, Vol. I, the difference in tone between the analytical 'The Ancient Tragical Motif' and the 'lyrical' 'Diary of the Seducer' (which Mrs Stobart praised in 1902 as 'the literary gem of Kirkegaard's masterpiece').[49] Both modes are often present alternately in a single essay. Kierkegaard himself functioned most freely when alternating analysis and lyricism. Vol. II of *Either/Or*, the presentation of the 'ethical case', deliberately eschews the lyrical and is one of his dullest works stylistically.

but that with experience and growth Stephen will find it inadequate himself . . . what [the aesthetic theory in the *Portrait*] leaves out [is] precisely the moral responsibilities Stephen has still to learn that his vocation entails. . . . Stephen's militant Aestheticism and its collapse under the pressure of the social conditions and beliefs he had violently rejected, was a symbol such as Ibsen might have used.[50]

Kierkegaard, however, having divided the human character into the two nodal types of personality, aesthetical and ethical, hesitated to assign to any one person the abstract qualities of the type, and in so doing elevated the problem to the fuller paradoxical level. This 'existential' recognition first forces itself upon the ethical spokesman, in Volume II of *Either/Or*:

That a man may thus suffer damage to his soul is certain; how far such is the case with the particular individual can never be determined, and let no man venture on this point to judge another. A man's life may appear strange, and one may be tempted to believe that such is the case with him, and yet he may possess an entirely different interpretation which assures him of the contrary.[51]

This view is of course correlative to Kant's insistence that morality can be judged by intention only, not by effects;* a romantic ethic, certainly, called out when men feel their values thwarted by the social nexus. Kierkegaard used this transcendentalizing insight more systematically in *Fear and Trembling*, where the burden of his argument is: I do not know what motivated the historical Abraham to offer up Isaac at God's command, but if he was acting 'religiously', his motivation would have to be as follows. Denomination of motive withdraws into the subjunctive mood; a particular motive cannot be assigned to a particular character definitely. The philosopher only says *if* he acted from a particular motive, *then* the meaning of his action is such and such.†

Stephen's view of his own experience, as it develops in the *Portrait of the Artist*, projects a Kierkegaardian aesthetical

* 'Truth for Kierkegaard, lies in Subjectivity alone. "Subjectiviteten, Inderligheden er Sandheden." Objective faith, objective works, are of no avail. To *will*, not do, the good, is all important' (Stobart, 'New Lights', p. 228).

† For claiming that the Pope could condemn heresy abstractly, but had no power to decide whether the particular heresy was lodged in a particular work, the followers of Jansen were declared heretics.

trajectory, a subjectivist interpretation in which outer events serve merely to display basic unchanging characteristics in a permanent and static complex. This is not, however, the only possible understanding of the nature of his experience. It calls into being, logically, an alternative view which is a permanent complementary possibility in the interpretation of the action. We may not be able to adjudicate in a particular instance whether Stephen Dedalus is *really* 'fixed' or 'free'. In the absence of a definitive judgement by Joyce, we are forced to carry the alternative explanations forward to the novel's end, to maintain what Kierkegaard called 'dialectical suspense'. They are equally possible interpretations at each stage of Stephen's career and one's full understanding of *A Portrait of the Artist as a Young Man* depends upon our ability to perceive and sustain the nature of the paradox and contrasting alternatives it presents.

IV

ULYSSES: STYLES

I understand that you may begin to regard the various styles of the
episodes with dismay and prefer the initial style much as the wanderer
did who longed for the rock of Ithaca.

—Joyce to Harriet Shaw Weaver,
August 6th, 1919 (*Letters,* p. 129)

THE CRITICISM OF *Ulysses,* like that of *A Portrait,* subdivides cleanly in respect of Joyce's attitude towards his major
characters and towards the *direction* in which they are assumed
to be heading. The direction of the plot, the end to which it
apparently moves, is often assumed to be the most telling
means of assessing the characters, for by it is constituted a
judgement on them *by their world,* and not immediately by their
author. Thus we might expect the 'end' of *Ulysses* to have
become a moot issue, and William Schutte's review of the
various attitudes critics have taken to Stephen and Bloom's
meeting alone proves it has.[1]

Kierkegaardian categories help arrange the critical responses.
Stephen is 'liked' by those who feel he is moving from his
'aesthetic' phase into an ethical one, in which he gains sympathy
with the common life of mankind from his contact with
Leopold Bloom. He is disliked by those who think—with,
say, Hugh Kenner—that he is fixed in the aesthetic mode of
experience.

Bloom's detractors think him fixed in the ethical mode,
albeit unhappily. His today was as his yesterday and is the

prevision of his tomorrow. There, as here, he will be doggily humane and equally ineffectual, his ghosts unexorcized. Bloom's supporters—Ellmann would, I suppose, be the most prominent example—find Bloomsday a crucial turning-point for Bloom. In it he transits from the purely bourgeois ethical existence into the category of the 'religious'. He accepts; he becomes resigned. Here, the meeting with Stephen is perhaps a contributory event, but Bloom's crisis is his response to Blazes Boylan and the adultery which occurs at four o'clock in the afternoon:

> With what antagonistic sentiments were his subsequent reflections affected?
> Envy, jealousy, abnegation, equanimity.   (864/717)

The first two are in the realm of the ethical the true Kierke-gaardian aesthete would feel no such breathing human passions. But the final two *may* belong to another realm entirely. The context which in the text helps define 'abnegation' and 'equanimity' does not shut the door on speculation. In each case varying and 'exclusive' meanings are given to the terms.*

I will continue to emphasize the 'religious' possibility, as it is generally more slighted, while logically it is required as an equal counterweight.

Bloom's newly found 'equanimity' is, I think importantly, not handled quite as ironically by Joyce as are the catechistical responses to the three previous terms, where, for example, Bloom's desire to cash in on Molly's projected 'provincial musical tour' is listed alongside less disreputable reasons for 'abnegation'. His feelings of equanimity arise from reflecting that the adultery was 'natural', 'not as calamitous as a cataclysmic annihilation of the planet', 'less reprehensible than theft, highway robbery, cruelty to children and animals [etc., etc.]', 'As more than inevitable, irreparable' (864/717–18). This sentiment dies away and is replaced by others 'antagonistic' (864/717) to it, but neither the statistical norm of Bloom's thoughts nor their 'curve' are the same as the meaning of the action and a possibility has been planted.

---

* By exclusive is meant that any one but not the others could be, indeed must have been the true explanation; or, that the terms we use to describe such actions are too imprecise and cut, in their definitions, across the integral whole of meaning.

The defence of Bloom cannot be conducted on the ethical plane. Those who find him unsatisfactory (as a man, not a literary creation, which is another matter) judge his resignation merely a rationalization, a self-delusion. They hold him, that is, to the ethical level, on which he is a failure. Those who accept the resignation as a responsible gesture in the face of reality move him on to a quasi-religious plane of existence.

Kierkegaard's 'knight of faith' has many of the outward line-aments of a Bloom. 'Having made the movements of infinity' (that is, of 'infinite resignation'), faith 'makes those of finite-ness'.[2] Having given up all expectations ('by virtue of the absurd' in all existence), they are entitled to return to the everyday world:

> The knights of the infinite resignation are easily recognized: their gait is gliding and assured. Those on the other hand who carry the jewel of faith are likely to be delusive, because their outward appearance bears a striking resemblance to that which both the infinite resignation and faith profoundly despise ... to Philistinism.
>
> I candidly admit that in my practice I have not yet found any reliable example of the knight of faith, though I would not therefore deny that every second man may be such an example. ... As was said, I have not found any such person, but I can well think him. Here he is. ... 'Good Lord, is this the man? Is it really he? Why, he looks like a tax-collector!' However, it is the man after all. ... I examine his figure from tip to toe to see if there might not be a cranny through which the infinite was peeping. No! He is solid through and through. ... [He] belongs entirely to the world, no Philistine more so. ... He takes delight in everything he sees, in the human swarm, in the new omnibuses, in the water of the Sound; when one meets him on the Beach Road one might suppose he was a shop-keeper taking his fling, that's just the way he disports himself, for he is not a poet, and I have sought in vain to detect in him the poetic incommensurability. ... As it happens, he hasn't four pence to his name. ... On the way he comes past a building site and runs across another man. They talk together for a moment. In the twinkling of an eye he erects a new building, he has at his disposition all the powers necessary for it. ... [He] is interested in everything that goes on, in a rat which slips under the curb, in the children's play, and this with the nonchalance of a girl of sixteen. And yet he is no

genius, for in vain I have sought in him the incommensurability of genius.[3]

Again, on the ethical plane Bloom is merely condoning adultery, sin or shabbiness. His rescue is attempted only after the example of Kierkegaard. For Kierkegaard, Abraham's offer to sacrifice Isaac, considered ethically, was a sin, 'for the ethical had for Abraham no higher expression than the family life'[4]; but considered religiously, it was right.

If Kierkegaard is interested in the creation of categories, he is, when he comes to discuss human beings, even more interested in those who exist in border-states, 'between' categories. That is, he devotes his attention to those who may be moving from one to another. He has a high sense of the difference between abstraction—characters invented to fit categories—and existentiality—'real' characters who give every appearance of being in either of two categories. Allegorical characters are definite and fixed; real ones most often permit of a dual, and opposed interpretation.

A description similar to this one of Kierkegaard's 'knight' has been applied to Bloom by Father Noon, who proceeds to apply Kierkegaard's definition of irony to *Ulysses*.[5] Let us note in our context that 'irony' is the mode which Kierkegaard applies to the boundary between the aesthetical and the ethical, while 'humour' applies to that between the ethical and the religious.[6] The Kierkegaardian ironical mode—which Noon calls 'specifically Christian satire'[7]—could best be applied to the parts of *Ulysses* concerned with Stephen alone. Humour, which Noon finds lacking in the novel, is more the mode of approach to Bloom.

This suggests that a critical synthesis, rather than a particular determination among already existent views, is to be sought. We need not dismiss, in the main, any of the major critical positions which have been taken up, if we argue that Stephen and Bloom, being 'real' in the context of the fiction, exist not as illustrations of particular categories, but as border-figures. As such, they are *either* figures moving from one condition to another *or* fixed in one realm. Further, either one of these two possibilities may be true or it may be our own modes of analysis which so divide experience in itself unitary. The novelist, working from the *outside*, must create the whole possibility and

77

need not determine which of these things is finally *true* of his characters. In fact, he would wish to prevent us from being able to say, being as interested in creating the whole structure of possible meanings, with its particular internal dialetic, as in deciding which of the possibilities to make true in the individual case. Diagrammatically, *Ulysses* appears like this:

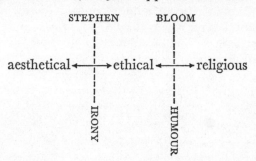

Kierkegaard later complained that the picture he had given of the 'knight' in *Fear and Trembling* was presented 'in a state of completeness [i.e. as an allegorical figure] and hence in a false medium, instead of in the medium of existence'.[8] In the medium of existence, the picture demands *incompleteness*— that is to say, radical ambiguity. Such a presentation, in the words of Reuben Brower commenting on the 'double vision' of *A Passage to India*, 'enjoys to the full the freedom of giving varied and even opposite meanings' to the action of the novel.[9] If *Ulysses* is such a presentation, we do not wish to strike through the mask to discover which of the alternatives is right, we wish to enjoy the drama of the alternatives.

To consider next the way Joyce has created these alternatives, will also adumbrate the particular ontological status of the action and characters in *Ulysses*.

The first six chapters of *Ulysses* excite no especial concern in us respecting differences between the ways in which the protagonists, Dedalus and Bloom, perceive their worlds and the ways in which we ourselves might be assumed to perceive it had we been present at the scene. The style 'indirectly free' at the beginning of the novel will modulate into something different, what Ellmann calls 'the undependable narrator'.[10] But for six chapters it is not undependable, and for a purpose.

78

When the voice of the narrator is a mimic of his characters—
a systematization of a possibility always latent in indirect
discourse—it is, as already discussed, extremely difficult to make
definitive descriptions. Any particular instance not part of
actual dialogue may be Stephen thinking, Joyce describing
Stephen thinking, Joyce describing how Stephen might have
thought, or some indeterminate state between these. The
method is not, of course, original in Joyce, nor is its systematic
application, which is to be found, for instance, in *The Ambassadors*. A single passage taken from the first chapter of *Ulysses*
can be used to illustrate it and also to suggest the purpose which
the technique has in respect of the whole:

> Stephen, an elbow rested on the jagged granite, leaned
> his palm against his brow and gazed at the fraying edge of
> his shiny black coatsleeve. Pain, that was not yet the pain of
> love, fretted his heart. Silently, in a dream she [his mother] had
> come to him after her death, her wasted body within its loose
> brown graveclothes giving off an odour of wax and rosewood,
> her breath, that had been bent upon him, mute, reproachful,
> a faint odour of wetted ashes. Across the threadbare cuffedge
> he saw the sea hailed as a great sweet mother by the wellfed
> voice beside him. The ring of bay and skyline held a dull green
> mass of liquid. A bowl of white china had stood beside her
> deathbed holding the green sluggish bile which she had torn
> up from her rotting liver by fits of loud groaning vomiting.
>
> (4/7)

Though there is no indication, one can only assume that
Stephen had some thought of the 'bowl of white china',
however *wordless* it might have been. The rhythms, which here
shape indigestible material rhetorically to the point at which
they assume a *fin-de-siècle* beauty, may belong to Stephen or to
Joyce or to both in common. More importantly, while this
indeterminateness invites a suspension of judgement, it is
never broken, suggesting the existence of a real action being
filtered through a particular consciousness. It is to the establishment of this real action as a substructure which will lie beneath the
technical presentations to follow that the first chapters function.

The introduction of Bloom in the fourth chapter alters our
expectation radically. It is, in all but pagination, a new beginning to the novel. The fourth, fifth and sixth chapters retrace

79

the first, second and third in time (one and four, 8 a.m.; two and five, 10 a.m.; three and six, 11 a.m.) and this is the only time in the novel which such chronological retracing occurs. It has, in fact, to be *avoided* elsewhere, when Stephen and Bloom are not together, and the decision to omit Stephen's day at 1 p.m. (when Bloom is seeking lunch), 4, 5, and 8 p.m. (Bloom at the Ormond, Barney Kiernan's and at the beach) is deliberately taken.

The fourth, fifth and sixth chapters do over what the first three had done. Joyce adjusts his own tone (however much one can ascribe directly to him) to suit Bloom. Bloom's rhythms, his syntax, his vocabulary all differ significantly from Stephen's. Again, a passage can illustrate:

> Gentle sweet air blew round the bared heads in a whisper. Whisper. The boy by the gravehead held his wreath with both hands staring quietly in the black open space. Mr Bloom moved behind the portly kindly caretaker. Well cut frockcoat. Weighing them up perhaps to see which will go next. Well it is a long rest. Feel no more. It's the moment you feel. Must be damned unpleasant. Can't believe it at first. Mistake must be: someone else. Try the house opposite. Wait, I wanted to I haven't yet. Then darkened bedchamber. Light they want. Whispering around you. Would you like to see a priest? Then rambling and wandering. Delirium all you hid in your life. The death struggle. His sleep is not natural. Press his lower eyelid. Watching is his nose pointed is his jaw sinking are the soles of his feet yellow. . . . People talk about you a bit: forget you. Don't forget to pray for him. Remember him in your prayers. Even Parnell. Ivy day dying out. Then they follow: dropping into a hole one after the other. (139–40/109)

Stephen's meditation on death had been centripetal: all day he will be haunted by the deathbed scene.[11] All things conspire to remind him of it: Dublin Bay becomes the white china bowl at the bedside holding the 'green sluggish bile'. (It is interesting to note that the symbolic 'correspondence' is a function of an anxiety-state.) Stephen's mind cannot move forward—it can only circle round and round, to perch at last on the ghastly memory. Bloom, on the other hand, knows that 'people'—if not Stephen—do forget. His attitude permits even humour over the thought of the deathbed, where the dying man cries out to Death, 'Mistake must be: someone else. Try the house opposite'. Bloom's mind here can move forward, noting details carefully, arranging a little drama, concluding with a reflection on the transitoriness of grief, a reflection which incidentally does not encompass the Stephen Dedaluses of the world. Bloom of course has had his own point of repair, which turns his otherwise linear, though not passive, flow of consciousness inward: Molly's tryst with Boylan.

But here I am interested primarily in pointing the magnitude of the difference between points of view on which Joyce insists. For three chapters we follow Stephen, at the Martello Tower in Sandycove, at Deasy's, along Sandymount Strand, until the rhythms of his mind, his way of looking at things, are firmly present to us. Joyce abets this effect by consistently aping his character's own mode of apprehension. These first three chapters give us a norm for Stephen. They involve us in the postulation of a real and human action for *Ulysses*. The introduction of Bloom does not detract from this postulation, but submits us to an awareness of an equal and opposite apprehension, another way of looking at what is by now assumed to be going on. Had both Stephen and Bloom been introduced, antiphonally, into the first chapter—or, further, had any of the technical experimentation with narration been introduced at that point—the effect would have been far different. (Nabokov's lightning shifts of the substantive level in certain of his novels have the effect of attenuating the credibility of any primary level.)

Only with the existences of Stephen and Bloom clearly established does Joyce begin, in the seventh chapter, the systematic exploitation of technical experimentation in his narrative.* But the major arbitrary narrative intrusions—the newspaper headlines, the illustrations of rhetorical devices, the

---

* The 'flower' motifs of Chapter Five are almost unique in this respect. They were added between periodical publication and the final text. It is difficult for someone who knows that they were added to comment on how far they stick out in the final version. That they should not seem to emanate from a source other than Bloom's consciousness [or Joyce's redaction of it] I would think desirable. The method of accretion to his text which Joyce followed sometimes makes Bloom seem a more *abstracted* man from his surroundings than he did in the earlier version. This can be seen, I think, in the passage quoted on p. 80, where 'Try the house opposite' through 'yellow . . .' and 'Don't forget to pray' through 'Ivy day dying out' are additions.

'wind' motif—however obvious and prepossessing they now are, were also added after the first publication in the *Little Review* for October 1918. Thus they are not as integral to the chapter as certain of the tehniques to follow—'Circe' cannot be imagined apart from its technique—and the chapter forms a kind of half-way stage between what has preceded and what is to come. In it we may read the continuing human action, in which the events in Dublin are a *mimesis*, behind the narrative presentation. Besides the sixty-three newspaper titles, which, as has been noticed, generally reproduce a history of titles from 'dignified' Victorian to modern 'slickness',[12] there are passages like the following:

> Under the porch of the general post office shoeblacks called and polished. Parked in North Prince's street His Majesty's vermillion mailcars, bearing on the sides the royal initials, E.R., received loudly flung sacks of letters, postcards, lettercards, parcels, insured and paid, for local, provincial, British and overseas delivery. (147–8/115)

This is, of course, neither Bloom's stream of consciousness nor any analogous representation of it. The voice is 'Joyce's', and while it appears at times to combine the rhythms of Stephen with the observation of Bloom, it is capable of shading into various parody languages, such as *no human voice* would speak: the non-human voices of public notices, bills of lading, legal writ.

The newspaper titles are also an example of the non-human voice, in so far as their *origin* is not vocal. While figures of speech and 'wind' allusions are generally worked into the dialogue, and ideally, one might suppose, would not stand out, functioning equally as part of the human action, I doubt if this is the experience of most readers. They do call attention to themselves, which makes 'fusion' of symbolist techniques and human action a practical failure I cannot help but think part of the book's meaning. We experience both reactions, and keep them distinct. It is one of a large number of instances in which the book forces us to keep separate the way it talks about things and the things it is talking about.

More important, for example, than the notation of the particular rhetorical figure being employed at any one moment is the recognition that the symbolist techniques in *Ulysses*, with which Joyce has had little to do for six chapters, begin in 'Aeolus' to gather head, initiating a process by which we are to be progressively *detached* from the mimetic action of the novel, from the primacy of the Dublin scene. But because of the preparation we do not thereby reject the reality of that scene; though the events may come to be described in hallucinatory terms, we do not therefore assume that the dead really walk in the Dublin of 1904. Though a chapter is written entirely in clichés, we do not believe that the characters spoke entirely in clichés. The opening chapters—and there are strategic returns to their styles, to remind us of the *real* Stephen and the *real* Bloom—have predisposed us to assume we are reading about '*an action* at a *real* place at a *real* time',[13] and so we assign the symbolist techniques entirely to the narrative voice. In this way *Ulysses* can incorporate surrealism without becoming (in its entirety) a surrealistic fantasy.

We begin, in Chapter Seven, to grasp that the words (and techniques) of *Ulysses* stand between us and the Dublin action. The voice which is speaking to us for much of the time is speaking about that action, but it is not representing that action. There is a deliberately played-on gap between the narrative styles and the material which is their subject.

The eighth ('Lestrygonians') and ninth ('Scylla and Charybdis') chapters return us to the styles of the first six chapters, reacquainting us with the 'styles' of first Bloom and then Stephen. (It was perhaps the problem of what to do when both, or neither, figured in one chapter, which suggested to Joyce the extensive use of symbolist techniques—a voice or voices not belonging to the human context—as an aesthetically consistent *retreat* from that context, and which occasioned the back-writing of the additions to Chapter Six.) Bloom's mind, as he searches for lunch, is perhaps at its most active in the day, compared to its early morning sluggishness ('Calypso', Chapter Four) and the soporific overtones of 'Lotos-eaters' (Chapter Five). The problem of the adultery is an accelerating excitation for him, and Chapter Eight ends—Joyce's attempt to make each chapter a self-contained unit in itself is very evident in this and the next—with Bloom's near meeting with Blazes Boylan:

Mr. Bloom came to Kildare street. First I must. Library.
Straw hat in sunlight. Tan shoes. Turnedup trousers. It is.
It is.
His heart quopped softly. To the right. Museum.
Goddesses. He swerved to the right. . . .
Didn't see me perhaps. Light in his eyes.
The flutter of his breath came forth in short sighs. Quick.
Cold statues: quiet there. Safe in a minute.
No didn't see me. After two. Just at the gate.
My heart!
. . . Hurry. Walk quietly. Moment more. My heart.
His hand looking for the where did I put found in his hip
pocket soap lotion have to call tepid paper stuck. Ah, soap
there! Yes. Gate.
Safe! (234/180–1)

Bloom's excitement, whether over hunger or Boylan, permitted
Joyce, I think, the latitude for the stylistic 'return' at this
point. Because of the excitement, the danger of anti-climax,
of there being just more of the same of old Bloom, was mini-
mized. Similarly, the set-piece quality of Stephen's 'lecture'
on *Hamlet* and Shakespeare constitutes an increase in vitality
and agility on his part. Here too tension is maintained. Wyndham Lewis complained at the lethargy of Stephen in the novel's
first chapter,[14] but this is explained enough by the hour of the
morning after what must have been for Stephen as sleepless as
it was an upsetting night.

Chapter Nine ('Scylla and Charybdis') compares only with
Chapter Three ('Proteus') as an exploitation of Stephen's
brilliance. The problem was, at this stage, once more to present a
character whose mental life would have to be recognizably the
same in quality as it had been in the earlier chapters, and at
the same time, without offending that expectation, to present
enough new material from it not to bore. I expect it was done,
for one last time in the novel, only by arbitrarily withholding
and segregating the materials used. There is justification for this
withholding in that 'Proteus' presents Stephen alone, as 'Scylla'
presents him in the Dublin literary context, each levying
different requirements on him. Yet it may seem lingeringly odd
that the mind so intent on certain metaphysical speculations
earlier intrudes so few three hours later—this is obscured by
the intervention of five whole chapters—or, perhaps more

telling, that so few of the allusions available to him in Chapter Nine occur in Chapter Three.*

Still, there are important, and even overriding relationships between the 'Shakespeare' chapter and the rest of Stephen's day which minimize the *tour de force* aspect of the chapter, though by this point in the novel any 'jarring'—such as a recognition of a disparity between the postulated human action and the manner of its presentation, however accidentally come by—represents a foretaste of more systematic detachments to come. Like the noticeable flower-imagery of Chapter Five, imagery which threatens to break the bounds of Bloom's consciousness (or Joyce's narrative mimicry of it), the presentation of Stephen's Shakespeare tends to threaten the integrity of Stephen's imagination. Each represents a shadow-version of later, more systematic breakage. Like 'Lestrygonians', which ended with Bloom's evasion of Boylan, 'Scylla' has a 'form' and a climax to enforce its self-containedness. The whole chapter has a tendency to approach drama, which it actually does for two pages (268–9/206–7)—parodied by *'Ballocky'* Mulligan's *'Everyman His Own Wife, or, A Honeymoon in the Hand (a national immorality in three orgasms)'* (278/214). As the parody suggests, it is Mulligan who represents Stephen's adversary and potential 'usurper'—as Boylan is Bloom's—and the *'Entr'acte'* which occurs at the moment of his entrance—

> —Amen! responded from the doorway.
> Hast thou found me, O mine enemy?
> *Entr'acte.*
> A ribald face, sullen as a dean's, Buck Mulligan came forwards then blithe in motley, towards the greetings of their smiles. (252–3/195)—

corresponds to the 'quopping' of Bloom's heart at the sight of Boylan.† It is a kind of 'arrest' or *dis*enchantment of the heart, to misquote the *Portrait*, and its place, if not its meaning, will be taken in *Finnegans Wake* by the hundred-letter thunder-words.

* Perhaps I overstate. Stephen quotes from Shakespeare fifteen times, according to Schutte,[15] in his walk along the beach. Ten of these are from *Hamlet*. But the effect of comparison is lessened by Joyce's determination almost never to quote the same line twice in the novel.

† Joyce added the word *'Entr'acte'* after the *Little Review* publication in April 1919, presumably after abandoning the plan outlined to Budgen on October 24th, 1920, of writing an actual *entr'acte* to follow the chapter (*Letters* p. 149).

Mulligan's 'playlet' is the outcome of his wilful misinterpretation of Stephen's *finale:*

> The playwright who wrote the folio of this world and wrote it badly (He gave us light first and the sun two days later), the lord of things as they are whom the most Roman of catholics call *dio boia*, hangman god, is doubtless all in all in all of us, ostler and butcher, and would be bawd and cuckold too but that in the economy of heaven, foretold by Hamlet, there are no more marriages, glorified man, an androgynous angel, being a wife unto himself.
>   —*Eureka!* Buck Mulligan cried. *Eureka!*   (273–4/210–11)

Mulligan has been trying to interrupt—to ruin—Stephen's flow of argument, and it is difficult to know whether he has here succeeded. It is a satisfaction Stephen would not give him, and the lack of knowledge is as much his as ours. Stephen leaves Mulligan to his travesty ('Jest on. Know thyself.' [277/213]), which is functionally a satyr-play, and his last thought is a resignation which parallels the scene in *Portrait* (236/273) when he suspects Cranly of having to do with E[mma] C[leary]. There he had resigned his 'girl' to his 'friend'; here he realizes it is futile to joust for the good graces of literary Dublin:

> Cease to strive. Peace of the druid priests of Cymbeline, hierophantic: from wide earth an altar.   (280/215)

The tenth chapter of the novel ('Wandering Rocks') is the last in which the narrative stance—or better, style—bears obvious relation to what has preceded. Once more, after alternate chapters devoted mainly to Stephen and Bloom— Bloom does put in a momentary appearance in the ninth chapter, as had Stephen in 'Hades'—there is a 'Dublin' chapter, here not the confined (if micro-urban) newspaper office, but the entire city. The stance gives Joyce the opportunity to choose anyone he wishes—within limits, as the viceregal cavalcade touches upon many, but not all of the sketches—and while it may turn out that each person chosen will seem to have a particular relevance to the story, it cannot be allowed to seem so at first. Thus a tension must be set up between freedom (even randomness) and necessity, a tension which is to be found in

86

the book at large.* Here the appearance of chance and arbitrariness must be preserved to suggest the convincingness and completeness of the picture of Dublin, at the same time that coincidence must be permitted to suggest a unity, as at the vanishing-point of a perspective.

At the same time that 'Wandering Rocks' takes a more extensive view of Dublin than 'Aeolus', it affords correspondingly less room for Stephen and Bloom, who appear in only four of the nineteen episodes. In a sense, this takes the pressure off Joyce's having to deal once more at length, and in the same 'style', with Stephen and Bloom, and he can turn to aping the speech and thought of Father Conmee, Miss Dunne, Tom Kernan, Martin Cunningham, Master Patrick Aloysius Dignam, *et al.* This widening out of the 'initial styles' of *Ulysses* to include, momentarily, many of the characters tangential to Stephen's and Bloom's 'stories' is partial acknowledgement that whatever persons Joyce chose to focus on here, the results would have been similar. After this Dublin panorama is completed in Chapter Ten, Joyce can return to Stephen and Bloom, having also reinforced, in one dimension, the notion of their representativeness. (In other dimensions, their singularity is emphasized, of course. It was this chapter which influenced John Dos Passos, to similar purpose, in *U.S.A.*) What has been done with Stephen and Bloom, individually, is now done with a 'cross-section' of Dublin. In one sense, this chapter marks the end of a whole phase of the novel. The next chapter will open with a startlingly new narrative technique, the page and a half of 'fugal' themes. Widened to include all Dublin, the common mimicking style, except for a shadow-appearance in the Ormond Bar (the converse of the previsions of symbolist techniques), is now done with.

The 'Wandering Rocks' contains one 'jarring' narrative technique, to imply the simultaneity of various of the occurrences. In the section on Corny Kelleher is inserted a reminder, carried over from three pages before, that Conmee was at that moment boarding a tram. The Elijah 'throwaway' skims down

---

* Cf. Gilbert, p. 235: 'Here, again, we see a reason for regarding this episode as the microcosm of the universe of *Ulysses*, inspired by its creator with the breath of life, yet fashioned by the practised hand of an artificer, maker of labyrinths: a living labyrinth.'

the Liffey at the end of the section on the Dedalus girls at home: it reappears to Mr Kernan. Also in that section is inserted a sentence out of the Conmee section. Something of this sort happens in nearly every section, and at least once the reference is to something occurring outside the whole chapter: 'Bronze by gold [etc.]' appears on p. 316/242, and, after a repetition in the nineteenth (summary) episode, begins the next chapter (328, 331/252, 253). When, elsewhere in the novel, a phrase of Stephen's—'In a rosery of Fetter lane of Gerard's, herbalist, he walks, greyedauburn' (259/199)—turns up as a separate paragraph between two which are clearly Bloom's 'consciousness' (362/276), at least one critic has been given pause, but the compositional principle is clearly the same,[16] only simultaneity of occurrence does not occasion the narrative 'reminder', which here points to a thematic parallelism.*

From the published letters, it would appear that Joyce began only at this point in the writing of *Ulysses* to run into troublesome opposition (or criticism) from the inner circle. On June 19th, 1919, Joyce wrote Budgen—who always stuck by him and soon, the Joyces removing first back to Trieste and then to Paris, began to bear the brunt of Joyce's correspondence on *Ulysses*—'Pound writes disapproving of the *Sirens*' and wishing to see more of Stephen and less of Bloom.'[17] On July 2nd, 1919, he confided to Harriet Shaw Weaver that he feared Pound 'does not like the book' and eighteen days later he was writing to her to answer her complaint that 'the last episode sent [*Sirens*] seems to you to show a weakening or diffusion of some sort'.[18] He goes on,

> Mr. Brock also wrote to me begging me to explain to him the method (or methods) of the madness but these methods are so manifold, varying as they do from one hour of the day to another, from one organ of the body to another, from episode to episode, that, much as I appreciate his critical patience I could not hope to reply. . . . If the *Sirens* have been found so unsatisfactory I have little hope that the *Cyclops* or later the *Circe* episode will be approved of. . . .[19]

This is the first time that Joyce broached, in a letter, the notions like 'organ[s] of the body' later enshrined in the

---

* When Stephen is thinking of his 'pawned schoolprizes', Joyce tells us what Conmee is doing at that moment (311/239).

'schema' that he gave Herbert Gorman.[20] It is not important whether Joyce had the entire scheme thought out before he began the novel. It is important that, though he revised the earlier chapters after their *Little Review* appearances, and in many cases added certain recognizably 'symbolic' tones to them, he did not recast them entirely to match the extravagances of 'Cyclops', 'Circe', 'Oxen of the Sun', 'Eumæus', etc., as he might have done. The style of the novel required a gradual *lead into* these extravagances. Despite the schema's listing of an 'art', 'colour', 'symbol' and 'technic', the appositeness of the particular determinations are much less taking with respect to the earlier chapters. Joyce did not even bother to list an 'organ' for the first three chapters, and the 'technics' of the early chapters (narrative, catechism, monologue, narrative) are so much more general and common than the terms he chose for the later chapters (like *fuga per canonem*, gigantism, tumescence detumescen[ce], embryonic development, hallucination) whose specificity and uniqueness can both be recognized.

On August 6th, 1919, Joyce wrote to Miss Weaver for one last time on the subject of what seems to have been her first boggling at *Ulysses*.[21] By this date he had settled on his phrase for the 'technic' of 'Sirens', *fuga per canonem*, and added the comparison of his reader with the 'wanderer' which is the epigraph to this chapter, implying that his decision to abandon the streams of Stephen's and Bloom's consciousnesses was deliberately taken and part of his plan. 'Such variation' he claimed was necessary and 'not capricious'.

The narrator's 'intrusions' in 'Sirens' are embodied in the text itself, not, as in 'Aeolus', as set-apart sub-titles. As such, they point up more clearly the extent to which significant comment and correlations are now made on the 'story' not by the free imitation of the characters but by a distinct voice which does not belong to the Dublin plot. Throughout the chapter, this voice threatens and breaks through the integrity of Bloom's consciousness—similar to the threatening of Stephen's (in a much less systematic way) in 'Scylla and Charybdis'. As this new voice, or variants of it, take over the management of the novel from the 'imitative' voice, a form of withdrawal is constituted. This is a secondary withdrawal, more radical than the one constituted by the mimicking of consciousnesses, in so far as neither characters *nor* novelist could there be held responsible for what was not direct speech.

Besides the 'overture' of *leitmotifs*—attacked by Curtius as meaningless without the following text (and supererogatory with it); defended by Gilbert as just as meaningful as any Wagerian overture of motifs[22]—what Gilbert called 'the hundreds of musical forms verbally reproduced in the course of this episode' are the main agent of the breaking of 'the initial style'. I use some of Gilbert's examples:

> Her wavyavyeavyheavyeavyevyevy hair un comb: 'd (*trillando*)
> Will? You? I. Want. You. To (*staccato*)
> luring, ah, alluring (*appoggiatura*)
> Rain. Diddle, iddle, addle, oodle, oodle, oodle (*portamento*)
> Blmstup (*quinto vuoto*)[23]

Gilbert has four pages of these, and we have Joyce's testimony that he worked hard at including them[24]—as compared to 'Aeolus' where the figures of 'rhetoric' could probably be found in any other chapter as well.

Despite Gilbert's claim that 'the meaning . . . is . . . intensified by the combination of the two arts [language, music]; sense is not sacrificed to sound but the two are . . . harmonized', and that the technique is 'evocative of the theme itself',[25] Curtius seems to have been, if pejoratively, on a better track: the technique produces not fusion but awareness of disparity in the reader, and the figure, here of Bloom, retreats. The 'meaning' of his day is becoming public property, as the voice which exists to point it up ceases to be the indeterminate author/character's voice/consciousness. As Simon Dedalus sings 'Martha', Leopold Bloom and he may become 'symbolically' *one*, 'high in the effulgence symbolistic' (355/271)—

> —*Co-me, thou lost one!*
> —*Co-me, thou dear one!* . . .
>
> —*Come!* . . .
>
> —*To me!*
> Siopold!
> Consumed.   (355–6/271)—

but this is not something which really occurs to either Simon or Bloom. Nor is the authorial voice of the 'initial style'

responsible. The voice which makes this 'symbolistic' correspondence is the 'effulgent' one of this particular chapter. The
version of the story's meaning which we are given belongs to a
particular kind of interpretation.

Goldberg, who appreciates the 'Siopold' correspondence,
nevertheless considers 'Sirens' as exhibiting 'that precarious
intellectualization of structure under which some of the later
writing collapses completely'. He then criticizes 'the attempt
at *fuga per canonem* form' as 'unsuccessful in practice' and 'meaningless in conception'.[26]

The phase '*fuga per canonem*' belongs, however, not internally
to the novel, but externally to the criticism, and it is unfair to
demand it precisely of the chapter. It does seem to me to bear
some convincing analogy, though, to the experience of the
chapter, if not in the supposed theory of simultaneity of
perception which writers like Gilbert hold to be desirable.
Gilbert insisted that one should *not* read the chapter 'with the
parts kept mentally distinct in four, or less, independent
horizontal lines of melody', but should read *chordally*, in order to
experience 'the curious emotive quality of Joyce's prose in this
episode'. 'The musical "high-brow" ', who keeps the parts
separate, misses 'most of the sensuous value of music, the en-
thralment of the Sirens' song'.[27] Despite the mocks at 'high-
brows', it was specifically Ulysses whose salvation lay in
resisting the Sirens' song, and we may be excused our own
attempt to fight against merging the horizontal lines, recognizing that 'Siopold', which is such a merging in the text, is part
of the 'symbolistic' Siren-song. Less metaphorically, we should
recognize that the chordal apperception (or presentation) is
the property of the narrator, and at the same time the separateness of the 'lines'—whether they are the barmaids' chatter,
Bloom, Boylan, etc. or not—also contributes to the progressive
withdrawal of the totality of the novel from presenting a
determinative interpretation of Bloom's day.

Despite, then, such critically orthodox pronouncements as:

> The truth is that the 'objects' are presented to us only as
> Stephen sees them [in Chapter Three] and they *are* what he
> sees. We are not given two separate bits of reality—the 'real'
> sea or midwives and the 'real' stream of subjective impressions
> —but one: Stephen's experience,[28]

it can be seen that however true this may be of the 'initial style', it is not true of much of the novel. Goldberg's dictum is *more* true in the earlier stages of the novel, and progressively *less* true in the later. There we begin to see the deliberately played-on gap between narrative style and the material which is its subject.

The new narrator of Chapter Twelve ('Cyclops') is, in his own voice, the most 'undependable' so far. But into his garrulous Dublin narrative are interlarded such passages as:

> For nonperishable goods bought of Moses Herzog, of 13 Saint Kevin's parade, Wood quay ward, merchant, hereinafter called the vendor, and sold and delivered to Michael E. Geraghty, Esquire, of 29 Arbour Hill in the city of Dublin, Arran quay ward, gentleman, hereinafter called the purchaser, videlicet, five pounds avoirdupois of first choice tea at three shillings per pound avoirdupois and three stone avoidupois of sugar, crushed crystal, at three pence per pound avoirdupois, the said purchaser debtor to the said vendor [etc., etc.,] . . .
>
> (377/287-8)

Strictly this is not 'parody': it is the thing itself, an invoice. No one reads it out; it is in the hands of the character who narrates the events in the pub. In a manner similar to *collage*, Joyce interrupts the flow of his narrative to give it to us.

The other kinds of interruption to the chapter are more 'human', or at least literary, being 'Homeric', 'Ossianic', newspaper reports, literary essays (on the 'verse' which Garryowen 'recites'), a report of a theosophical meeting. Besides keeping us at a distance from the 'action' in Barney Kiernan's pub—an action we remain convinced is going on—this chapter begins to exploit, for the first time in the novel, encyclopaedic dimensions. There are lists of fish, 'foison of the fields', farm animals, 'Irish' heroes, 'the picturesque delegation known as the Friends of the Emerald Isle' (397/302), clergy, the 'fasionable international world [who] attended . . . the wedding of the chevalier Jean Wyse de Neaulan' [i.e. various trees] (424/321), the scenes depicted on the 'muchtreasured intricately embroidered ancient Irish facecloth' (430/326), the 'blessed company' (440–2/332–4), and places where bonfires were lit to celebrate the eviction of Bloom from Kiernan's. All that distinguishes this chapter from many sections of *Finnegans Wake* is the sporadic appearance of the 'actual' scene in the pub. As in the *Wake*, the incipient encyclopaedism promotes a sense of the randomness and arbitrariness of any one particular 'interpretation' of the action, or direction of the narrative. Where so many are available at all times, the choice of one mode of vision (here, the straightforward action) is demoted in importance. At the same time, its difference from the various pseudo-heroic modes of apperception is emphasized. The thematic appropriateness of the 'heroisms' of the style is pointed by the deliberate underplaying of Bloom's 'opinions' (which are always voiced in the dialogue),

—But, says Bloom, isn't discipline the same everywhere? I mean wouldn't it be the same here if you put force against force? (427/323)

—Persecution, says he, all the history of the world is full of it. Perpetuating national hatred among nations. (430/325)

—I'm talking about injustice, says Bloom. (432/327)

—But it's no use, says he. Force, hatred, history, all that. That's not life for men and women, insult and hatred. And everybody knows that it's the very opposite of that that is really life.
—What? says Alf.
—Love, says Bloom. I mean the opposite of hatred. (432/327)

Bloom's loquacity may come as a surprise—we had not thought him so articulate. Feeling this is partly covered by the masses of material which surround each of Bloom's small outbursts, but the notion that what is here in direct quotation as Bloom's words may not have been said by him need not be suppressed, or written off as a fault in Joyce. It may point, rather, to just how 'undependable' the narrator of the scene in the pub—who is only one of the chapter's 'voices'—may be. That even what is here directly attributed to 'characters' may in fact be a *variation*, what Goldberg, referring to 'Circe' and 'Ithaca', calls an alteration of 'dramatic integrity'.[29] Like the 'interpolated' material in 'Cyclops', which represents various imaginative (and usually 'heroic') potentialities of the postulated human

93

action, the actual pub scenes supposedly related by the narrator may themselves be a 'literary' possibility of the scene which really took place. It is, possibly, only a 'realistic' literary version—infected by that *naïveté* which has characterized conversation in literary 'realism'—which accounts for the 'finished' quality of Bloom's remarks, as the other aspects of the chapter are 'Homeric' or 'Ossianic' literary *variations*. The simple dichotomy between the scene in Barney Kiernan's pub, which is what really happened, given to us in the actual words which were spoken, and the interpolated 'technic' of 'gigantism' is perhaps too simple. The scenes in Kiernan's related by the debt-collector are better seen as just one more version of what might have happened that day to Bloom. In this sense we are not alternately 'let in on' the action and pushed back from it, we are held uniformly at a distance. Only our own prejudice in favour of the superior reality of literary realism could think otherwise.

The style of 'Nausikaa' is, for a little more than half the chapter, similarly a literary parody. It bears some relation to certain of the parodies in 'Cyclops', and is, of course, handled at much greater length than any of them. While in 'Cyclops' the shorter parodies were punctuated by similarly short returns to a 'realistic' scene, here the longer single one is balanced by a full return to the opening treatment of Bloom. The latter part of the chapter is thus our last touching of the home base, preparatory to the launching out of the last six chapters (which take up roughly a little more than half of the novel's length).

The cento of romantic clichés—dangerously close perhaps to the style of 'Eumæus' (Chapter Sixteen)—is hardly to be considered the actual reportage of Gerty Macdowell's speech, stream of consciousness, or even mode of perception. The statement that this is the way Dublin girls think is, after all, a generalization from the text without its authority. It is, however, the way certain sub-literature presents certain material; or rather, that is the working hypothesis which permits us to recognize in Joyce's prose the standard equipment of the mock-'heroic'—here mock-romantic—stance: 'lower' material to work on and a more systematic application of the romanticization.

'Oxen of the Sun' contains no alternation of parodies with returns to earlier narrative modes, but rather a number of parodies, like 'Cyclops', here presented continuously and on a chronological plan, from pseudo-Anglo-Saxon through a large number of Romantic prose-writers to a kind of pidgin-English. This extends encyclopaedically the manner in which the action of *Ulysses* could be presented. It points up the arbitrariness of any particular presentation by showing that the individual interpretations of the action are part of the historical ethos of the writer—as, the *courtesy* of Bloom (his consideration for Mrs Purefoy's labour) is the Malorian interpretation, while to emphasize the ethical plight of Stephen is to bring a Bunyanesque allegorical presentation to bear on the subject. By presenting *all* interpretations (a very large number standing for 'all'), *Ulysses* contrives to subscribe to no one. It becomes therefore more concerned with the relatedness of the various versions. In this chapter, the spectrum of interpretations is presented as inherent in the literary-historical process.

Further, the styles in 'Oxen of the Sun' are the narrator's. They do not belong to Stephen or Bloom or Dublin. Nor are they approximations in other 'languages' of the way in which any one present may be supposed to have felt. This is to insist on the distance which we are being kept from the major characters and on the difference between the techniques which the artist has for presenting his material and that material itself. The theory of the 'organic whole' of style and subject will not work for *Ulysses*, whose symbolic dimension (including its 'styles') wars with its human dimension.

Ulysses seems to posit a *noumenal* level which does not deny the multiplicity of phenomenal interpretive ones, but which is behind and beyond them, necessary to them inasmuch as without it, they could not exist at all. As *Ulysses* proceeds, the phenomenal dimension discovers that it can enjoy itself almost, as it were, at the expense of the noumenal one, but only at the cost of relinquishing a denominative, or final interpretation of it. This is reflected in Stephen Dedalus's problem, here adumbrated by the Bunyan parody, the contention of 'the god Bringforth' and 'the hubbub of Phenomenon' (516/389). The method of *Ulysses* is an accommodation of the total potentiality of a subject and the particular version(s) of it brought into being. *Ulysses* is most particularly an encyclopaedic fiction in this respect. Its claims to be one on the basis of an encyclopaedic range of knowledge and information have been denigrated, and rightly. Nor is it a cosmological fiction, like *Finnegans Wake*, which would imply that the plot itself contains analogues to the beginning and ending of all things. The plot of *Ulysses* is extended not so much to cosmological dimensions, but by means of an encyclopaedia of styles, each of which implies a different approach to its meaning.*

While I have been insisting on the reality of a difference between 'subject' and 'style' in *Ulysses*, at a particular level of conception there is no difference. It is the juxtaposition of many episodes each of which cannot, as Goldberg points out of the early chapters on Stephen, be separated into matter and manner, which, taken together promote a further difference. The 'subject' cannot be projected from a scrutiny of each individual chapter, or portion of a chapter, by discounting in some manner from the style of it. Such subjects would be different in each case. The readings of Bloom's case according to the Anglo-Saxon or Malory or De Quincey parodies would be mutually exclusive.

'Circe', which is the most complex chapter in *Ulysses* ontologically, has always been in danger of oversimplification by way of a too narrow application of the notion of 'hallucination' taken over from the authorized 'technic'. And this oversimplification has been in the nature of precisely the making of simple differences between *what really happened* and Joyce's manner of telling. While a real difference exists—we do project that something really did happen—there is no use dividing 'Circe' up between what Bloom, Stephen or others really said in an around Bella Cohen's and what is hallucinatory. The only way to accommodate into one conception, into a single ontological level, the entire chapter is not to make such divisions (which won't work), but to assume that the whole is the surrealistic fantasy of a man who knows what went on in Nighttown on June 16th, 1904, and who has read (or written) the fourteen previous chapters of *Ulysses*. 'Circe' is, if we will, The Dream of James Joyce.†

---

* Cf. Joyce to Carlo Linati, September 21st, 1920: 'It is also a sort of encyclopaedia. My intention is to transpose the myth *sub specie temporis nostri*' (*Letters*, pp. 146–7). Not to transpose the story *sub specie aeternitatis*.

† See Wyndham Lewis, *Time and Western Man* (London, 1927), p. 121: 'the

There is no other way to explain certain things in the chapter other than to assume that nothing of what Bloom or Stephen 'really' said appears in it verbatim—or rather that nothing which we could prove does. As Harry Levin has noticed,[30] the 'Moorish' phrase which 'Molly' (who isn't, of course, *there*) shouts out at her camel, 'Nebrakada! Feminimum.' (570/432), is the talismanic phrase 'to win a woman's love' which Stephen has read in a book picked off a barrow in front of Clohissey's bookshop, Nos. 10–11 Bedford Row (312/239). Within *Ulysses*, only Stephen and the author know the phrase. It is a reasonable assumption that Bloom, who is tired but not drunk, would have no way of 'hallucinating' the phrase—he shouts it at the Nymph, later (662/540)—and there is no indication that this is Stephen hallucinating what Molly says to Bloom. The obvious conclusion is that the episode is the fantasy of their creator about them.

That Joyce began to so dream about his characters we know from his description to Gorman:

> I saw Molly Bloom on a hillock under a sky full of moonlit clouds rushing overhead. She had just picked up from the grass a child's black coffin and flung it after the figure of a man passing down a side road by the field she was in. It struck his shoulders, and she said, 'I've done with you.' The man was Bloom seen from behind. There was a shout of laughter from some American journalists in the road opposite, led by Ezra Pound. I was very indignant and vaulted over a gate into the field and strode up to her and delivered the one speech of my life. It was very long, eloquent and full of passion, explaining all the last episode of *Ulysses* to her. . . . She smiled when I ended on an astronomical climax, and then, bending, picked up a tiny snuffbox, in the form of a little black coffin, and tossed it towards me, saying, 'And I have done with you, too, Mr. Joyce'. I had a snuffbox like the one she tossed to me when I was at Clongowes Wood College.[31]

Within a general description much like 'Circe' we see the mixture of levels in which the author appears alongside his characters. Besides giving the appearance of independent existence to the fictional characters, it reduces the author's claim to controlling the interpretation of their action. The admirable Goya-like fantasia in the middle of the book, in which all the characters enjoy a free metaphysical existence.'

97

presence of strictly autobiographical elements in 'Circe'—not just ones which Stephen and the young Joyce shared, but ones unique to Joyce—such as the inclusion of 'My literary agent, Mr. J. B. Pinker' (585/451) and Carr and Bennett of the Zurich Consulate, helps underwrite the view that the chapter is Joyce's fantasia on his own novel.

There are many other sections in the chapter which can be best 'explained' in this way. Levin also noticed that,

> It was Bloom who noted at the funeral that Martin Cunningham's sympathetic face was like Shakespeare's ([120/]95), yet it is now to Stephen that Shakespeare appears in the guise of Cunningham. ([672/]554)[32]

J. J. O'Molloy's metamorphoses into John F. Taylor and Seymour Bushe (590–1/456)—triggered by the associative chain Agendath-Moses-Taylor—should not be available to Bloom's mind, as he was not present in the *Freeman's Journal* office when Molloy had quoted Bushe (as defence counsel in the Childs murder case) on Michelangelo's 'Moses' and Professor MacHugh had capped that with Taylor on 'The Language of the Outlaw' (176–81/137–41; see 'EXIT BLOOM', 164/128, and Bloom's phone call, 173/135). Stephen was then present, but in at least two similar instances he was not, and the substance of 'Circe' is there solely available to the narrator: (1) 'Paddy Dignam's spirit' appears to 'Bloom', and after exhorting him to keep Mrs Dignam 'off that bottle of sherry', '*He looks round him*', saying, 'A lamp. I must satisfy an animal need. That buttermilk didn't agree with me' (597/464). 'That buttermilk' —a whole quart of it—had been given 'the apparition of [Paddy's] etheric double' (389/296) in the theosophic parody which follows Alf Bergan's claim to have seen Dignam some hours *after* the funeral (388/295). Bloom is not even in the pub at the time; outside, pacing back and forth, he enters only two pages later. (2) When Zoe Higgins, reading Bloom's palm, points to his 'Short little finger' and says he is a 'Henpecked husband', '*Black Liz, a huge rooster*' appears, with the line, 'Gara. Klook. Klook. Klook' (668/549). Black Liz makes her other appearance in 'Cyclops' as a five-line parody amplifying the debt collector's unspoken reflection that Bloom would 'have a soft hand under a hen' (408/310).

We might say, then, that by its fifteenth chapter, *Ulysses* has begun to provide its author enough in the way of material to become self-perpetuating.* The cross-referencing which the author had injected before to remind us of similarities between characters (as, Stephen's 'Gerard's Rosery' inserted in Bloom's monologue) here takes on an appearance of autonomy, as 'characters' belonging to other contexts or even ontological levels rise up to confront the characters in the Dublin action, in the meeting ground of the author's imagination which is the true *locus* of 'Circe'. Yet this is merely one place among many in the novel, and it does not provide a skeleton key to the true inwardness of the characters. On the assumption that the fantasies are really Bloom's hallucinations, S. L. Goldberg has argued that 'Bloom is finally unable to sustain any of his visions [sic] because none of them is finally adequate to his real character'.[33] This is equally true if we are not dealing with *Bloom's* 'hallucinations' and is, further, transferable to the whole conduct of the novel. Like each of the other 'styles' in *Ulysses*, which approach, more and more radically, discrete and often incompatible modes of vision, the 'Circean' style appears inadequate as a comprehensive explanation of the protagonists. The inadequacy is suggested by consideration of the whole; in the part, the claims of each style become progressively more importunate.

It is significant that the strongest line of interpretation which 'Circe' puts on *Ulysses* draws extremely close to the conduct of *Finnegans Wake*. As in the *Wake*, the protagonist (here, Bloom) is successively accused of sexual misconduct, tried, condemned to death, elevated to Messianic status, turned against—like Parnell first by the Church ('Father Farley') and then by Mrs Riordan—immolated; then, in a new 'incarnation', turned into a woman—Bella/Bello Cohen, who accomplishes this, enters pat upon Bloom's unmanning suspicion that Blazes

---

* In 'Ithaca', Bloom is described as having earlier 'proceeded towards the oriental edifice of the Turkish and Warm Baths, 11 Leinster street, with the light of inspiration shining in his countenance and bearing in his arms the secret of the race, graven in the language of prediction' (789–90/660). In 'Aeolus', MacHugh had recited Taylor's speech, describing Moses' descent from Sinai, 'with the light of inspiration shining in his countenance and bearing in his arms the tables of the law, graven in the language of the outlaw' (181/141). Bloom was not then present, and the pun on 'race' (Jews, Ascot Cup) is available only to author and reader.

Boylan is at the brothel (640–1/514–15 and 652–3/529)—humiliated, sacrificed. The cyclic pattern, the hero-god status—'THE VEILED SIBYL' '*Stabs herself* and *dies*' with the words 'My hero god!' addressed to Bloom (612/482) when the populace turns against the founder of the New Bloomusalem—the trial for sexual misdemeanor, the metamorphoses of costume and character, all combine to make 'Circe' a close approximation to the *Wake*, a *Wake*'s-eye view of *Ulysses*.

A. Walton Litz, discussing the 'designs' in *Ulysses*—'a network of interlocking motifs and cross references'—concludes that 'the principles which governed [Joyce's method of composition] in 1920 and 1921 did not differ greatly from those he followed in writing *Finnegans Wake*'.[34] This may be extended beyond Joyce's method to his basic conception, although it need not involve him in any ultimate aesthetic botch, a position Litz gets close to at times. Conflict has been transferred in *Ulysses* from a struggle between characters who represent opposed ways of envisioning one and the same event to a struggle between these opposing modes themselves, as part of the way of telling the story.

The closer Joyce comes to specifying the 'meaning' of *Ulysses*, the more hedged is the mode of presentation chosen. In 'Circe', while the springs of Stephen's and Bloom's motives are laid most bare, we are prevented by the ontology of the presentation—its relation to the Bloom and Stephen of the first chapters—from asserting its right to control our view of the whole. While we may wish to recognize the relationship of the manner of presentation to a mode of perception congenial to Joyce, who later spent seventeen years 'mining' it, we must simultaneously acknowledge its logical function in *Ulysses*' spectrum of styles. The 'interpretation' it presents has no unique claim to determine the situation—this should, by now, be clear of all the 'styles'—but rather it belongs to the structure of suppositions which the totality of styles provides.

The 'tired' clichés of 'Eumæus' strike most readers as a letdown. Probably this was in the nature of the case, after the pyrotechnics of 'Circe', and it must be acknowledged that Joyce has not gone out of his way to prevent the reaction—rather the opposite. The effect of the 'imitative form' (tired characters: tired prose) appears disastrous—though perhaps we ought to abandon any notion that *Ulysses* makes, read cover to cover, a beautiful experience—mainly because the style chosen contains little by way of density in itself. It was approached by certain of the parodies in 'Cyclops' (the ones which seem to be newspaper reports) and by Gerty Macdowell's 'reflections'. The effect of parody of a literary (or sub-literary) source, whose major point lies in showing the inability of the rhetoric to encompass the human content—this is especially true of 'Ithaca'—seems to be inversely proportional to length, as it is only the same effect gotten over and over again. Nevertheless, in the spectrum of styles there is a clear place for it.

There are attempts within the chapter to exploit its general mode, as when Stephen answers Bloom's loquacious 'I don't mean to presume to dictate to you in the slightest degree but why did you leave your father's house?' (713/603) with a blunt 'To seek misfortune'. ('Bloom', I assume, speaks 'in the style' of the chapter: that is, Bloom did not really say this in this way. Stephen's answer, on the other hand, very probably is in his own words.) Here the effect is gotten by the breaking in upon the 'style', not by any effect inherent in the style itself. Thus, while the 'style' is devoid of much local interest, its existence is available to induce a maximum effect from the material within it which is not *sui generis*. This happens tellingly in at least three other places:

> the other [Bloom], who was acting as his [Stephen's] *fidus Achates*[,] inhaled with internal satisfaction the smell of James Rourke's city bakery, situated quite close to where they were, the very palatable odour indeed of our daily bread, of all commodities of the public the primary and most indispensable. Bread, the staff of life, earn your bread, O tell me where is fancy bread? At Rourke's the baker's, it is said.   (706/598)

The second occurs when the sailor mentions his 'little woman' in Carrigaloe whom he has not seen in seven years. Mr Bloom 'could easily picture' the sailor's 'advent on this scene', but that 'picture', which begins in the cliché-style of the whole, shortly becomes a little drama on the same model as the graveyard meditation quoted before:

> The face at the window! Judge of his astonishment when he finally did breast the tape and the awful truth dawned

upon him anent his better half, wrecked in his affections. You little expected me but I've come to stay and make a fresh start. There she sits, a grass widow, at the selfsame fireside. Believes me dead. Rocked in the cradle of the deep. . . . No chair for father. Boo! The wind! Her brandnew arrival is on her knee, *post mortem* child. With a high ro! and a randy ro! and my galloping tearing tandy O! Bow to the inevitable. Grin and bear it. I remain with much love your brokenhearted husband, W. B. Murphy.   (719–20/608–9)

'That particular Alice Ben Bolt topic' (719/608), as told in Bloom's interior monologue, owes more to clichés ('Bow to the inevitable. Grin and bear it.') than most of his 'thoughts', but it still rises to an interest above that of many passages of similar length in 'Eumæus'. As it is directly concerned with the 'Penelope theme', it has obvious relevance to Bloom's own plight and presents a version of his own later 'abnegation', if an interpretation at the level of cliché. The subject crops up again momentarily in another example of a 'fracturing'—the term is R. M. Adams's[35]—of the fictional surface of the chapter:

> Nevertheless, he [Bloom] sat tight, just viewing the slightly soiled photo [of Molly which he is showing to Stephen] creased by opulent curves, none the worse for wear, however, and locked away thoughtfully with the intention of not further increasing the other's possible embarrassment while gauging her symmetry of heaving *embonpoint*. In fact, the slight soiling was only an added charm, like the case of linen slightly soiled, good as new, much better, in fact, with the starch out. Suppose she was gone when he? . . . I looked for the lamp which she told me came into his mind but merely as a passing fancy of his because he then recollected the morning littered bed etcetera and the book about Ruby with met him pike hoses (*sic*) in it which must have fell down sufficiently appropriately beside the domestic chamberpot with apologies to Lindley Murray.
> (759–60/637–8)

The sudden welling-up of a thought about Molly, not as she was in the picture but as she might be in the present, seems to unfix Bloom's mind. The phrase 'Suppose she was gone when he? . . .' discomposes Bloom. The paragraph continues in a jumble of phrases and finally regains a precarious balance at the level of cliché.*

Another kind of diversion from the main style of the chapter occurs when Corley accosts Stephen in the street for a handout: 'Lord John Corley, some called him, and his genealogy came about in this wise' (709/600), which is followed by a fourteen-line 'genealogy'. After the chapter has returned from this epical *excursus* to the matter at hand, there is intruded, on no pretext whatever, a hashed and bathetic counter-genealogy:

> No, it was the daughter of the mother in the washkitchen that was fostersister to the heir of the house or else they were connected through the mother in some way . . . if the whole thing wasn't a complete fabrication from start to finish. . . .
>
> (709/601)

Both the pseudo-heroic and the botched comedown are not cliché-ridden. This is a unique example in 'Eumæus' and it may be questioned whether it really belongs in the chapter, being more in the style(s) of 'Cyclops'. There seems, for instance, no intention to recall 'Cyclops' at this point, which would constitute an aesthetic defence. It suggests once again that the ground-style of 'Eumæus' has little local interest of its own, that what interest is present is manufactured by using devices not inherent in the general manner of presentation—as, for instance, the 'lics' which Joyce told Budgen he put 'into the mouth of that sailorman'.[36]

When Joyce wrote Harriet Shaw Weaver on July 12th, 1920, announcing his arrival in Paris from Trieste and his intention 'to remain here three months in order to write the last adventure Circe in peace (?) and also the first episode of the close', he added that 'A great part of the Nostos or close was written several years ago and the style is quite plain'.[37] Whether any material later used in 'Ithaca' is here intended is doubtful. In any case, Joyce seems to have hit on the 'styles' of the 'Nostos' quite late, as he announced that of 'Ithaca' to Budgen only in February 1921, in words which suggest that Budgen would have seen no earlier version. 'Circe' was 'finished'

---

* Lindley Murray, the grammarian, is mentioned in *Finnegans Wake* (269:69); see also *Letters*, p. 278. Murray's *A New English Grammar* proceeds largely by *exempla* barely above the level of cliché. It may have fertilized Joyce's imagination much as the Assimil *L'Anglais Sans Peine* did Ionesco's in *La Cantatrice Chauve*.

by Christmas 1920. 'Ithaca' was begun almost immediately afterwards. On December 10th, 1920, Joyce had said in a letter to Budgen, '*Eumeus* you know, and in February he was telling him about the 'lies'.[38]

This suggests that the basic style of 'Eumæus', the accumulation of clichés, existed from the start, and that the 'quite plain' style was not later rewritten. In so far as the major stylistic features of *Ulysses* developed in the course of writing and were perceived by Joyce as 'necessary' only as he came, as it were, to review his existing achievement, it seems to suggest itself that 'Eumæus' does not participate in the logic of styles to the same extent that other chapters do. Fabricated in advance, and programmatically fashioned (with additions—a letter of 'Early 1921' to Claude Sykes calls it 'about 30 pp.'),[39] 'Eumæus' may seem to jar. Mainly, it seems to have been *done* already in the novel. Given its early composition, one can begin to speculate about the chapter as a practice run for Joyce, and as providing yet another medium of existence for Stephen and Bloom.

In the logic of styles, 'Eumæus' is a reduction of the action to a superficial account, and the manner of it only exposes its own inability to encompass the matter. 'Ithaca', on the other hand, represents an attempt to probe the significance of the action to a great depth by the assumption of an apparently 'objective' method. This method too exposes its own short-comings. Whether *Ulysses* is itself a deterministic novel, as Clive Hart asserts[40] and others imply, the parody of 'Ithaca' maintains an ambivalent relationship with determinism: in so far as it is parodic, it is critical of determinism; in so far as it is not, determinism is presented as adequate to understand the meeting of Bloom and Stephen. Internally there is perhaps no way to decide, except in certain cases; externally, as we cast our eye over other 'versions' of the situation, we may be inclined to take at discount the 'Art' of the chapter, 'Science' (in the Schema).

Oddly enough, the scientific rationalism (or literary naturalism) of the chapter, which ought on the face of it only to *report*, seems to run off into mythologizing. This paradox is notable, for instance, in Zola, where avowedly repertorial novels like *Germinal* tend to develop a 'mythic' dimension, or in

Frank Norris's *MacTeague* and *The Octopus*, where an anti-mythic naturalistic programme cannot banish mythic (nature-cycle) structural elements. This myth/fact paradox enters 'Ithaca' with Joyce's very first announcement of the chapter in the letter of February, 1921, to Budgen:

> I am writing *Ithaca* in the form of a mathematical catechism. All events are resolved into their cosmic, physical, psychical, etc. equivalents, e.g. Bloom jumping down the area, drawing water from the tap, the micturating in the garden, the cone of incense, lighted candle and statue so that the reader will know everything and know it in the baldest and coldest way, but Bloom and Stephen thereby become heavenly bodies, wanderers like the stars at which they gaze.*

Between the baldness and coldness and the 'heavenly bodies, wanderers' falls the 'but', which acknowledges the anti-thetical potentiality of the form, yet another instance of radical ambiguity in the novel.

Critics have emphasized one or another of the poles of this fact/myth ambiguity according to their particular interpretation of Bloom's and Stephen's characters. Deprecators of Bloom and Stephen emphasize the validity of the 'baldest and coldest way'. Hugh Kenner, though seeing humour in it, thinks it always shows up the characters: the 'periphrastic absurdities' may be 'sometimes pathetic', but they reflect accurately *Joyce's* judgement of Bloom, 'the epiphanization of industrial man'.[41] Supporters of Bloom and Stephen are, on the other hand, drawn to exposing the shortcomings of the method, and this is often accompanied by an elevation of the 'mythic' dimension. S. L. Goldberg, who takes particular concern to emphasize the vitality of Bloom and the 'potentiality' of Stephen, is most articulate in formulating this position:

> 'Ithaca'. . . turns back on the action and forms an abstract, choric commentary on it as a whole. . . . In 'Ithaca' the action may be said to reach towards a conscious statement of itself. . . .
>
> [The] narrative must now move outside the consciousness of the characters altogether—not merely outside the 'stream-of-consciousness' (which disappears between 'Nausicaa' and

---

* *Letters*, pp. 159–60. In spring 1921 Joyce called 'Ithaca' 'A mathematico-astronomico-physico-mechanico-geometrico-chemico sublimation of Bloom and Stephen' (Ibid., p. 164).

'Penelope', and is used only intermittently in any case), but even outside any reflecting consciousness in Henry James's sense. . . . Now the 'reflector' is replaced by an intelligence utterly superior to the whole action, an ironic *persona* directing us from beyond or above it. . . .[42]

Goldberg then quotes from Joyce's letter to Budgen on 'Ithaca' and comments,

> The cold, catechistic, 'objective' style is indeed a parodic mask, as for example Mr Kenner has so pertinently shown. But the point of the chapter is the difference between what the mask represents and its actual dramatic *effect*. The mask proceeds with its ruthless vivisection of the 'scientific' facts of modern society and of the sensibility characteristic of that society—*a sensibility, of course, that Bloom largely shares*. This vivisection, however, is not the final comment on Bloomsworld; it is only one term in the dialectic of the chapter. For its effect is again like that of the pervading irony of the whole work, not to demolish Bloom and Stephen into scattered, fragmentary 'facts', but rather to show their ultimate invulnerability to this view of them. . . . The deeper affirmation does emerge nevertheless. . . . In the event, the 'scientific' perspective only heightens our sense of an imperishable dignity and vitality in the two characters . . . it points to what it cannot reduce to its terms . . . it parodies the method and outlook of naturalistic Realism in order to suggest what lies beyond its grasp.[43]

Goldberg's own grasp of 'the dialectic of the chapter' is less than sure, for while he posits one, and admits Bloom's 'share'— that is, the *adequacy* of the 'mask'—he is clearly more drawn towards the pole of 'affirmation'. Ultimately, Goldberg's view empties 'Ithaca' of ambiguity by denying the supremacy of 'fact'. But he does perceive the significance of the 'mathematico-astronomico-physico-mechanico-geometrico-chemico' myth as the extrapolation of the affirmative pole of meaning:

> Stephen's departure leaves Bloom alone once more. . . . We begin here to see him completely objectively and representatively; the narrative moves us away from all sympathetic identification *with* him towards a more abstract, depersonalized perception *of* him. He becomes less himself and more a symbol, now consciously and explicitly abstracted from the action. Only his most general outlines—or rather, his most essential

qualities—now remain. We examine him as a symbol of his society and its material ideals; then reduced . . . 'to a negligible negative irrational unreal quantity' . . . then as a prospective wanderer and exile from home . . . become at last an inter-stellar wanderer. . . .

[We] see them as a completed *action*, which is fulfilled both by the book itself to which it points as its goal and in the silent luminous *stasis* wherein all men appear as adventurers, all adventurers appear as one, and all adventure, all process, a simultaneous, static, eternal pattern—the entelechy of all history. . . . It is thus that Stephen and Bloom achieve their apotheosis, 'wanderers like the stars at which they gaze'.[44]

Because Goldberg is unwilling to admit that in true 'dialectical suspense' the opposing forces exist in permanent contradiction, he too easily assimilates the darker side of the progressive mythicizing of 'Ithaca' and the 'entelechy of all history' appears as a kind of liberal humanism—or worse as the 'one great goal, the manifestation of God' which is Mr Deasy's definition. The staticness of his picture might have put Gold-berg on his guard, but the term is part of his vocabulary of praise. Just as Kenner's praise of 'Ithaca' for reducing Bloom and Stephen hovers on the edge of acknowledging that the prose can only reflect on itself—the 'pathetic' and 'peri-phrastic absurdities'—Goldberg's patronage of them comes near to evidencing the hopelessness and cyclic fixity of the total pattern. Neither the approach from 'fact' nor the approach from 'myth' can alone satisfy our experience, nor can an approach which pretends to a comfortable synthesis—the celebrated 'fusion', *correspondance* or parallelism.

What both critical versions of 'Ithaca' share, however, is an emphasis on isolation, a separation between persons and things, or the reduction of persons to things. The language of 'Ithaca', in terms of a subject/object relationship, is at the furthest remove from that of the first six chapters, what Joyce called 'the initial style'. There, as Goldberg insists, subject and object are indistinguishable. In dialectical terms 'Ithaca' is the logical extremity of the separation of subject and object which, in one manner or another, by one literary strategy or another, has become increasingly prominent since Chapter Seven ('Aeolus'). *Ulysses'* final chapter, 'Penelope', describes one last swing of the pendulum, all the way back to the indistinguishability of subject and object of the first chapters.

The vein of 'Ithaca' has been re-opened in recent French novels. There the entire novel may be in the style of Joyce's chapter, the programmatic intention of the artist being to circumvent the metaphysical antinomy of subject and object by treating everything as an object. For example, from Alain Robbe-Grillet's *Jealousy*:

> [A] sits down in front of the dressing-table and looks at herself in the oval mirror, motionless, her elbows on the marble top and her hands pressing on each side of her face, against the temples. Not one of her features moves, nor the long-lashed eyelids, nor even the pupils at the centre of the green irises. Petrified by her own gaze, attentive and serene, she seems not to feel time passing.
>
> Leaning to one side, her tortoise-shell comb in her hand, she fixes her hair again before coming to the table. A mass of the heavy black curls hangs over the nape of her neck. The free hand plunges its tapering fingers into it.
>
> A . . . is lying fully dressed on the bed. One of her legs rests on the satin spread; the other bent at the knee, hangs half over the edge. The arm on this side is bent toward the head lying on the bolster. Stretched across the wide bed, the other arm lies out from the body at approximately a forty-five degree angle. Her face is turned upward toward the ceiling. Her eyes are made still larger by the darkness.
>
> Near the bed, against the same wall, is the heavy chest. A . . . is standing in front of the open top drawer, on which she is leaning in order to look for something, or else to arrange the contents. The operation takes a long time and requires no movement of the body.
>
> She is sitting in the chair between the hallway door and the writing table. She is rereading a letter which shows the creases where it has been folded. Her long legs are crossed. Her right hand is holding the sheet in front of her face; her left hand is gripping the end of the armrest.
>
> A . . . is writing, sitting at the table near the first window [etc., etc.]. . . .[45]

The supposed effect of 'objectivity' is secured in part through a sympathetic subject-matter ('requires no movement of the body', etc.), but also through continual reference to portions of the body ('her hands pressing', 'the free hand plunges', etc.)

used as attenuated metonymic subjects, generally with active verbs. The verbs attached to 'A . . . ' or 'she' are more often than not neutral ('seems', 'is lying', 'is standing'). The effect of reducing the integrity of personality to components no different in status from other objects in the room is additionally secured by the absence of verbs to follow A . . . 's movement from one place or position to another. (Robbe-Grillet and his 'school' have eschewed the use of active verbs in occasional manifestos.)

The whole procedure, in terms of the scale of 'styles or genres in description' suggested by W. K. Wimsatt, constitutes a diminution of the use of both 'the abstract or less than specific-substantive style' and the 'extra-concrete, the detailed, or more than specific style' in favour of a 'minimum concrete or specific-substantive style' neither '*implement*' nor '*rusty garden spade*', but '*spade*'.[46] Wimsatt calls 'the purely specific or substantial' level probably the rarest, citing Hemingway's 'The Killers' and the description of Brobdingnag in Book II of *Gulliver's Travels* as examples. While he does not define the effect of the use of this level, it may be inferred from his description of the others:

> Both the more than substantive style and the less than substantive are pre-eminently internal and reflexive modes of description—expressing on the one hand the intricately sensitive, Proustian awareness of experience in detail, and on the other the dreamy abstractness, the suffused vagueness of reverie.[47]

These descriptions of style touch, at their outer limits, on philosophical, if not metaphysical positions. It is doubtful, of course, that a particular technique alone could secure the intended effect, and congenial subjects—such as *human* apathy and alienation—help. Similar effects have been gained without the stylistic (or quasi-metaphysical) programme, as in Camus's *L'Etranger*.* On the other hand there is little doubt that particular 'styles', as can be seen from Wimsatt's comment on his three-part scale ('Proustian awareness . . . dreamy abstractness'), seem likely conventions for certain 'interpretations' of their subjects.

---

* Sartre's analysis makes Camus' style the father of Robbe-Grillet's and finds its origin in the 'American neo-realists' and Hemingway (Sartre, p. 39).

As Robbe-Grillet may be said to embody an Ithacan mode, Virginia Woolf may be said to have used the stream of consciousness to Penelopean purpose, *subjectifying* all.[48] The *'Ithaca episode'*, Joyce wrote Harriet Shaw Weaver on October 7th, 1921, 'is in reality the end [of *Ulysses*] as *Penelope* has no beginning, middle or end'.[49] It is perhaps best conceived as a process which goes on all the time during the novel, not just in Molly Bloom and between waking and sleeping. The style of 'Penelope' is, then, an approximation to a level of consciousness (or *un*consciousness) which is during the day working below the level of the 'stream' reproduced for Stephen and Bloom in 'the initial style'. Its verbalization by Molly is something of a pretext, but acknowledgement of the style's function in the logic of *Ulysses*' styles may help divert attacks from Molly herself by those who object to her supposed Great Motherishness.

The reasons why Joyce allowed 'the last word'[50] to Molly, rather than to Bloom, may be manifold, but like so much in the novel it functions to protect Joyce from appearing to put a definitive stamp upon his portrait of Bloom. To have exhibited Bloom's psyche at this level at this point without appearing to commit himself to one or another 'interpretation' he may have felt beyond him. He could go all down the line in presenting particular interpretations in various parody-styles, because our recognition of their 'literary' origins prevents us from ascribing the interpretations at face value to Joyce, but in the matter of an apparently direct representation of consciousness, no immediate similar recognition is possible. As it is, Molly seems, by virtue of her presentation in the last chapter, too programmatic for many tastes, the springs of her behaviour only too clearly revealed.[51] We are not yet so conditioned as to regard an author's presentation of consciousness as a literary mode, though 'Joyce himself came later to regard the interior monologue as a stylization, rather than a total exposition, of consciousness'.[52]

Whether in this instance Joyce's avoidance of telling us, in the manner of Molly, what Bloom was then 'thinking' constitutes an arbitrary refusal, whether the author has led us to ponder questions and entertain expectations whose answers and satisfactions he then deliberately withholds is a perennial question in dealing with the ellipticality of many modern 'story-telling' methods. As V. S. Pritchett has remarked of the method of Ford Madox Ford:

> His art—particularly the theory of the time-shift—was in part based on an analysis of talk, the way it plunges back and forth. . . . It often becomes a device for refusing to face a major scene.[53]

Joyce has the right to make 'Ithaca' the *end* of his story of Bloom: the often unprinted egg-shaped full-stop may be said to underscore this intention. It is equally allowable that, as Joyce has already in the novel suggested the infinite extensibility of the potential treatments of his story material, we be shown one of these extensions—to stand for a potentially large number—that of entry into the consciousness of another character. There is more justification here, perhaps, than for Joyce's ducking the 'very unpleasant scene at Westland Row terminus' (713/604).

Mulligan had presumably made a 'Gothic' exit from the Holles Street hospital, saying, 'Meet me at Westland row station at ten past eleven' (539/405). Bloom, arriving in Nighttown, 'thinks', 'Scene at Westland row' (579/444). The matter is broached again only by Bloom, with the suggestion that what has happened must mark a turning-point in Stephen's relations with Mulligan, and by implication with all his Dublin contemporaries. Asking Stephen where he will sleep that night, Bloom appears to suggest that even if Sandycove were not out of the question because it would be too long a walk, 'you won't get in after what occurred at Westland row station' (713/604). Bloom's 'interpretation' is a recognizable cliché, and therefore to be taken at discount: 'Except it simply amounts to one thing and he is what they call picking your brains, he ventured to throw out' (715/605). Stephen's mind, however, never seems, in 'Eumæus' or 'Ithaca', to run on the subject. Thus, when he has turned down Bloom's offer to let him stay the night at Eccles St, 'Promptly, inexplicably, with amicability, gratefully' (815/680), and has gone off into the night, the extent to which 'Westland row' is important to him remains undefined. To withhold information as to whether Stephen felt the 'scene' significant, even determinative, may constitute a 'refusal' (in Pritchett's terms). Or, if Stephen had just not yet thought

about the matter, then he is not brought, in *Ulysses*, to a
personal impasse of the magnitude of Bloom's in respect of his
marriage.*

That Joyce intended to present Stephen in this novel as
heading towards but not *yet* arrived at a clear predicament may
appear doubtful.† It seems clear that Bloom arrives at a defined
predicament on Bloomsday, never before having had to contemplate his position *vis-a-vis* Molly as he does on it. In this
respect the 'ordinary day' theories of *Ulysses* seem deficient
and it is more likely that both Bloom and Stephen were to be
presented as in individual moments of crisis, Stephen facing
what the psychologist Erik Erikson calls an 'identity crisis' and
Bloom the second of the major crises of adult life, the 'integrity
crisis'.‡

The stylistic manipulations of *Ulysses* to which the previous
pages have been devoted, all that which deviates from 'the
initial style' (and in particular ways) are part of the symbolist
dimension of the novel and cumulatively suggest what Ortega y
Gasset has called the 'dehumanization of art': the use of style
to 'deform reality' and to 'shatter its human aspect'.[54] S. L.
Goldberg, writing of *Ulysses*' 'Ithaca' chapter, alludes to Ortega;
he believes that Joyce 'drifted towards' dehumanization (or
abstractionism).[55] But that *Ulysses* (or Joyce) moves towards it is
no indication that the structure of *Ulysses* cannot accommodate
the movement. *Ulysses* does not begin as a 'dehumanization',
as its first chapters *humanize* the subject-object totality by lend-

* Joyce told Budgen that Ulysses was a more rounded character than Christ,
because Christ 'never lived with a woman[, s]urely . . . one of the most difficult
things a man has to do' (quoted by Ellmann, p. 449). 'Which domestic problem
as much as, if not more than, any other frequently engaged his mind? What to do
with our wives,' (*Ulysses*, 802/670).

† See Stephen's advice to Corley, in the cabman's shelter, to seek a job 'tomorrow
or the next day . . . in a boys' school at Dalkey for a gentleman usher' (709–10/601),
and on the other hand, William Empson, 'The Theme of *Ulysses*', in *A James Joyce
Miscellany, Third Series*, ed. Marvin Magalaner (Carbondale, 1962), pp. 127—54,
esp. p. 136.

‡ Erik Homburger Erikson, 'The Problem of Ego Identity', *Journal of the American
Psychoanalytic Association*, No. 4 (1956), pp. 56–121; *Childhood and Society* (London,
1961), chapter on 'Integrity'; and *Young Man Luther* (London, 1959), pp. 38–9,
248–56, which uses Stephen Dedalus's religious crisis in the *Portrait* to adumbrate
particular points. Erikson's whole exposition of the two complementary crises
bears striking resemblances to Kierkegaard on the transitional stages of experience.

ing support, alternatively, to Bloom's and Stephen's recognizably human versions of experience.

The encroachment of modernist stylistic experimentation into the novel can, at one extreme, be seen as attacks on the characters. According to Goldberg, Joyce 'does the worst that can be done to the characters and yet in doing so reveals their human validity'.[56] Having established the 'human validity' of Stephen and Bloom in the early chapters, Joyce initiates a process whereby he criticizes them, ethically, psychologically, ontologically, with all the weapons of 'modern art'. Whether they survive is moot and perhaps the only success desirable is that their survival remain an open question, providing the kind of drama of point of view discussed in respect of the *Portrait of the Artist*.

Symbolism (or, as Ortega has it, 'stylism') has, of course, not merely a destructive force, for 'dehumanization' can involve a super- or supra-humanization as well, as in the suggestions that Bloom *is* the Christ (745/627), though these are carefully guarded by being made part of Stephen's consciousness— Stephen sees Bloom as 'The traditional figure of hypostasis', but it is only a 'quasisensation' (808/674). Dehumanization has, then, both a depreciative and an appreciative pole. Corresponding 'naturalistically' to the depreciative is the sense of the way *things* weigh the characters down, the predicament outlined in Chapter Two, where Stephen's difficulty in finding a field of action for himself in Dublin was discussed. This was George Bernard Shaw's point about *Ulysses* when in the Preface to *Immaturity* he wrote,

> In 1876 I had had enough of Dublin. James Joyce in his Ulysses has described, with a fidelity so ruthless that the book is hardly bearable, the life that Dublin offers to its young men, or, if you prefer to put it the other way, that its young men offer to Dublin. . . . A certain flippant futile derision and belittlement that confuses the noble and serious with the base and ludicrous seems to me peculiar to Dublin.[57]

Shaw's subordinate alternative ('if you prefer to put it the other way') suggests that the 'derision and belittlement' may belong equally to Stephen.* Questions of responsibility aside, Goldberg notes the same of Bloom:

* It is questionable whether Shaw read beyond the first chapter.

113

What Joyce portrays is a man whose genuine impulse is toward Love but who can not discover any adequate image of himself as a social being practising it. . . . The process points to his essential humanity as well as to the absence of any available idea of social or personal relationships adequate to it.[58]

The issue Goldberg's arguments raise is whether *Ulysses*, by moving towards more and more radical stylistic versions as the novel proceeds, commits itself to the *direction* of these chapters. Goldberg obviously thinks not ('essential humanity'), but to arrive there he attributes the accumulating symbolisms to Joyce personally. 'Trust the tale', he quotes from Lawrence: but the teller *is* the tale.

Kenner, discussing the 'technics' of the novel, is almost alone in taking up the question of the styles as structuring the novel. He sees a *progression* of styles in *Ulysses*:

As the day runs on, everything moves towards death. Entanglement in matter, in cliché, and in weariness. . . .

Epilogue is not simply to Prologue as parody to exemplar. It is also as *reductio ad absurdum* to thing reduced. The social matter (Bloom's menage) vulgarizes the intellectual matter (Stephen's mind) because the latter already contains seeds of perversion.*

Kenner erects a structure for the 'technics': the 'Telemachia' and the 'Nostos' are mirror-versions, 'Eumæus' is a hyperbole of the 'parodied theological clichés of "Telemachus"', the 'impersonal' catechism of 'Ithaca' 'perfects' the 'personal' one of 'Nestor', ' "Proteus" circles around its protagonist just as does "Penelope" ', 'Molly has merely resolved the tensions of the earlier episode by accepting with smug satisfaction the body with which Stephen is at once so obsessed and so displeased.'[59] The structural parallels may be more convincing than the judgements of value which Kenner places on them, and once again the question of whether that which occurs later demolishes that which appears earlier cannot be finessed: it is a general problem inherent in the nature of romantic irony.[60]

Presently more important is Kenner's belief that by inspecting the 'technics' of 'the Odyssey' proper (Chapters Four to

---

* Kenner, p. 241. As the last sentence shows, Kenner's subscription to the primacy of an allegorical substantive level allows him to assert that 'vulgarization' is not merely a description of 'Bloom's menage'. It is for him a reflection back upon Stephen, whose prior imperfection ('seeds of perversion') is thereby proved.

Fifteen) 'we can see that the progression of styles enacts a drama even at this tabular level of abstraction'.[61] His 'table' is reproduced on the next page (p. 116); the prose explication he offers of it hardly seems adequate to the logical rigour the table itself suggests. His conclusion—'Thus the action of the book resembles the running down of an immense clock'[62]— merely echoes what he has said about 'mirror' chapters. His claim here, however, as it concerns *progression* and therefore the internal dialectic of the whole novel, is wider. If a single progression can be determined in the style, it may well amount to the most persuasive definite comment on the action available. On the other hand, the usual objections suggest themselves: *Ulysses* concerns the action of only one day—there will be others; the progression of different styles may only be an imitative approximation to ordinary diurnal psychic change and therefore make no individual comment on the human action. The situation is analogous to the variety of response possible to romantic irony, only in respect of point of view rather than subject-matter.

In the Byronic irony, Don Juan protests eternal fidelity to his first love as he becomes progressively more seasick.[63] If a Kenner would claim that Juan's 'retching' 'vulgarizes' his protestations—because these 'already contain seeds of perversion'—a Goldberg would hold that the passage, while 'doing its worst' to Juan 'yet reveals his human validity' (or 'essential humanity'). It would appear that a permanent 'dialectical suspense' of these views offers the only firm ground, however indeterminate it might leave particular cases. While earlier romantic ironists might embody suggestions of each view in the text itself (protestations *v.* retching), others might carefully avoid reference to either. If it seems possible to say of *Ulysses* that one can see in it either no progression or progression in two major, though contrary directions, the whole of the proposition must be the novel's 'structure'.

Another pattern than Kenner's is, however, perceptible in the progression of styles, a further refinement of the pattern of 'resonance' described earlier. Here resonance is not particularly to be found either in the order of plot incidents or directly in the contents of the characters' consciousnesses. It has moved outwards to the narrative technique.

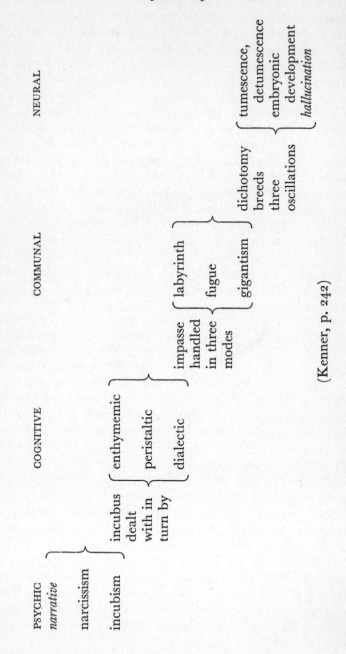

(Kenner, p. 242)

Seven chapters introduce Stephen, then Bloom, then Dublin, 'realistically', and three more recapitulate these, in characteristic activity (Bloom hunting lunch, Stephen expounding Shakespeare), with the Dublin scene then widened from the synecdoche of the newspaper office. Henceforth the chapters, or their parts, oscillate more and more strongly between 'symbolic' and 'realistic' presentation, between literary parody (of high and low literature) and the parody, or extension of common speech, between the super-conscious and the subconscious. The final swing has been characterized by Ian Watt as explicitly fulfilling the major implicit concern of the novel form in English:

> Joyce's *Ulysses*, which is in so many ways the climax of the novel's development, is certainly its climax in the treatment of the dualist extremes: in its last two books [sic] the graphic presentation of Molly Bloom's daydream and the cataloguing of the contents of her husband's drawers are defiantly unadulterated examples of the adjustment of narrative manner to the subjective and the objective poles of dualism.[64]

Progressive withering away of 'adulteration' is perhaps the key to the order of styles in *Ulysses*. And further, the progressive approach to—and, according to Watt, touching of—the ultimate extremes of 'the internal and the external approach to character' or 'the reality . . . of the ego [and] of the external world' demonstrates the limited efficiency of extreme presentations in *wholly* accounting for the human action related according to that 'narrative adjustment' which constitutes 'formal or presentational realism' in literature.[65] In this way, the 'styles' of *Ulysses* clearly demonstrate the 'limits' of the novel.

V

ULYSSES: THE SYMBOLIC
SCENARIO

---

his farced epistol to the hibruws. . . . a most moraculous jeeremyhead
sindbook for all the peoples.

—Finnegans Wake (228–9)

THE QUESTION OF progression in *Ulysses* may be further investi-
gated in reference to the homogeneous symbolist texture of the
novel (as distinct from the 'styles' of particular chapters). Here,
we may allow full play to our perception of such symbolist
paradigms as 'cyclic return'. Joyce's structural use of 'cycles' in
Finnegans Wake is well known and undisputed, though their
source, whether in Vico or elsewhere, is often a point at issue.[1]
Besides the numerous smaller cycles in the *Wake*, the hundred-
letter thunder-words end major cycles and initiate the next.

The notion of cyclic experience is double-faced. That
nothing is ever 'new', that every action is destined to be
repeated over and over again may suggest on the one hand
Sisyphus at his eternal task. We have already had occasion
to glance at this possibility in earlier chapters. On the other
hand, cyclic return can be taken, as does Mircea Éliade, to
represent a flight from 'the terror of history', towards 'the
"staticisation" of becoming, toward annulling the irreversibility
of time'.[2] In this view of 'archaic ontology', the reintroduction
of the new cycle brings a 'regeneration' and:

it is justifiable to read in this depreciation of history (that is, of events without transhistorical models), and in this rejection of profane, continuous time, a certain metaphysical 'valorization' of human existence.[3]

Thus, 'cyclic periodicity'[4] can represent either the 'bad karma'* in which repetition in history is seen as a futility of the spirit's expense from which the wise man attempts to detach himself, or the regenerativeness of which Éliade and some anthropologists write. And while Éliade finds

> that the work of two of the most significant writers of our day —T. S. Eliot and James Joyce—is saturated with nostalgia for the myth of eternal repetition and, in the last analysis, for the abolition of time,[5]

it is not incumbent on us to believe that in the developed dialectic of these two writers 'eternal repetition' will be as unambivalent as Éliade apparently believes.

Not only is the use of cyclism, then, uncommitted to either a cosmic optimism or pessimism—and we may compare the debate over the comic or tragic import of *Finnegans Wake*—but there is a further sophistication available for its mode of existence in a work of art: in *Ulysses* Joyce manages both to suggest the presence of cyclic return and to limit its warrant to exclusive control of his meaning.

There are many evidences of Joyce's predilection for the 'end' of a cycle. His personal interest in the Mass of the Presanctified—historically celebrated just prior to the Easter resurrection, during which time Christ is harrowing Hell and the Church awaits his 'return'—is discussed later in this chapter.[6] As early as the story 'Counterparts', whose scope does not invite allegorical expansion into the full 'myth of eternal return', Joyce was observing the repetitiveness of experience: Farrington, bullied at his office, fortifies himself at Davy Byrne's and totters home to bully and strike his son, the two bullyings being the 'counterparts' of each other. In 'Ivy Day in the Committee Room', six men (and the caretaker) celebrate the anniversary of Parnell's death, both deliberately and unconsciously. But the Uncrowned King will not, like the Christ

---

* *Ulysses*, 237/183; and see 233/180, Bloom's 'Holocaust. Karma they call that transmigration for sins you did in past life the reincarnation met him pikehoses'.

with whom Mr Hynes's poem compares him (*Dubliners*, 151/169), rise again. Their 'celebration' is ambivalent, both containing and lacking the psychic regeneration of which Éliade writes.* The reading of Hynes's 'The Death of Parnell' lifts the assembled out of the small-minded political bickering in which they have been engaged and even compels the respect of Crofton, the 'Conservative'. Another 'tak[es] out his cigarette papers and pouch the better to hide his emotion' (152/170). The story ends before their emotion is either eroded by the re-introduction of their more mundane interests or allowed to spill over into sentimentality. We know of course that this annual observance will have no outward effect on Irish political life—in *Ulysses* Bloom notes, 'Ivy day dying out' (140/109)—and so the outer 'cycle' will not renew; but the potential for inner renewal is suggested in 'Ivy Day in the Committee Room'. It is the same Hynes who, at Paddy Dignam's funeral in *Ulysses*, suggests,

—Let us go round by the chief's grave. . . . We have time.
. . . With awe Mr Power's blank voice spoke:
—Some say he is not in that grave at all. That the coffin was filled with stones. That one day he will come again.
Hynes shook his head.
—Parnell will never come again, he said. He's there, all that was mortal of him. Peace to his ashes. (142–3/111)

The use of cyclic experience in two other stories in *Dubliners*, 'Clay' and 'The Dead', is equally significant. Both these stories are set at what, in the 'archaic ontology' is the end of the old cycle or the 'threshold' of the new. This is what Frazer calls the 'intercalary' episode, to which he devoted a whole section of *The Golden Bough*.† Various cycles imply, naturally, various intercalary periods, as Shrove Tuesday/Ash Wednesday, Hallowe'en, the days between Christmas and Epiphany

* Thomas Mann, in 'Freud and the Future', makes a similar point about 'lived myth', quoting Ortega to the effect that 'the man of antiquity, before he did anything, took a step backwards, like the bull-fighter who leaps back to deliver the mortal thrust. He searched the past for a pattern. . . . For life in the myth, life, so to speak, in quotation, is a kind of celebration, in that it is a making present of the past, it becomes a religious act . . . it becomes a feast . . . (in *Essays*, trans. H. T. Lowe-Porter [New York, 1958], pp. 319–20).

† Part VII ('Between Old and New'), pars. 471–81; see *The New Golden Bough*, ed. Theodor H. Gaster (New York, 1959), pp. 559–78. This portion of *The Golden Bough* was first published in *The Fortnightly Review*, n.s. 68 (July–December 1900), pp. 653–76, 825–49.

(Twelfth Night), the days between Good Friday and Easter Sunday; but what Éliade calls the 'scenario of the end and the beginning of the year'[7] has a number of recurrent features. In speaking of 'the relations between the New Year ceremonies and the cult of the dead', Éliade notes,

> the beliefs, held almost everywhere, according to which the dead return to their families (and often return as 'living dead') at the New Year season (during the twelve days between Christmas and Epiphany) signify the hope that the abolition of time is possible at this mythical moment, in which the world is destroyed and recreated.* The dead can come back now, for all barriers between the dead and the living are broken (is not primordial chaos reactualized?), and they will come back because at this paradoxical instant time will be suspended, hence they can again be contemporaries of the living. . . .
>
> How could the invasion by the souls of the dead, for example, be anything but the sign of a suspension of profane time, the paradoxical realization of a coexistence of 'past' and 'present'? This coexistence is never so complete as at a period of chaos when all modalities coincide. The last days of the past year can be identified with the pre-Creation chaos, both through this invasion of the dead—which annuls the law of time—and through the sexual excesses which commonly mark the occasion. . . . [t]he abolition of all norms and . . . an overturning of values . . . in a word a reversion of all forms to indeterminate unity.[8]

The 'invasion of the dead' in Joyce's 'The Dead', whether tropically in the memories of the past during the dinner party or more pointedly in that of the 'ghost' of Michael Furey—who, in so far as his spirit contends with Gabriel Conroy for the possession of Gretta, becomes the 'carnival king' temporarily enthroned, with Gabriel the ousted sovereign 'humiliated' by him[9]—is a noted feature of the story. 'Clay', too, being set on Hallowe'en, when witches or ghosts are said to walk among the living producing 'inversions of rank',[10] forms a secular trope for the mysterious and dread time in which normal categories of experience are jeopardized and the conditions for the 'karma'

* Cf. C. J. Jung's initial reaction to *Ulysses*, that it is 'creative destruction' in a world given over to 'eternal repetition' which has 'no place for value', written in 'a mood befitting a cosmic Ash-Wednesday' ('*Ulysses*, A Monologue', trans. W. S. Dell, *Nimbus*, Vol. 2, No. 1 [June–August, 1953], pp. 9, 13, 18); his subsequent discovery of the creative aspect of *Ulysses* is discussed below, pp. 160–1.

of the next cycle are posited and potentiated. Maria, who has seemed to some a kind of 'witch', picks 'clay' in the fortune-telling game, which is the neutral substance, and the 'death' which is her 'fortune' has radiations of possible meaning.

During the Hallowe'en party Maria has dreams of reinstating remembered conditions, which she unconsciously projects by singing 'I Dreamt that I Dwelt'—

> But I also dreamt, which pleased me most
> That you loved me still the same. (118/132)—

and of restoring the antagonistic brothers Joe and Alphy, the first of a line culminating in Shem and Shaun, to friendship. It is the task of an ALP (as at *Finnegans Wake*, 194) and Maria fails:

> So Maria let him have his way and they sat by the fire talking over old times and Maria thought she would put in a good word for Alphy. But Joe cried that God might strike him stone dead if ever he spoke a word to his brother again and Maria said she was sorry she had mentioned the matter. Mrs Donnelly told her husband it was a great shame for him to speak that way of his own flesh and blood but Joe said that Alphy was no brother of his and there was nearly being a row on the head of it. But Joe said he would not lose his temper on account of the night it was and asked his wife to open some more stout. The two next-door girls had arranged some Hallow Eve games and soon everything was merry again.
>
> (116/130)

But the girls play an unsentimentalized version of their game, and Maria chooses 'death', the clay. After this she sings, her song affecting Joe as does Mr Hynes's poem the men in the Committee room; but here the effect is pointedly sentimental, and ironic on Joyce's part:

> Joe was very much moved. He said there was no time like long ago and no music for him like poor old Balfe, whatever other people might say; and his eyes filled up so much with tears that he could not find what he was looking for and in the end he had to ask his wife to tell him where the corkscrew was.
>
> (118/132)

And so with Joyce's deliberate delay of the word 'corkscrew' the story ends. 'Clay' is an end-of-the-year celebration gone sour, and no 'regeneration' may be assumed to have taken place. The stories in *Dubliners* are usually more open-ended than 'Clay', more ambivalent in their outcomes, like the remembrance ceremony (or mass) for Parnell dead but not risen in 'Ivy Day', and this is especially true of 'The Dead'.*

'The Dead' is set on the last night of the twelve-day 'intercalary' period following Christmas, that is, on the Feast of Epiphany itself. The night is the traditional European analogue of the Saturnalia[11] and socialized versions of all Éliade's conditions for the Epiphany feast are realized in Joyce's story. Kate and Julia Morkan's 'annual dance' 'was always a great affair' (199/224). Gabriel Conroy, a teacher in 'the college' (214/241),† prepares his usual speech for people whose 'grade of culture differed from his' (203/229). His disaffection from Dublin provinciality he bears like a chalice through the crowd, but the 'bitter and sudden retort' of a serving-girl discomposes him (202–3/227–9) and the banter of Miss Ivors, a nationalist, unnerves him further, perhaps by forcing him to formulate for the first time the precise nature of his disaffection, his un-'Irishness':

> 'O, to tell you the truth,' retorted Gabriel suddenly, 'I'm sick of my own country, sick of it!' (216/243)

His self-possession gutters in the course of the story and the ghosts of the past begin to assume more tangible shape than 'those great singers' (232/261) discussed by the guests and recalled by Gabriel in his speech. When Bartell D'Arcy sings 'The Lass of Aughrim' for Gretta Conroy, the spectre of yet another singer from the past arises. Perhaps the extent to

---

* As we have seen in the first chapter, many hover on the edge of 'entrapment', but by one means or another Joyce usually contrives to suspend judgement, to avoid blank failure for the characters. In the case of 'The Boarding House', the usual strategy seems to be reversed, and we watch the setting of the trap and its jaws closing. Joyce underlined his meaning by recreating Bob Doran, the trapped suitor, as a drunkard in *Ulysses*. He goes on 'periodical bends' (89/72) and is blind drunk by five in the afternoon (386ff./294ff.). On the other hand, to strike a balance, there is a suggestion that Martin Cunningham (in 'Grace') may be more 'free' in the novel than in the short story. Cf. *Dubliners*, 177/199, on Cunningham's wife, with *Ulysses*, 672/554, where he gazes 'impassivel[y]' at her and says, 'Immense! Most bloody awful demirep!'.

† Frazer notes the custom of colleges appointing a Lord of Misrule for the Twelve Nights (or from the Eve of All Saints' Day to Candlemas, February 2nd [Joyce's birthday] or from St Stephen's Day), 'to regulate the games and diversions' (Frazer, p. 566).

which his wife's memory of the boy who 'died for [her]' (252/283) humiliates Gabriel goes beyond Gretta's intruding Michael Furey into the current of egoistic possessiveness in which Gabriel is just at the moment enveloping her, remembering 'moments of their life together, that no one knew or would ever know of' (244/275). 'He longed to be master of her strange mood' (248/279), only to discover that she was engrossed with a buried life in which he had no part. Perhaps Gabriel's own previous refusal to come to terms with 'Irish' Ireland, with what Ellmann calls 'the primitive, untutored, impulsive country'[12]—

> 'Well, we usually go to France or Belgium or perhaps Germany,' said Gabriel awkwardly.
> 'And why do you go to France and Belgium,' said Miss Ivors, 'instead of visiting your own land?' (215/242)—

precipitates his discomfiture by the memory of Michael Furey of Galway. For whatever reasons, 'the dead' come to control Joyce's story, first the old singers and old Patrick Morkan, and lastly Michael Furey, all walking among the living.

David Daiches has written, 'The theme of "The Dead" is the assault on the walled circle of Gabriel's egotism'.[13] In this account the story is a parable of the breaking down of the 'norms' of Gabriel's life and a 'reversion to indeterminate unity'.[14] 'The Dead' ends with the completion of this process of destruction and we do not see the further outcome of Gabriel's new recognition of the separateness of his wife's existence, of the world outside whose claims he has resisted. We know only that he becomes 'shy of intruding on her grief', that he 'looked for a few moments unresentfully on her tangled hair and her half opened mouth', that 'It hardly pained him now to think how poor a part he, her husband, had played in her life' (253–4/285). A trace of sentimentalizing grows as his meditation extends. This tone becomes clearest in

> One by one, they were all becoming shades. Better pass boldly into that other world, in the full glory of some passion, than fade and wither dismally with age, (255/287)

and the rising tide of sentiment must be borne in mind as a paradoxical alternative to Richard Ellmann's summarization:

> The tone of the sentence, 'The time had come for him to set out on his journey westward', is somewhat resigned. It suggests

a concession, a relinquishment, and Gabriel is conceding and relinquishing a good deal—his sense of the importance of civilized thinking, of continental tastes, of all those tepid but nice distinctions on which he has prided himself. The bubble of his self-possession is pricked; he no longer possesses himself, and not to possess oneself is in a way a kind of death. It is a self-abandonment not unlike Furey's, and through Gabriel's mind runs the imagery of Calvary.[15]

'The final purport of the story' for Ellmann is 'the mutual dependence of living and dead'.[16] He points out that 'Ivy Day', 'A Painful Case' and the fantasias of both Bloom and Stephen in 'Circe' concern the relationship of the living and the dead.[17] He might have added, as we have seen, 'The Sisters' and 'Eveline'.

But if Gabriel's unresentfulness approaches Bloom's 'abnegation' and 'equanimity' or the advice Stephen gives to himself as he leaves the library ('Cease to strive'), we might expect to see it surrounded by the same ethical paradoxes as theirs. The suspicion of sentimentality—the gratuitous *Shropshire Lad* heroics of 'better pass boldly'—is a part of this paradox, as is the ambiguity of the 'death' Gabriel suffers. For we see the death only, and not the rebirth. The action at the end of a year-cycle culminates in the unfixity of the period 'between old and new'.*

Many items from the 'scenario' of cyclic ontology dot the texture of *Ulysses*. They help suggest that the action of the novel, like that of 'The Dead', takes place in the interim between periods of clearer definition—between Stephen as he appears to himself at the end of *A Portrait* and Bloom untroubled by the 'wife's admirers' (405/307) and whatever conditions appertain from June 17th, 1904, onwards. During this time we may expect problems latent in the former precarious equilibria to be sharpened to clearer focus, with a corresponding unfixity, a moment of crisis where the conditions out of which the future will arise are searched for their prediction—the period between crucifixion and resurrection; a chronological analogue for Kierkegaard's 'dialectical suspense'.

---

* J. V. Kelleher suggests to me that the Celtic myth of 'The Destruction of Da Derga's Hostel' influenced Joyce in 'The Dead'. 'The Destruction' relates the death of a king (Conaire > Connery > Conroy) and the end of a cycle. Other parallels may represent conscious influence or may testify to both stories' belonging to the same portion of a 'cycle'.

This scenario would suggest items concerned with the 'eleventh hour', the moment-before-the-last, the questioning of the present for the future as its emblems; and to these, as they appear in *Ulysses*, I now turn.

In this connection, two regular features of epic which concern the replacement of one order by another—in the *Aeneid*, the supplanting of Turnus; in *The Faerie Queene*, from Elizabethan England to the New Jerusalem; in *Paradise Lost* a reverse movement, from pre-lapsarian existence to the human condition—are the visit to the Underworld and the vision of the future. *Ulysses* has its 'Hades' (the sixth chapter), but it is to the emblem of augury, occurring as it does just before the end of epics, that our attention must be directed. Adam on 'a Hill/Of Paradise the highest',[18] the Redcrosse knight on 'the highest Mount'* find their counterpart in *Ulysses* in Stephen's 'DUBLINERS' story which he would title '*A Pisgah Sight of Palestine*' (189/148). 'I see,' says Professor MacHugh, 'Moses and the promised land. We gave him that idea, he added to J. J. O'Molloy.'

O'Molloy and MacHugh had been reciting from memory great Dublin orations, and O'Molloy's remembrance of Seymour Bushe on the law of evidence had recalled Bushe's remarks on 'the Moses of Michelangelo in the Vatican' (177/

---

* Spenser encyclopaedically assimilates Redcrosse's Mount to its analogues:

> That done, he leads him to the highest Mount;
> Such one, as that same mighty man of God,
> That bloud-red billowes like a walled front
> On either side disparted with his rod,
> Till that his army dry-foot through them yod,
> Dwelt fortie dayes vpon; where writ in stone
> With bloudy letters by the hand of God
> The bitter doome of death and balefull mone
> He did receiue, whiles flashing fire about him shone.

> Or like that sacred hill, whose head full high,
> Adorned with fruitfull Oliues all arownd,
> Is, as it were for endlesse memory
> Of that deare Lord, who oft thereon was fownd,
> For ever with a flowring girlond crownd:
> Or like that pleasaunt Mount, that is for ay
> Through famous Poets verse each where renownd,
> On which the thrise three learned Ladies play
> Their heavenly notes, and make full many a louely lay.
> (*The Faerie Queene*, I, x, liii–liv.)

138; it isn't). This had prompted MacHugh's recital of John F. Taylor's defence of the Irish language, ending,

> had the youthful Moses . . . bowed his will and bowed his spirit . . . he would never have brought the chosen people out of their house of bondage nor followed the pillar of the cloud by day. He would never have spoken with the Eternal amid lightnings on Sinai's mountaintop nor ever have come down with the light of inspiration shining in his countenance and bearing in his arms the tables of the law, graven in the language of the outlaw. (181/141)

This passage, which Joyce, as we have seen, later applies to Bloom, has its relevance for Stephen, who feels that he is being asked to accept 'our culture, our religion and our language'—versions of the *Portrait's* 'nets'. But if Taylor's vision of Moses ends in a kind of triumph, the triumph of the restored law ('the tables'; for Stephen, art), it also suggests personal 'failure': J. J. O'Molloy breaks the silence that follows with, 'And yet he died without having entered the land of promise' (181/141).* Success in the task and personal disappointment. Stephen thinks to himself,

> Gone with the wind. Hosts and Mullaghmas and Tara of the kings. Miles of ears of porches. The tribune's words howled and scattered to the four winds. A people sheltered within his voice. Dead noise. Akasic records of all that every anywhere wherever was. Love and laud him: me no more, (181–2/141–2)

and '[to] free his mind from his mind's bondage' (272/209), he suggests going for a drink. But MacHugh returns him to the subject:

> —Come along, Stephen, the professor said. That is fine, isn't it? It has the prophetic vision. *Fuit Ilium!* The sack of windy Troy. Kingdoms of this world. The masters of the Mediterranean are fellaheen today, (183/142)

and Stephen thinks, 'Dublin. I have much, much to learn'.† He then launches '*A Pisgah Sight of Palestine or the Parable of the Plums*', in which 'Two Dublin vestals' (183/143), having climbed the local 'highest Mount', Nelson's Pillar, take fright,

---

* The reference is to *Deuteronomy* 32:52 and 34:4. Joyce's title for the section is 'OMINOUS—FOR HIM!'.

† See, 'And here what will you learn more?' (43/35) and 'What here I learned? Of them? Of me?' (276/212).

'afraid the pillar will fall' (187/146). 'It makes them giddy to look up' at 'the statue of the onehandled adulterer'[19] Nelson:

—It gives them a crick in their necks, Stephen said, and they are too tired to look up or down or to speak. They put the bag of plums between them and eat the plums out of it, one after another . . . spitting the plumstones slowly out between the railings. (187–8/146)

It is, as Kenner comments, 'a parable of infertility',[20] * an aborted epic vision. Bloom, later hearing Stephen retell the 'parable' (and other 'scenes'), realizes the relief Stephen finds in the telling, 'by which potential narration was realized and kinetic temperament relieved' (802/669). Here MacHugh proposes that Stephen title his story, in part self-reflexively, *'deus nobis haec otia fecit'* (189/147). For the story is also a reproach to 'the life that Dublin offers to its young men', a personal *Improperia*.

Here a complex association begins to form. Stephen's story, being a reproach, can be titled *A Pisgah Sight of Palestine* by analogy to Moses' own report of the original sight, 'The Song of Moses' (*Deuteronomy* 32), which he delivers as a reproach to the people of Israel just upon his ascent to the top of Pisgah (*Deut.* 34:1), where he will receive his vision of the Promised Land and die. Stephen is shortly concerned to connect Moses with Shakespeare—each with a 'celestial phenomenon' to guide him (270/207)—and with Aristotle (805/671), but he is equally aware of the assimilation at this point to Christ.† His longest speech in the 'Oxen of the Sun' begins in the style of the Authorized Version (514/387) and recalls 'in structure and theme . . . the *Improperia* of the Catholic liturgy for Holy Week'.[21]

In the *Improperia*—or Reproaches—during the Adoration of the Cross in the Good Friday Office, the identification of Moses with Christ is explicit and sustained—e.g. Christ's *'Quia eduxi te de terra Aegypti: parasti crucem Salvatori tuo.'* The *Improperia* are, of course, Christ's reproaches addressed to the Jews, read out each year in the period between his death and resurrection.

---

* A Pisgah view is defined by *The Oxford Dictionary of the Christian Church* as 'any vision or hope of which a man will not see the realization'.

† The biblical locus is *Hebrews* 3:1–6. Cf. Spenser, quoted above p. 126.

Stephen's own explicit reproaches to 'Erin' conflate, in part, the *Improperia* with its sources in *Deuteronomy*:

> Remember, Erin, thy generations and thy days of old, how thou settedst little by me and by my word and broughtest in a stranger to my gates to commit fornication in my sight and to wax fat and kick like Jeshurum. Therefore hast thou sinned against the light and hast made me, thy lord, to be the slave of servants. Return, return, Clan Milly: forget me not, O Milesian. . . . Look forth now, my people, upon the land of behest, even from Horeb and from Nebo and from Pisgah and from the Horns of Hatten unto a land flowing with milk and money. But thou hast suckled me with a bitter milk: my moon and my sun thou hast quenched for ever. And thou has left me alone for ever in the dark ways of my bitterness: and with a kiss of ashes hast thou kissed my mouth. (514/387)*

Stephen extends his reproaches into a Brownean encapsulation of man's (and Moses') life, 'First saved from the waters of old Nile, among bulrushes' to 'at last the cavity of a mountain,

---

* Joyce may also have known the apocryphal 'Assumption of Moses', which contains among other things Satan's interruption of the Archangel Michael at his task of burying Moses and a disputation over the body (Michael wins)—but I cannot discover any use of this apt item in *Finnegans Wake*.

The 'Assumption of Moses' contains an important development of the notion of the Kingdom of God, for in Ch. 10 we are given to understand that 'The reign of God will not only be established by a judgement (and destruction) of men and nations. Evil is conceived as a cosmic force and the world as the Kingdom of Satan and his demonic powers (an idea found also in the new Hebrew [i.e., "Dead Sea"] scrolls); and the final triumph of the reign of God will bring the total destruction of the reign of Satan' (M. Black, 'The Development of Judaism in the Greek and Roman Periods', in *Peake's Commentary on the Bible*, eds. Black and Rowley [London, 1962], p. 698).

There was an edition of 'The Assumption of Moses' in 1897 by R. H. Charles, in which the text was first translated into English from the Latin text of 1861, its first publication. Charles was Professor of Biblical Greek at Trinity College, Dublin, from 1898 to 1906. He was 'the greatest authority of his day . . . in matters of Jewish eschatology and apocalyptic' (*The Oxford Dictionary of the Christian Church*, ed. F. L. Cross [London, 1957], p. 268) and he published editions in English of the whole *corpus* of late Jewish writings between 1893 and 1913.

Stuart Gilbert comments of the present passage in *Ulysses*, '[it is] undoubtedly personal, a remonstration in which, perhaps, many another artist out of Ireland might join. There is no blasphemy here, only a great sorrow which, in solitude, invokes its greatest prototype'. Gilbert connects the last words of the passage with Stephen's mother, to whom he 'for a moment likens his country' and points ahead to the appearance of the 'phantom of his mother' in 'Circe' (Gilbert, p. 302).

Cf. '[The] Eighth and ninth books of Moses' which Stephen sees on a book barrow (311/239). *Finnegans Wake* (4), alludes to the first *seven* books of the Old Testament, to Moses and to the Pentateuch.

an occulted sepulchre' (515/387). The 'Pisgah' material is thus the formal conclusion of the 'Exodus' (or life-journey) theme in the novel. The association of Ireland under the British yoke with Israel in Egypt is a Celtic commonplace: 'those that came to the land of the free', says the Citizen of Irish emigrants to America, 'remember the land of bondage' (428/324), and a mental slip of Bloom's associates the Exodus with the Odyssean journey of life:

> That brought us out of the land of Egypt and into the house of bondage. Something in all those superstitions [the *mezuzah* 'poor papa's father had on his door to touch'] because when you go out never know what dangers. (494/372)

Just as he cannot remember the word *mezuzah*, Bloom has earlier failed to remember Jewish lore in a striking instance of the presence and use of cyclic materials in the novel. 'AND IT WAS THE FEAST OF PASSOVER' reads the 'newspaper headline' of a section of 'Aeolus' in which the backwards distribution of type—'mangiD. kcirtaP.'—prompts Bloom to remember the Hebrew of his fathers:

> Poor papa with his hagadah book, reading backwards with his finger to me. Pessach. Next year in Jerusalem. Dear, O dear! All that long business about that brought us out of the land of Egypt and into the house of bondage *alleluia. Shema Israel Adonai Elohenu.* No, that's the other. Then the twelve brothers, Jacob's sons. And then the lamb and the cat and the dog and the stick and the water and the butcher and then the angel of death kills the butcher and he kills the ox and the dog kills the cat. Sounds a bit silly till you come to look into it well. Justice it means but it's everybody eating everyone else. That's what life is after all. (155/121)

The Passover (Pessach) *seder* (ritual meal) remembers the 'day in which ye came out from Egypt, out of the house of bondage; for by strength of hand the Lord brought you out from this place: there shall no leavened bread be eaten'.* In the Roman Catholic liturgical year, the place of this remembrance is the Second Lesson in the Good Friday Office; Bloom's recall of Passover is his analogy to Stephen's *Improperia*. The meal itself commemorates and recapitulates the

---

* *Exodus* 13:3. Bloom remembers the 'mazzoth' (unleavened bread) on p. 99/79.

Exodus whose story is told in the special prayer book used, the *Haggadah*. The word '*haggadah*' means a 'telling', and specifically in this context, the passing on of the history of the Jews from fathers to sons:

> In every generation, one ought to regard himself as though he had personally come out of Egypt. As it is said: 'And thou shalt tell thy son on that day, saying: This is on account of what the Lord did for me when I went forth from Egypt.' Not only our forefathers did the Holy One, blessed is He, redeem, but also ourselves did He redeem with them. As it is said: 'And us did He take out from there, in order to bring us hither, to give us the land which he had sworn unto our fathers.'*

The 'hither' of the *Haggadah* began to have a bitter sound to the Jews of the Diaspora, and the Passover *seder* came to have two complementary aspects, a strong sense of the weariness of a yearly repetition which did not regenerate in the wilderness of Europe—had not the Lord brought them 'into the house of bondage' after all?—and a messianic yearning for a time when the exodus of history would end—'Next year in Jerusalem' ('*L'shonoh ha'bo-oh beeroosholoim*').

Ashkenazic copyists added to the end of the *Haggadah* the children's song '*Chad Gadya*' ('One only Kid') which Bloom is attempting to recall. The song is a house-that-Jack-built with an allegorical history:

> [It is] interpreted as the history of successive empires that devastate and swallow one another (Egypt, Assyria, Babylon, Persia, etc.). The 'kid', bottom-most and most injured of all, is, of course, the people of Israel. The killing of the Angel of Death marks the day when the Kingdom of the Almighty will be established on earth: then, too, Israel will live in perfect redemption in the Promised Land.[22]

Bloom has remembered the song only as far as the *next-to-last* verse, in which the Angel of Death kills the butcher. Stopping here he may indeed ruminate on 'everybody eating everybody else'. Once again in *Ulysses* we are left one before the last term of a series, suspended between the apparently unalterable human condition where 'Next year in Jerusalem' is like 'jam

---

* *The Haggadah of Passover* (New York, 1956), p. 31. After this is said, the cup is lifted, and then praise is said, concluding with the *alleluia* Bloom remembers.

tomorrow' and the tantalizing possibility of regenerative change when,

> the Holy One, blessed is He, came and killed the Angel of Death, that slew the slaughterer that slaughtered the ox that drank the water that quenched the fire that burned the stick that beat the dog that bit the cat that ate the kid that father bought for two zuzim. One kid. One kid.[23]

Bloom's 'association' with Charles Stewart Parnell in *Ulysses* comprises an equally striking instance of Joyce's employment of the emblem of cyclic *transit*, representing a fusion of the materials already considered as well as an important addition to them.

'Parnell will never come again', Hynes had said at the Chief's grave (143/111). But his memory returns again and again in *Ulysses*. Bloom's own denunciation in 'Circe' follows the pattern of Parnell's 'fall'—

> FATHER FARLEY: He is an episcopalian, an agnostic, an anything-arian seeking to overthrow our holy faith.
> MRS RIORDAN: (*Tears up her will.*) I'm disappointed in you! You bad man!
> MOTHER GROGAN: (*Removes her boot to throw it at Bloom.*) You beast! You abominable person! (611/481)

After midnight the cabman announces,

> —One morning you would open the paper . . . and read, *Return of Parnell*. He bet them what they liked. . . . Dead he wasn't. Simply absconded somewhere. The coffin they brought over was full of stones. . . . He made a mistake to fight the priests. (753/633)

Bloom thinks it 'highly unlikely' that Parnell was not dead and 'even supposing' he was alive, that 'a return [was] highly inadvisable, all things considered'.

Still, the cabman's words set Bloom off on a train of thoughts about the Uncrowned King and twice over we are told (754, 760–2/634, 639)—and at extraordinary length—of the single occasion on which Bloom and Parnell 'met'. It was precisely at the time when Parnell was suffering, in a complex figuration which can be limned in Joyce's imagination, his 'agony' or 'Passover'.

132

When Parnell led his men in an attack on the offices of the *United Ireland*,

> His hat (Parnell's) was inadvertently knocked off and, as a matter of strict history, Bloom was the man who picked it up in the crush after witnessing the occurrence meaning to return it to him (and return it to him he did with the utmost celerity) who, panting and hatless . . . turned round to the donor and thanked him with perfect *aplomb*, saying: *Thank you, sir. . . .*
>
> (761–2/639)

This 'Homeric struggle'—Kitty O'Shea (Parnell)'s phrase[24]—occurred in December, 1890, *after* the meeting in Committee Room 15, when his 'trusty henchmen round[ed] on him with mutual mudslinging' (*Ulysses*, 754/634), but while he yet fought on, refusing to submit to demands for his resignation as leader of the Parliamentary party.

The image of the leader, 'falling, falling, but not yet fallen, still unfallen, but about to fall' exercised a hold hardly to be underestimated on Joyce's imagination. Perhaps even more central than the theme of *betrayal*—we remember

> This lovely land that always sent
> Her writers and artists to banishment
> And in a spirit of Irish fun
> Betrayed her own leaders, one by one.
> Twas Irish humour, wet and dry,
> Flung quicklime into Parnell's eye[25]—

is the notion of the leader who works on in the face of betrayal, knowing he will be betrayed but carrying on nevertheless. The explicitness of such an interpretation can be assigned directly to Joyce, from the article '*L'Ombra di Parnell*' which he contributed to *Il Piccolo della Sera* (Trieste) in May 1912:

> The melancholy which invaded his mind was perhaps the profound conviction that, in his hour of need, one of the disciples who dipped his hand in the same bowl with him would betray him. That he fought to the very end with this desolate certainty in mind is his greatest claim to nobility.[26]

Stanislaus Joyce has commented on the relevance of this view of Parnell in *My Brother's Keeper*:

> My brother was always of the opinion that a dramatist could understand only one or two of life's tragedies, and that he

133

always presented different aspects of the few he understood. One of the tragedies that obsessed my brother's imagination, beginning from the time when he first understood the Mass as drama, was the tragedy of dedication and betrayal. In later life, the story of Parnell became for him another aspect of that tragedy.[27]

Earlier, Stanislaus outlined just what 'the Mass as drama . . . the tragedy of dedication and betrayal' had signified to his brother:

On one of these strolls [across Dublin] I announced out of the blue that I would refuse to do my Easter duty. Jim made a half-hearted attempt to dissuade me from my purpose. . . .

—Don't you think, said he reflectively, choosing his words without haste, there is a certain resemblance between the mystery of the Mass and what I am trying to do? I mean that I am trying in my poems to give people some kind of intellectual pleasure or spiritual enjoyment by converting the bread of everyday life into something that has a permanent artistic life of its own . . . [sic] for their mental, moral, and spiritual uplift, he concluded glibly.

—I don't know, I said . . . what symbolical significance the Mass may be made to bear . . . and in any case it is quite impossible now to sift the ounce of truth from the bushel of legend.

—What do you consider legendary?

—The virgin birth, for example. In Roman history, long before Christianity was heard of, the legend was told of a vestal virgin, Rhea Silvia, and the alleged father was a god.

—The Christian legend is more interesting, said Jim. The Mass on Good Friday seems to me a very great drama. . . .

The mention of the Mass of the Presanctified was not made with the intention of diverting the discussion. . . . He understood it as the drama of a man who has a perilous mission to fulfil, which he must fulfil even though he knows beforehand that those nearest to his heart will betray him. The chant and words of Judas or Peter [it is Peter] on Palm Sunday, '*Etsi omnes scandalizati fuerint in te, ego numquam scandalizabor*', moved him profoundly. He was habitually a very late riser, but wherever he was, alone in Paris or married in Trieste, he never failed to get up at about five in all weathers to go to the early morning Mass on Holy Thursday and Good Friday.[28]

And in *Stephen Hero*, Stephen had described the Good Friday Mass to Cranly thus:

Isn't it strange to see the Mass of the Presanctified—no lights or vestments, the alter naked, the door of the tabernacle gaping open, the priests lying prostrate on the altar steps? . . .

—Don't you think the Reader who begins the mass is a strange person. No-one knows where he comes from: he has no connection with the mass. He comes out by himself and opens a book at the right hand side of the altar and when he has read the lesson he closes the book and goes away as he came. Isn't he strange? . . .

—You know how his lesson begins? *Dixit enim Dominus: in tribulatione sua* [*mane*] *consurgent ad me; venite et revertamur ad Dominum. . . .*

—He pleads, said Stephen. He is what that chalk-faced chap was for me, *advocatus diaboli*. Jesus has no friend on Good Friday. Do you know what kind of a figure rises before me on Good Friday?

—What kind?

—An ugly little man who has taken into his body the sins of the world. Something between Socrates and a Gnostic Christ— a Christ of the Dark Ages. That's what his mission of redemption has got for him: a crooked ugly body for which neither God nor man have pity.[29]

For young Stephen interest in the Resurrection is over-shadowed by the tragic nature of the 'Christian legend' or 'drama'. Holy Saturday, by comparison, has an altogether different effect: it is a comedy, which Stephen 'likes', but as a comedy.

[T]he Church seems to have thought the matter over and to be saying, 'Well, after all, you see, it's morning now and he wasn't so dead as we thought he was.' The corpse has become a paschal candle with five grains of incense stuck in it instead of its five wounds. The three faithful Mary's [sic] too who thought all was over on Friday have a candle each. The bells ring and the service is full of irrelevant alleluias. It's rather a technical affair, blessing this, that and the other but it's cheerfully ceremonious.

(122/117)

The 'lesson' Stephen quotes is the 'Prophecy from *Osee*' (*Hosea* 6:1–6). The Second Lesson is the institution of the Paschal meal (*Exodus* 12:1–11) and makes even clearer the extent to which Christ is friendless,* for many Missals print at

---

* Some of the force of this enters Cranly's 'Not only to be separate from all others but to have not even one friend' (*Portrait*, 251/292).

its head the allegorization, 'The children of Israel are to sacrifice the Paschal Lamb; the Israelites will put the Lamb of God to death on the Cross'.[30] The passage describes God's orders to Moses and Aaron when they were yet in Egypt, containing instructions as to the sacrifice of the Paschal lamb (the blood to be smeared on door-posts and lintel), and concludes (in the *Vulgate*), '*est enim Phase (id est transitus) Domini*'.[31] The Gospel which follows is St John's version of the crucifixion, after which the *Improperia* are recited.

The association between Moses and Parnell and their typification of Christ thus formed an unbroken circle for Joyce, for whom Parnell was 'like another Moses, [and] led a turbulent and unstable people from the house of shame to the verge of the Promised Land.'[32] Each is seen at the moment of his *Pasce*, which is his agony and only triumph—or rather, since the technical outcome is less important than the present reality, his 'nobility'. The place of the Passover in the cyclic ontology is as a 'borderline or transitional situation'.* The action of *Ulysses*, in so far as it partakes of cyclism, is positioned in the Paschal phase, and this extends to Stephen and Bloom alike. They celebrate it by initiating an Exodus of their own as Stephen departs from Bloom's:

In what order of precedence, with what attendant ceremony

---

* I use the phrase to denominate a portion of the complete cycle, but I have borrowed it from another context. It is J. N. Findlay's, from his discussion of Hegel's notion of 'becoming', which 'involves a perpetual borderline hesitation or vacillation between notions, which never settles down to a harmonious compromise. Hegel is not wrong in pointing out that our thought hates borderline or transitional situations, that it is averse to anything that would now be called a three-valued logic, and that it seeks to break up its subject-matter into mutually exclusive aspects or phases, so that the conceptual position of anything is immediately clear' (*Hegel, A Re-examination* [London, 1958], p. 158).

If this points to an alignment of ontological and metaphysical notions, one further extension may be relevant. Richard B. Sewell uses the notion of a 'boundary-situation' to describe the nature of tragedy and traces its origins as follows: 'Karl Jaspers has used the phrase since 1919, obviously inspired by his reading of Kierkegaard. It has had some currency, notably in Paul Tillich, *The Protestant Era*, University of Chicago Press, 1948: "The human boundary-situation is encountered when human possibility reaches its limit, when human existence is confronted by an ultimate threat" (p. 197)' (*The Vision of Tragedy* [New Haven and London, 1962], p. 151). Just as the Hegelian 'borderline' is an approach to the kind of 'drama' I have been arguing for Joyce, so the tragic 'boundary' may apply equally to the cyclic *phase* and the human action involved.

was the exodus from the house of bondage to the wilderness of inhabitation effected?

Lighted Candle in Stick borne by

BLOOM

Diaconal Hat on Ashplant borne by

STEPHEN

With what intonation *secreto* of what commemorative psalm? The 113th, *modo peregrinus: In exitu Israël de domus Jacob de populo barbaro.** (818/682)

Bloom is 'the centripital remainer' and Stephen 'the centrifugal departer' (826/688). Bloom has walked through his days and his crisis is domestic; Stephen exits to begin his odyssey, wandering, exodus.

Stephen's class-riddle was set when 'The bells in heaven / Were striking eleven' (32/27), and when he remembers it in Bella Cohen's, he initiates the train of fantasies which culminate in the appearance of 'THE MOTHER':

Why striking eleven? Proparoxyton.† Moment before the next Lessing says. Thirsty fox. (*He laughs loudly.*) Burying his grandmother. Probably he killed her. (666/545)

For it is the extent of his own responsibility in his mother's death ('Cancer did it, not I. Destiny' [681/565]) which is the ground of Stephen's 'remorse of conscience' in *Ulysses*. Just as the emblemata of the Bloom-plot bring their protagonist to a crisis of integrity over his relationship with his wife, so the Stephen-plot brings him to an eleventh-hour crisis in respect of his identity, past, present and future.

---

* This psalm is also liturgically commemorative of Christ's passion.

† In the *Portrait*, Stephen thinks of the Greek for a word with its accent on the antepenultimate syllable in connection with 'the first words of a woman which pierce the gloom and clamour of the first chanting of the Passion:—*Et tu cum Jesu Galilæo eras*' (248/288).

VI

ULYSSES: PHILOSOPHICAL
THEMES

MERCIUS (of hisself): *Domine vopiscus!* . . . Pariah, cannibal Cain,
I who oathily forswore the womb that bore you .., haunted by a
convulsionary sense of not having been or being all that I might
have been of you meant to becoming. . . .

—*Finnegans Wake* (193)

THE 'STYLES' AND THE SYMBOLIC TEXTURE of *Ulysses*, then,
both assume 'structural' importance. In so far as the former
draw further and further away from Stephen and Bloom as
presented in the first chapters, they constitute a progressive
withdrawal from a determinate judgement on the human
action of the novel. In so far as the latter locates the action and
problems of the novel in a 'boundary' near the end of a cycle—
but before the beginning of any next cycle—it inhibits the
elimination of possibilities of meaning and indeed promotes
their 'suspense'. The full spectrum of critical opinion is, as is
usually true of the hyperbolic literary forms,* a projection
of thematic conflicts within the work.

Three examples may be taken. (1) Critical views of Melville's
Moby-Dick tend to embody projections of the attitudes to the
whale and the chase entertained by Ahab, Starbuck, Stubb, etc.
The nine ships which the *Pequod* meets, as W. H. Auden has
pointed out, present spectra of views about the White Whale.[1]

* Cosmological, encyclopaedic, ontologically and epistomologically dialectical;
see Northrop Frye, *Anatomy of Criticism* (Princeton, 1957), pp. 315–26 and *passim.*

This diagrammatic quality is repeated at other points in the novel, in respect of other matters, sometimes—as in the cases of the doubloon which Ahab hammers into the mast, which the crew interpret each according to his own nature (Chapter 99), the picture on the wall of the Spouter Inn (Chapter 3), and the markings on Queequeg's body—suggesting not only an entire range of possible interpretation but an imperilling relativism and cancellation of views.

(2) The pursuit of his various 'educations' leads Henry Adams in a similar direction, and the cartoon (possibly) by Raffaello[2] is accorded the same treatment as the picture in the Spouter Inn in *Moby-Dick*. The tendency to treat the meaning of experience as an unknowable *noumenon* evidenced—if at all —by indeterminate phenomena pervades both books. Adams presents a neat emblem of the extent to which experience becomes a neutral Rorschach 'blot' when he describes the St Gaudens monument over his wife's grave, suggesting that one sees in it only a reflection of one's personal bias.[3]

(3) In Forster's *A Passage to India* the characters again represent the spectrum of possible attitudes to the 'mystery' (or 'muddle') of India. Reuben Brower claims that the logic of the alternatives requires that no single interpretation prevail and that when, at the novel's end, Forster appears to present a particular one as having primacy, he is betraying the integrity of his conception.[4]

Where Melville and Forster use individual characters to represent the spectrum, in the manner of a 'philosophical' novel like Camus' *La Peste*, Joyce in the first instance does not. In *Ulysses*, as in the *Portrait*, the paradoxes and mutually exclusive interpretations exist largely as a function of 'style' or point of view. As a result, each of the major characters, instead of being clear and agreed representations of particular positions, have clustered about them those wider antinomies which are involved in one's perception of the novel's meaning. (See the Diagram, p. 140.)

Novels whose 'meaning' seems to embrace paradoxes of a wide nature, especially epistomological and ontological paradoxes, run peculiar dangers. As the alternative interpretations they bring to notice are below the level, as it were, of what novels are often taken to be about, as they imperil the very postulates which can be assumed for most novels—proceeding *from* which ordinary critical statement is made—they are liable to misunderstanding of various kinds. Most prominent is the assumption that the ordinary postulates are still there (as, that Joyce's *world* is 'fixed'). Passing over objections which are based only on a resistance to these kinds of fiction, there is yet a special risk of over-generalization. An implied ontology or epistomology may possibly be extrapolated from every work of art: it may, however, turn out to be the merest of common-places. Only the particular finding can justify the procedure.

THE PHILOSOPHICAL NOVEL:

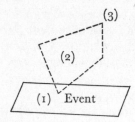

(3)   Interpretation (synoptic of
characters' responses)

(2)   Characters (take distinctive
response)

(1) Event   Action

ULYSSES:

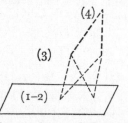

(4)   Interpretation (synoptic of
alternative responses)

(3)   Alternative responses to
Character/Events, made by
reader (or by chapter-styles)

(1–2)   Action: Character/Event

The alternatives of Stephen's and Bloom's future selves, being simplifying projections of their present states, are reflections of the opposing metaphysical positions from which they can be inspected. The alternatives of stagnation (or repetition) and development are mirrored by the metaphysical terms *stasis* and *kinesis* used by Stephen in the *Portrait*. Stephen had espoused *stasis* as a condition both of art and life, to the exclusion of any kinetic response.

S. L. Goldberg has prepared the best case for the rightness of Stephen's choice,[5] but he does not relate the terms precisely to ideas of actuality and possibility. In some unspecified manner a successfully achieved *stasis* is supposed to release the best possibilities into a condition of actuality. But Goldberg's conclusion is lame—'The development of the soul is thus the sequence of the epiphanies [=*stases*] it discovers'—because it must smuggle in the back way the terms ('development', 'sequence'=*kinesis*) earlier ushered out the front.[6]

In construing Stephen's cogitations on time, actuality and possibility—

> Had Pyrrhus not fallen by a beldam's hand in Argos or Julius Caesar not been knifed to death. They are not to be thought away. Time has branded them and fettered they are lodged in the room of the infinite possibilities they have ousted. But can those have been possible seeing that they never were? Or was that only possible which came to pass? (30/26)—

it is well to look to the 'answer' which Stephen himself gives a few moments later, apropos of the paradox of Lycidas, 'Sunk . . . beneath the watery floor' (actuality), yet 'not dead' (his drowning has not 'ousted' his alive-ness):*

> It must be a movement, then, an actuality of the possible as possible. Aristotle's phrase formed itself within the gabbled verses and floated out into the studious silence of the library of Saint Genevieve. . . . Thought is the thought of thought. Tranquil brightness. The soul is in a manner all that is: the soul is the form of forms. Tranquillity sudden, vast, candescent: form of forms. (30-1/26-7)

Goldberg has traced the 'form of forms' to Aristotle's *De Anima*,[7] but he ignores the beginning of Stephen's train of thought, which is Aristotle's (and his) explicit 'solution' to the problem of possibility in conflict with actuality: 'It must be a movement, then, an actuality of the possible as possible.' 'Aristotle's phrase' is in the *Physics*[8] and the word 'movement' in Stephen's translation stands for Aristotle's *kinesis* (κίνησις) which, far from being banished as the disreputable alternative, is thereby elevated to a key role in synthesizing the possible and actual:

> 201ª10 Definition. The fulfilment [Stephen says actuality] of what exists potentially [S: of the possible], in so far as it exists potentially [S: as possible], is motion [*kinesis*, movement]. . . .

* Young Talbot, who is reciting the poem, quotes the Christian 'solution' to this paradox,
  —*Through the dear might of Him that walked the waves.*
Only the 'dear might' of Christ guarantees that one may be 'sunk' yet 'not dead'.

201^b . . . clearly it is the fulfilment of what is potential as potential that is motion.

202^a Hence we can define motion as the fulfilment of the movable *qua* movable. . . .^{9}

In transferring, as he does, this 'definition' of motion from a physical plane to the metaphysical and ethical, Stephen Dedalus is following the main Aristotlian philosophical tradition. Aristotle repeats his definition of movement in the *Metaphysics* (1065^{b}15—1066^{a}5) and its place there, as Werner Jaeger has stated, is central:

> The whole first book of the *Metaphysics* . . . would collapse if the aetiology of the *Physics* were not behind it in every line. . . . [I]ts whole philosophical conception presupposes the *Physics* and develops out of it. Two of the foundations of Aristotle's first philosophy belong to the *Physics*, and they are the most important of all, namely the distinction between matter and form and the theory of motion . . . even that pair of conceptions by means of which motion is linked up with form and matter, namely potency and entelechy, is not foreign to the *Physics*.^{10}

Jaeger's exposition of Aristole's metaphysics at one point follows the precise course which underlies Stephen's stream of consciousness, and is worth extended quotation, showing as it does the Aristotelian dialectic which lies behind Stephen's movement from the 'actuality of the possible as possible' to soul as 'the form of forms', from *kinesis* (*Physics*) to entelechy (*De Anima*):

> Metaphysics is based on physics according to Aristotle in the first place because it is nothing but the conceptually necessary completion of the experimentally revealed system of moving nature. The prime task of physics is to explain motion. . . .
>
> Aristotle anchors this branch of knowledge still more firmly in physics by means of his analysis of the conception of substance. . . .
>
> [He] considered it axiomatic that nothing universal possesses independent existence. . . . Matter is the remnant, the nonexistent, in itself unknowable and alien to reason, that remains after [the] process of clarifying the thing into a form and a conception. . . . Hence no matter is just matter . . . it is matter for this definite form. . . . Nothing absolutely formless 'is' at all. . . .
>
> In this way form comes to explain motion as well. . . . The aim of Aristotle's theory of motion is to invent a logic of it. . . .

With reference to motion the form is the entelechy (ἐν–τελ–έχια), inasmuch as in its form each thing possesses the end of motion realized within itself. For the heavenly bodies this is their eternal circular revolution, but Aristotle carries over the principle to earthly things as well. . . . [T]he fundamental principle of change in the organic world is the same as it is in the heavens, namely locomotion, to which all kinds of motion are to be referred. Locomotion here serves the special laws of organic coming-to-be and passing-away, which in their turn depend on the form. The entelechy of beings that come to be and pass away is the height of this organic development. In them form appears as an orderliness and determinateness building from within and unfolding itself from the matter as from a seed. . . .

[But] the meaning of 'entelechy' is not biological; it is logical and ontological. In every kind of motion Aristotle's gaze is fastened on the end . . . that something fixed and normative is making its way into existence—the form. . . . The notions of potency and act [also] . . . must be taken from human power or δύναμις, which now remains latent and now becomes active (ἔργου), attaining its end (entelechy) only in this activity (ἐνέργεια). . . .

The higher we ascend in the cosmos, the more purely the motion expresses the form that is its end. As a whole the motion of the world is the effect and expression of a form that is absolute and free of all matter. . . . Reality is in its determinateness and in its essence necessarily what it is. It cannot be explained from mere possibility and chance, for then it might as well not be or be otherwise. There must be form at the head of motion, and the highest form must be pure act, through and through determination and thought.* This thought cannot think anything more perfect than itself, for as the end of the motion of the whole world it is necessarily the most perfect thing existing, since everything aims towards it. Nevertheless, the thought that thinks itself is not a merely formal self-consciousness devoid of content. . . . In Aristotle's teleology substance and end are one, and the highest end is the most determinate reality there is. This substantial thought possesses at one and the same time the highest ideality as conceived by Plato and the rich determinateness of the individual.[11]

---

* This is the essential paradox—that form must not destroy the reality of motion, nor motion the reality of form, but both must coexist. What follows can best be regarded as a postulation of the necessary condition for such a conclusion.

Jaeger is hard-pressed at times to rescue his exposition from determinism (especially in the denial of the 'organic' origin of the terms).[12] His 'argument' is finally less a 'proof' than a series of contingent paradoxes; all the same, it demonstrates the clear Aristotelian line from 'movement' to the 'thought of thought' and 'form of forms', by way of notions of substance and entelechy.

The bridge notions are not raised to consciousness in Stephen's classroom musings, but his possession of them is borne out later in the day. 'But I, entelechy, form of forms,' he thinks in the library, 'am I by memory because under everchanging forms' (242/187).* The notion of entelechy is combined with that of substance in a personal comic tableau concerning a pound note which A. E. (George Russell) had lent Stephen:

> Wait. Five months [have passed since the loan]. Molecules all change. I am other I now. Other I got pound.
> Buzz. Buzz.
> But I, entelechy, form of forms, am I by memory because under everchanging forms.
> I that sinned and prayed and fasted.
> A child Conmee saved from pandies.
> I, Land I. I.
> A.E. I.O.U.   (242–3/187)

The expression is comic, but the 'applied Aristotle' has its point: Stephen accepts his indebtedness. It is Aristotle who 'proves' that he is now the person he then was, despite physical change.†

Moments later, attempting to 'shake [Eglinton's] belief that Shakespeare is Hamlet', Stephen transfers the notion to that of artistic creation:

> —As we, or mother Dana, weave and unweave our bodies, Stephen said, from day to day, their molecules shuttled to and fro, so does the artist weave and unweave his image. And as the mole on my right breast is where it was when I was born, though all my body has been woven of new stuff time after time, so through the ghost of the unquiet father the image of the unliving son looks forth. In the intense instant of imagination,

* See also 564/425: 'the first entelechy, the structural rhythm' (a translation of the paradox of 'formal motion').

† Cf. Bloom's more mundane version: 'I was happier then. Or was that I? Or am I now I?' (213/165).

144

when the mind, Shelley says, is a fading coal[,] that which I
was is that which I am and that which in possibility I may come
to be. So in the future, the sister of the past, I may see myself
as I sit here now but by reflection from that which then I shall
be. (249/192)

The Shakespeare who has lived through 'the hell of time',
Stephen assimilates to Pericles, 'shipwrecked in storms dire,
tried, like another Ulysses' (ibid.). (This is Stephen's only
reference to Ulysses in the course of the novel.)*

The version of Stephen's predicament according to Bunyan
(in 'Oxen of the Sun') makes it clear that the earlier metaphysical speculations have personal ethical relevance:

Heard he then in that clap the voice of the god Bringforth or,
what Calmer [Bloom] said, a hubbub of Phenomenon?
Heard? Why, he could not but hear unless he had plugged up
the tube Understanding (which he had not done). For through
that tube he saw that he was in the land of Phenomenon where
he must for a certain one day die as he was like the rest too a
passing show. And would he not accept to die like the rest and
pass away? By no means would he. . . . (516/389)

Here the narrator posits Stephen's problem as precisely that of
possibility—or potentiality—(Bringforth') *versus* actuality
('Phenomenon'),† concluding that Stephen's difficulty lies in a
refusal to resign himself to the latter and to mortality. Stephen's
own conclusion about Shakespeare had been similarly gloomy:

He found in the world without as actual what was in his world
within as possible. Maeterlinck says: *If Socrates leave his house
today he will find the sage seated on his doorsteps. If Judas go forth
tonight it is to Judas his steps will tend.* Every life is many days,
day after day. We walk through ourselves, meeting robbers,
ghosts, giants, old men, young men, wives, widows, brothers-
in-love. But always meeting ourselves.‡ (273/210)

* The allusion is taken over from Georg Brandes: 'Pericles is a romantic
Ulysses, a far-travelled, sorely tried, much-enduring man' (*William Shakespeare: a
Critical Study* [London, 1898], p. 585). See also Eglinton's 'Ulysses quote[s] Aris-
totle' (*Ulysses*, 271/209).

† Or, 'Believe-on-Me' (the New Testament) *versus* 'the book Law' (the Old)
(517/389).

‡ Cf. Bloom, 491–2/370: 'The year returns. History repeats itself. Ye crags and
peaks I'm with you once again. Life, love, voyage round your own little world. . . .
'The new I want. Nothing new under the sun. Care of P.O. Dolphin's barn. . . .

Stephen is here captured by repetitveness and by the assimilative tendencies of the human animal *never* to 'encounter reality'—as had been his fond hope at the end of the *Portrait*—but only to meet self-projections.* Giddily reviewing the problem some hours later in the brothel he thinks,

(*Abruptly.*) What went forth to the ends of the world to traverse not itself. God, the sun, Shakespeare, a commercial traveller, having itself traversed in reality itself, becomes that self. Wait a moment. Wait a second. Damn that fellow's noise in the street. Self which it itself was ineluctably preconditioned to become. *Ecco!* (623/494)

'That fellow' is the '*dio boia*, hangman god' (274/210) who arranges that we always meet ourselves in a personal history which is always and only a 'hubbub of Phenomenon'. Here he is associated with the 'shout in the street' Stephen had called 'God', identifying for himself God and 'history' as equally tending towards the inertness of mere phenomena:

—History, Stephen said, is a nightmare from which I am trying to awake.

From the playfield the boys raised a shout. A whirring whistle: goal. What if the nightmare gave you a back kick?

—The ways of the Creator are not our ways, Mr Deasy said. All history moves towards one great goal, the manifestation of God.

Stephen jerked his thumb towards the window, saying:

—That is God.

Hooray! Ay! Whrrwhee!

—What? Mr Deasy asked.

—A shout in the street, Stephen answered.† (42/35)

Thus Stephen's conclusions are that the God of this world is a version of Blake's Nobodaddy—his thunderclap precipitates

So it returns. Think you're escaping and run into yourself. Longest way round is the shortest way home. And just when he and she.'
The whole of this passage is rich in texture: It gathers up the notion of 'always meeting yourself' with a handful of prominent themes, including the repetitiveness of history, disappointment, the Ulyssean travel-motif, and Bloom's personal fantasies, memories and anxiety.

* Ellmann and Mason (*Critical Writings*, p. 130) note the reappearance in 'Scylla and Charybdis' of Joyce's 1903 remark that 'Leonardo . . . has noted the tendency of the mind to impress its own likeness upon that which it creates'. Cf. '[*Ulysses* is] a parable of solipsism' (D. S. Savage, *The Withered Branch* [London, 1950], p. 169).

† See also 238/184: 'God: noise in the street: very peripatetic', and 676/599: 'Hark! Our friend, noise in the street!'

the parable of Bringforth and Phenomenon*—and that He insures that 'history' is no more than a phenomenal repetition of 'day[s] after day[s]' in which we 'walk through' only ourselves. 'What went forth . . . to traverse not itself', 'to encounter . . . the reality of experience'? Neither himself nor any man.

'Ineluctability', inescapability has played through Stephen's mind most of the day, growing to include various aspects of his experience. First it extends to space, the 'modality of the visible', and time, the 'modality of the audible', which he calls the *nebeneinander* and the *nacheinander*.† Stephen hates the temporal extension of things, one after another, 'history', 'He hates past time because it would bind him with present duties'.[13] Throughout the *Portrait* he has courted the *nebeneinander*, space, the static dimension. Now it is the other dimension which menaces him, the 'back kick' (42/35) of 'history'.

There is, however, a significant counterpoint to Stephen's pessimistic view of the 'nightmare of history' in *Ulysses*. Before Stephen arrives at the Maeterlinckean formulation of experience as a mere mirror, the notion had occurred to him apropos of Lyster's commonplaces on the interpretations of *Hamlet*:

> Harsh gargoyle face that warred against me over our mess of hash of lights in rue Saint-André-des-Arts. [Stephen is thinking of his meeting with Synge in Paris.] In words of words for words, palabras. Oisin with Patrick. Faunman he met in Clamart woods, brandishing a winebottle. *C'est vendredi saint!* Murthering Irish. His image, wandering, he met. [I.e., his experience was 'Syngian'.] I mine. I met a fool i' the forest.
> —Mr. Lyster, an attendant said from the door ajar.
> — . . . in which everyone can find his own [face]. So Mr Justice Madden in his *Diary of Master William Silence* has found the hunting terms. . . . Yes? What is it?
> —There's a gentleman here, sir, the attendant said, coming forward and offering a card. From the *Freeman*. (256/197–8)

* Cf. *Finnegans Wake*, p. 221: 'the Pageant of Past History worked up . . . by Messrs. Thud and Blunder.' The 'thunderwords', of course, open (and close) historical cycles, and 'Sandhyas' (593) are 'period[s] which precede a Yugareon, the period[s] intervening between the expiration of one Yuga and the commencement of another' (B. P. Misra, 'Sanskrit Translations', *A Wake Newslitter*, n.s. Vol. I, No. 6 [December, 1964], p. 8).

† The terms are in fairly common usage, but the *Concordance* to Hegel does not list them. In *Finnegans Wake* it is Shem who is associated with time and Shaun, who can't 'keep time', with space (see 152–9, 'The Mookse and the Gripes'). Joyce prided himself on his 'definitions' of space and time; see Budgen, p. 49.

A moment later, Buck Mulligan pounces on the 'card' and we learn that the 'gentleman' is Bloom. It is the first time in the novel that his path has crossed Stephen's.* The significance of his entry upon the note of 'self-meeting'—'His image, wandering he met. I mine. . . . in which everyone can find his own'—will shortly become apparent.

Leaving the library in the company of Mulligan, Stephen recalls Maeterlinck on Socrates meeting only himself and thinks of parting from his own appointed betrayer:

> Part. The moment is now. Where then? If Socrates leave his home today, if Judas go forth tonight. Why? That lies in space which I in time must come to, ineluctably.
> My will: his will that fronts me. Seas between.
> A man passed out between them, bowing, greeting.
>
> (279/214)

There is no reason to part, even if 'where' to go is unknown, if space/time 'lies' (like the Leviathan) ineluctably ahead. The 'Scylla and Charybdis' of the chapter, usually construed as signifying 'the stability of Dogma, of Aristotle and of Shakespeare's Stratford . . . contrasted with the whirlpool of Mysticism, Platonism, the London of Elizabethan times',[14] between which Stephen must pass, here becomes 'My will' and 'his will [Mulligan's] that fronts me'. Given 'ineluctability', the choice seems illusory, but precisely at this moment 'a man' does *pass between* them: it is Bloom.

Stephen is standing at the portico of the National Library, the place from which, in the *Portrait*, he had watched the birds in the sky for an omen of his future—'Then he was to go away? . . . Symbol of departure or of lonliness' (230/265). Bloom passes between him and Mulligan, he is again at the portico and he remembers this previous search for an omen:

> A man passed out between them, bowing, greeting.
> —Good day again, Buck Mulligan said.
> The portico.
> Here I watched the birds for augury. Ængus of the birds.
> They go, they come. Last night I flew. Easily flew. Men

---

* On the way to Dignam's funeral, Bloom had noticed Stephen in the street and pointed him out to Simon Dedalus (109/87). They miss being in the newspaper office together by minutes. Their 'previous encounters' (two—Stephen aged five and ten) are detailed in 'Ithaca', 795/664.

wondered. Street of harlots after. A creamfruit melon he held to me. In. You will see. (279/214–15)

Casting about for a present omen, he remembers his dream of the previous night. This dream, which Stephen apparently had before and after Haines had awakened him screaming about the black panther, has prepared us for the significance of a meeting with a stranger:

> After he woke me up last night same dream or was it? Wait. Open hallway. Street of harlots. Remember. Haroun al Raschid.*
> I am almosting it. That man led me, spoke. I was not afraid.
> The melon he had he held against my face. Smiled: creamfruit smell. That was the rule, said. In. Come. Red carpet spread.
> You will see who. (58–9/47–8)

William Empson has been alone among critics in considering Stephen's dream a crucial element in the novel. (He finds the dream confirmed by what he calls 'the Bloom offer'[15] of Molly to Stephen.) In 'Circe' it is when Stephen remembers his dream that Bloom approaches him:

> STEPHEN: Mark me. I dreamt of a watermelon. . . .
> (*Extending his arms.*) It was here. Street of harlots. In Serpentine Avenue Beelzebub showed me her, a fubsy widow. Where's the red carpet spread?
> BLOOM: (*Approaching Stephen.*) Look. . . .
> STEPHEN: No, I flew. My foes beneath me. And ever shall be. World without end. (*He cries.*) *Pater!* Free!
> BLOOM: I say, look. . . . (674/556–7)

Stephen seems too much within his own world to hear or see that which lies unineluctably outside it. What rises to him is not the 'reality' of Bloom but that other '*Pater*', Simon Dedalus, '*on strong ponderous buzzard wings*' (674/557).

What Joyce's carefully drawn 'exposition' of the gradual meeting of Bloom and Stephen suggests is that Bloom might be for Stephen an instance of the 'not [him]self', the unineluctable, an opportunity to break the cycle of 'assimilation'. That Bloom is a 'challenge' to Stephen has general credence, even if his

---

* In 'Circe' 'VOICES' call Bloom 'Haroun Al Raschid' (652/528) and leaving the brothel, Bloom momentarily metamorphoses into Haroun (685/570).

success or failure is often prejudged. In the words of R. P. Blackmur,

> [Stephen's] hope is to make an epiphany of the darkness shining in brightness. . . . Bloom is that darkness projected. . . .
> Stephen has somehow to become Bloom, or see the need of it.[16]

Stephen may or may not make of his meeting with Bloom a 'charismatic' incident, *bringing forth* a new attitude in him, and even if he does, Joyce is at pains to point out that his 'success' is not thereby assured. Just prior to Bloom's addressing Stephen, Joyce projects a fantasy in which Stephen and Bloom literally become 'one'. The emblem of their one-ness is the 'face of William Shakespeare', which seems to suggest that a 'synthesis' of Stephen and Bloom would qualify one for artistic triumph, but something is awry:

> (*Stephen and Bloom gaze in the mirror. The face of William Shakespeare, beardless, appears there, rigid in facial paralysis, crowned by the reflection of the reindeer antlered hatrack in the hall.*)   (671/553)

S. L. Goldberg feels that this passage represents a kind of immanent success for Stephen, for the face of Shakespeare, though 'rigid in facial paralysis'—that dire word in Joyce's vocabulary—is 'yet triumphant' by virtue of the cuckold's 'crown'.[17] (The mirror 'reflection' is taken as a symbol for 'art'.) But the crucial word 'paralysis' seems a clear indication that the 'face', the hypothetical Stephen-cum-Bloom, is yet locked in the ineluctable world of Phenomenon.

Previously Stephen's Shakespeare met himself, 'day after day'. To that image we might apply the phrase Goldberg uses of the mirror-image, 'kinetic bondage',[18] by which we may understand the ceaseless non-developmental change of the karmic cycle. The paralysed face in the mirror is, however, in *static* bondage, incapable of change. Neither state implies the potentiality of vital, meaningful change,[19] the charismatic interinanimation of subject and object which the Aristotelian notion of *kinesis* labours so hard to postulate.

In *Portrait of the Artist*, Stephen Dedalus maintained his notion of *stasis* optimistically in respect of himself—though we have noted the pessimistic implications available to the 'symbolist' reading which static postulation projects (art as *nebeneinander*). In *Ulysses*, both responses (*static* and *kinetic*) are exhibited dramatically. According to Stuart Gilbert,

> The conflict of deliberate indifference (*stasis*) with the loathing of disgust (*kinesis*) is apparent throughout *Ulysses*. Of this conflict in the mind of Stephen Dedalus the author of *Ulysses* is fully aware.[20]

Disgust as response to present condition resulting in indifference assumed as self-protection; indifference assuring that no response whatever is possible, reacted against as life-killing. Absolute paradox and a vicious circle.

Given Stephen's redefined situation, in which both static and kinetic response are brought up short against an existential paradox, is any further development of the subject, in respect of art or of life, either possible or brought to bear in *Ulysses*?

In the *Ethics* Aristotle, perhaps seeking to circumvent the necessitarian bias which clings to his attempted metaphysical transcendence, makes a single special exemption from ordinary human conditions, not, however, for any human action ('doing') but for Art ('making'):

> Among things liable to change we count (a) articles manufactured [including *techne*, art], (b) actions done. Making and doing are different activities. . . . Consequently the rational faculty exercised in doing is quite distinct from that which is exercised in making. Moreover, they are mutually exclusive, for doing never takes the form of making, nor making of doing. . . . The business of every art is to bring something into existence, and the practice of an art involves the study of how to bring into existence something which is capable of having such an existence and has its efficient cause in the maker and not in itself. This condition must be present, because *the arts are not concerned with things that exist or come into existence from necessity* or according to Nature, such things having their efficient cause in themselves. . . . We may even say that in a manner art and chance work in the same field.[21]

Stephen had, in the *Portrait*, conceived of art and life in transposable terms. In *Ulysses* there is a suggestion that he would raise art into freedom, leaving life behind in the ineluctable human condition. This is why *Hamlet* can be a triumph while Shakespeare,

> goes back, weary of the creation he has piled up to hide him from himself, an old dog licking an old sore. But, because loss is his gain, he passes on towards eternity in undiminished personality, untaught by the wisdom he has written or by the laws he has revealed. (252/194)

Stephen's Shakespeare creates from himself—

> He drew Shylock out of his own long pocket. The son of a malt-jobber and moneylender he was himself a cornjobber and moneylender (262/202)—

but unremittingly—

> All in all. In *Cymbeline*, in *Othello* he is bawd and cuckold. He acts and is acted upon. Lover of an ideal or a perversion, like Jose he kills the real Carmen. His unremitting intellect is the hornmad Iago ceaselessly willing that the moor in him shall suffer.* (272—3/210)

Soured by life, Shakespeare returns to Stratford, 'and there, his journey of life ended, he plants his mulberry-tree in the earth. Then dies. The motion is ended' (273/210).

Aristotle's notion of art, while restoring art to freedom, binds the artist as man to 'Nature' and the laws of necessity. By analogy, the 'maker' of an artifact is the God of his creation, being to it what the Unmoved Mover is to the Creation itself. Just as the whole of nature cannot have its cause in itself, so the work of art cannot. Its cause resides in its author.

The artist's position is dual, therefore, for he cannot 'sink' himself in his artistry. As a man he is, like Shakespeare, subject to 'ceaselessly willing' his own suffering even in the creation of his art, but by the laws of its coming-to-be that art is free. The romantic artist's possession by the notion of the high cost of a life of art lived that the art-object may be free and the notion of the freedom of the death-in-life status of the art-image have been detailed at length by Frank Kermode in his *Romantic Image*. Kermode uses Stephen's 'Thomism' in the *Portrait* to adumbrate his subject, deciding,

---

* Thus, the facially paralysed 'Shakespeare' who is the mirror reflection of Stephen and Bloom 'crows' 'Iagogo! How my Oldfellow [Othello] chokit his Thursdaymomum [Desdemona]. Iagogogo!' (671/553).

One such conclusion is that the artist who is vouchsafed this
power of apprehending the Image—to experience that
'epiphany' which is the Joycean equivalent of Pater's 'vision'—
has to pay a heavy price in suffering, to risk his immortal soul,
and to be alone.[22]

But Stephen's 'Aristotelianism' in *Ulysses* suggests a considerable
realignment. 'The Image' may yet be 'a radiant truth out of
space and time' (i.e. the order of nature), but its 'inextricabl[e]
associat[ion]' with 'the necessary isolation or estrangement of
men who can perceive it' has been broken.[23] The 'Romantic'
artist's 'estrangement' was an inhumanity; the artist, as
Stephen presents him in *Ulysses* and as he is himself presented,
is as a man no more and no less isolated and estranged than
others. Stephen's kinship with Bloom, while it may or may not
come to him as the day wears on or after June 16th, 1904, has
ended, is in a manner present all through the day, not least in
Stephen's 'Shakespeare theory'.

When Shakespeare appears in the brothel's mirror, he shouts
'With paralytic rage', the Player Queen's 'wormwood' sentence,
'Weda seca whokilla farst' (762/554)—'None wed the second
but who kill the first'.* Here Stephen's Shakespeare and Bloom
intersect in the figure of the cuckold, 'Shakespeare' being
present as both Old Hamlet and Othello, 'hornmad'.

What Stephen phrases of Shakespeare—and it is equally a
self-admonition—'One life is all. One body. Do. But do',
Joyce inserted into a section of Bloom's monologue. The
relevance exists in the mind of the maker, or more precisely in
the 'making' itself. For Aristotle this is exactly what is left to
man in the order of nature:

> Virtue, then, is of two kinds, intellectual and moral. Of these
> the intellectual is in the main indebted to teaching for its
> production and growth, and this calls for time and experience.
> Moral goodness on the other hand, is the child of habit, from
> which it has got its very name, ethics being derived from
> *ethos*, 'habit'. . . . This is an indication that none of the moral
> virtues is implanted in us by Nature, since nothing that Nature
> creates can be taught by habit to change the direction of its
> development. . . .

* Stephen had earlier applied this to the accusation brought against Shakespeare's
grand-daughter Elizabeth, about which he had read in Sidney Lee (260/200).

[Unlike 'natural' faculties like sight or hearing, which 'we had . . . before we used them',] the moral virtues we do acquire by first exercising them. *The same is true of the arts and crafts in general.* The craftsman has to learn how to make things, but he learns in the process of making them. So men become builders by building. . . .

Men will become good builders as a result of building well, and bad builders as a result of building badly. Otherwise what would be the use of having anyone to teach a trade? Craftsman would all be born either good or bad. Now this holds also of the virtues. It is in the course of our dealings with our fellow-men that we become just or unjust.*

Still, the exhortation to virtuous action does not determine whether such action is even possible, and to explore this in relation to Aristotle we must make an excursion into Kierkegaard's analysis of the question. The 'Interlude' of Kierkegaard's *Philosophical Fragments* is a discussion of the Aristotelian definition of motion on which Stephen meditates, relating it to the moral life. We may abstract his argument largely in his own words:

Is the past more necessary than the future? or, When the possible becomes actual, is it thereby made more necessary than it was?

How does that which comes into being change? Or, what is the nature of the change involved in becoming (κίνησις)? . . . [T]he change involved in becoming is the transition from possibility to actuality.

Can the necessary come into existence? Becoming is a change; but the necessary cannot undergo any change. . . . Everything that comes into being proves precisely by coming into being that it is not necessary; for the necessary is the only thing that cannot come into being, because the necessary is.

* *The* [*Nichomachean*] *Ethics*, Book II, Ch. 1, trans. J. A. K. Thompson (Harmondsworth, 1953), pp. 55–6. This passage attempts to apply to ethics the transcendental 'movement' (*kinesis*) which was required in physics to circumvent the paradox of the possible and the actual, and Aristotle has used the same analogy (of building) to express it. Cf.,

The actuality of the buildable as buildable is the process of building. For the actuality of the buildable must be either this or the house. But when there is a house, the buildable is no longer buildable. On the other hand, it *is* the buildable which is *being* built (*Physics*, in *Works*, ed. W. Ross [Oxford, 1930], Book III, 1 [201^{a}15 and 20, 210^{b}5, 10]).

The metaphor of 'building' is Aristotle's vehicle at *Met.* 1065^{b}15ff. as well.

Is not necessity then a synthesis of possibility and actuality?
[the Hegelian position, which Kierkegaard has set himself to
refute as leading to a determinism of ineluctable precondition-
ing]. . . .
      The actual is no more necessary than the possible, for the
necessary is absolutely different [in essence] from both [which
are determinants of being]. . . . [Aristotle's] mistake lies in his
beginning with the principle that everything which is necessary
is possible . . . he helps himself out by creating two species of
possibility [making a metaphysical confusion rather than admit
his terms are necessitarian].
      The change involved in becoming is an actual change; the
transition takes place with freedom. . . .
      All becoming takes place with freedom, not by necessity.[24]

The 'actual change' is Kierkegaard's terminus; notions of
actuality, change, possibility, necessity and history which
restrict his meaning he opposes. Becoming, transition (*kinesis*)
he will not define as metaphysically necessary, for it would
become, in the sphere of individual behaviour, conditioned
response.

      The past does not become necessary by virtue of its having
happened, nor is the future any more or less necessary than the
past.[25] Becoming 'is a change in actuality brought about by
freedom',[26] and any restriction of 'freedom' (by false concep-
tions of the problem) is metaphysically intolerable. Kierkegaard
then proceeds to attack the Hegelian 'Manifestation theory'—
which bears close relation to the theory of 'epiphany' discussed
in the first chapter—because mere knowledge does not confer
necessity on the thing known:

the certainty of the past is based upon an uncertainty, an uncertainty that exists for the past in precisely the same sense that
it exists for the future, being rooted in the possibility (Leibniz
and the possible worlds) [*Theodicée*, par. 42] out of which it
could not *emerge* into necessity.[27]

Kierkegaard recognizes the disjunction of two 'spheres' of
discourse, the logical and the 'sphere of freedom' (of time and
human action). He notes that 'Motion . . . is a concept which
logic cannot abide' but that it is part of the dialectic of time
as well, on the analogy of a correspondence between the point

in space and the instant in time.[28] Walter Lowrie cites Kierke-gaard's extended comment from the *Papers*:

> *transition is a becoming.* In the sphere of logic transition is mute, in the sphere of freedom it becomes. So when possibility in logic qualifies itself as actuality it merely disturbs the hushed reticence of the logical process by talking about motion and transition. In the sphere of freedom, on the other hand, there is possibility, and actuality emerges as a transcendency. Therefore when even Aristotle said that the transition from possibility to actuality is a KINESIS *he was not talking about logical possibility and actuality but about the possibility and actuality of freedom* [my italics], and therefore he quite rightly posits motion.[29]

Something of this last interpretation Joyce may be attributing to Stephen when he revises the 'actuality of the possible as possible' into

> Here he ponders things that were not:* What Caesar would have lived to do had he believed the soothsayer: what might have been: *possibilities of the possible as possible*: things not known: what name Achilles bore when he lived among women. (248/191) [my italics]

The establishment not of possibility but of the possibility of possibility is Kierkegaard's aim and it would equally provide a foothold for the reintroduction of vital change into Stephen's world.

'Repetition' is Kierkegaard's word for the perception of sameness which accompanies the souring of the fruits of the aesthetic mode of existence. Such 'repetition' assumes a quasi-categorical status as transitional stage between the aesthetical and ethical, or, in its 'later' reappearance as a disillusionment with the ethical, between the ethical and the religious stages. The perception of the apparently meaningless repetitiousness of life having come, there is no ignoring it; it must be accepted as a condition of existence:

> In the sphere of nature repetition exists in its immovable necessity. In the sphere of spirit the problem is not to contrive

---

* The syntax allows for this being either Stephen's interior monologue or Joyce's own comment on Stephen. 'What name Achilles bore [etc.]' is, of course, from Browne's *Hydrotaphia* (*Urn Burial*), Ch. 5, whose unspoken title suggests Stephen's next phrase, 'Coffined thoughts around me' (248/191) (*Religio Medici and Other Writings*, ed. Halliday Sutherland [London, 1906], p. 132). Stephen/Joyce has 'bore' for Browne's 'assumed' and 'lived' for 'hid himself'.

to get change out of repetition and find oneself comfortable under it . . . but the problem is to transform repetition into something inward, into the proper task of freedom.[30]

The 'transition' by which one comes to 'will' repetition, Kierkegaard calls the 'modern category' which corresponds to *kinesis*.[31]

Thus it is the soul's task to recognize the necessity of repetition in life, and to incorporate it internally into 'the sphere of freedom'. By doing so one is not thereby immanently freed, but one brings to life the paradox of being. The paradox is otherwise in danger of a kind of petrifaction, as when the aesthetic personality remains fixed in its *stasis* only. The internalization of repetition recognizes the equal necessity of both *stasis* and *kinesis*.

Leopold Bloom's reflections on repetition in life are poignant enough:

> Trams passed one another, ingoing, outgoing, clanging. Useless words. Things go on same; day after day: squads of police marching out, back; trams in, out. Those two loonies mooching about. Dignam carted off. Mina Purefoy swollen belly on a bed groaning to have a child tugged out of her. One born every second somewhere. Other dying every second. . . .
>
> Cityful passing away, other cityful coming, passing away too: other coming on, passing on. Houses, lines of houses, streets, miles of pavements, piledup bricks, stones. Changing hands. This owner, that. Landlord never dies they say. Other steps into his shoes when he gets his notice to quit. They buy the place up with gold and still they have all the gold. Swindle in it somewhere. Piled up in cities, worn away age after age. Pyramids in sand. Built on bread and onions. Slaves Chinese wall. Babylon. Big stones left. Round towers. Rest rubble, sprawling suburbs, jerrybuilt, Kerwan's mushroom houses, built of breeze. Shelter for the night.
>
> No one is anything.* (208/162)

* Bloom's detestation of the 'sprawling suburbs, jerrybuilt' should be compared with his supposed 'ultimate ambition' 'to purchase by private treaty in fee simple a thatched bungalowshaped 2 storey dwelling-house' (837/697)—with 'additional attractions' (839/698) and 'improvements' (840/699)—to be called 'Bloom Cottage. Saint Leopold's. Flowerville' (841/699). The apparent discrepancy can be resolved when we view 'Bloom Cottage' as the narrator's encyclopaedic extension of a much less articulate fantasy of Bloom's. It forms part of 'Ithaca's'

Never know anything about it. Waste of time. Gasballs spinning about, crossing each other, passing. Same old dingdong always. Gas, then solid, then world, then cold, then dead shell drifting around, frozen rock like that pineapple rock. The moon.* (212/164–5)

Bloom's contemplation of the 'series' of Molly's possible lovers, and his 'abnegation, equanimity' were discussed previously. The latter seems conclusively to represent a kind of acquiescence and detachment, however temporary, in respect of the single personal problem from which Bloom has been fleeing, mentally and even physically (when he sees Boylan) all day long. His resignation may be ethically suspect,† but it precisely enacts the inward transformation of 'repetition' and is Bloom's essential preparation to qualify for the position of the Kierkegaardian religious category, his becoming a 'knight of infinite resignation'.

Just after Bloom has passed between Stephen and Mulligan on the library steps, Stephen appears to attain a moment of peace from the tensions of the worlds inside and outside:

Kind air defined the coigns of houses in Kildare street. No birds. Frail from the housetops two plumes of smoke ascended, pluming, and in a flaw of softness softly were blown.

Cease to strive. Peace of the druid priests of Cymbeline, hierophantic: from wide earth an altar.

Laud we the gods
And let our crooked smokes climb to their nostrils
From our bless'd altars.‡ (279–80/215)

Cymbeline's added words—'Set we forward' (V. v. 480)—suggest the dimension of freedom towards which the detachment of ceasing to strive would attain.§ J. Mitchell Morse has given

'Utopian' counterpart to 'Circe's' 'Messianic' section, each version being fitted to its 'technic'.

* This provokes a memory of Molly and then Bloom pictures Molly and Boylan together, breaking off with 'Stop. Stop. If it was it was. Must' (212/165).

† Budgen points up the avoidance of Boylan and Bloom's decision not to 'interfere' and comments on Bloom's reasons (pp. 144–7, 261–2).

‡ The poised cigarettes in the newspaper office, while J. J. O'Molloy recites John F. Taylor's 'noble words', had first reminded Stephen of Cymbeline's words (180/140).

§ Much depends on one's reading of *Cymbeline*. To some the play ends in ignoble compromise between Roman and Englishman, to others this ending is 'beyond

the best description of the tension between this search for
detachment in Stephen and its opposite, noting that Stephen's
possession by remorse, his 'conviction of sin' is the way in which
'society binds him to itself and commits him to its values'. 'He
must, as an artist, overcome that conviction', gain 'liberation
from remorse', achieve detachment, and cease the 'violation
of his essence' which 'consists in not doing the work he is
destined to do'.[32]

In 'Circe' it is, of course, the apparition of 'The Mother' which
comprises the crisis of Stephen's 'hallucination'. Stephen is
'*Horror-struck*' and speaks to her '*Choking with fright, remorse and
horror*':

> They said I killed you, mother. He offended your memory.
> Cancer did it, not I. Destiny. (681/565)

One after another the nets are flung out by the dead mother—
mother love ('Years and years I loved you, O my son, my
firstborn, when you lay in my womb'), the Church ('Repent!
O, the fire of hell!'),* family ties ('Get Dilly to make you that
boiled rice every night after your brain work') (682/566). As
she prays for his soul, he resists, calling on 'The intellectual
imagination', standing on Brand's ground ('all or not at all')
and repeating the devil's '*Non serviam!*' (682/567). Calling on
them to 'Break my spirit all of you if you can! I'll bring you all
to heel!,'

> (*He lifts his ashplant high with both hands and smashes the chandelier.*
> . . .)† (683/567)

The connection Morse points between the struggle against
remorse and the need 'to be one's self', to do one's own appointed
work, is equally crucial in both Ibsen and Kierkegaard—
'*væresig selv*':

> For the purpose of becoming (and it is the task of the self freely
> to become itself) possibility and necessity are equally essential.

beyond', 'a vision,—of unity certainly, perhaps of the Earthly Paradise, perhaps
of the Elysian fields, perhaps, even, the vision of the saints. But whatever else, it is
assuredly a vision of perfect tranquillity . . .' (J. M. Nosworthy in the Arden
Edition [London, 1960], p. lxxxv).

* Expiring, she identifies herself with Christ: 'Inexpressible was my anguish
when expiring with love, grief and agony on Mount Calvary' (683/587).

† A page later the 'chandelier' is only a 'lamp' and Bloom points to 'a crushed
mauve purple shade' (684/569) claiming 'not a sixpenceworth of damage done'.

... A self which has no possibility is in despair, and so in turn is a self which has no necessity.*

In psychological terms, the crisis of 'identity' requires the eliciting of the 'necessary' self 'freely' from the welter of possible selves without injustice to the integrity of personality. Jung observes,

> Personality is the supreme realization of the innate idiosyncracy of a living being. It is an act of high courage flung in the face of life, the absolute affirmation of all that constitutes the individual, the most successful adaption to the universal conditions of existence coupled with the greatest possible freedom for self-determination.[33]

It will be no surprise that as we draw near to 'solutions' to metaphysical and existential antinomies of the order of freedom and necessity, the language of them should become more and more paradoxical. 'Adaption' 'coupled with' 'self-determination' is Jung's paradox: it is not only difficult to specify the precise nature of the 'coupling', it is more so to specify particular cases of success. The *logic* of these 'solutions' is, however, unimpeded by such existential difficulties, and returns us at last to a literary form.

Jung's essay on *Ulysses* revolves around two major points, that 'hopeless emptiness is the dominant note of the whole book', marked by an 'eternal repetition' which leaves 'no place for value',[34] while on the other hand—and this is a position Jung works himself into, laboriously, as he proceeds—the course of the novel marks a gradual *detachment* from the *impedimenta* of existence, not on the part of the characters particularly, nor yet on the part of Joyce, but in 'Ulysses',

> the sufferer who has often lost his way, [and] toils ever towards his island home, back to himself again, beating his way through the turmoil of eighteen chapters, and, free at last from a fool's world of illusions, 'looking on from afar' is not concerned. Therewith he achieves just that which a Jesus or a Buddha achieved —and that which Faust also strove to attain—the overcoming

---

* Søren Kierkegaard, *The Sickness Unto Death*, trans. Walter Lowrie, bound with *Fear and Trembling* (New York, n.d.), p. 168. Mrs Stobart's article on Ibsen and Kierkegaard ('New Lights', p. 235) stresses the need of 'true tragedy' to embody moments of both 'personal responsibility' and 'personal irresponsibility, a relativity to circumstances beyond personal control'. Kierkegaard's similar reflections on *Hamlet* are in *Stages on Life's Way*, trans. W. Lowrie (Oxford Press: London and Toronto, and Princeton, 1940), pp. 409–11.

of a fool's world, a liberation from the opposites. . . . [T]he groundwork . . . of Ulysses . . . [is] the detachment of the human consciousness. . . . Ulysses is the creative god in Joyce, a true demiurge who has succeeded in freeing himself from entanglement in the physical and mental worlds and in contemplating them with a liberated consciousness. . . . Ulysses is the higher self that returns to its divine home after a period of blind entanglement in the world. In the whole book no Ulysses appears; the book itself is Ulysses, a microcosm embraced by Joyce.[35] *

Jung makes clear the extent to which the energy of the novel —or if we prefer, the imagination of Joyce—is a participant in its total action, the one which embraces not only the Dublin 'story' but the modes of its telling as well. If this imagination secures 'a liberation from the opposites' and 'the detachment of . . . consciousness', as Jung claims, then that liberation and detachment stand at the vanishing-point of a perspective down which the major 'characters', Bloom and Stephen, are pointed. They, too, are entangled in the opposites, the philosophical antinomies of freedom and necessity, possibility and actuality, and for each paths, each to his own capacity, are laid out. Their situation in *Ulysses* remains dramatic precisely because 'inelectable preconditioning' to become one thing or another is not definitely posited by the text. The question of their being remains an open one, to the very end, one in which 'ineluctability' and 'fixity' are but one possibility.† In the novel as a whole, the possibility of possibility would remain open.

* For the history of the Neo-Platonic allegorization of epics as 'detachments' from the brute round of existence, see Graham Hough, *A Preface to the Faerie Queene* (London, 1962), pp. 116ff. Not only Odysseus but Aeneas received such treatment. Hough cites the interpretation attributed to the Florentine Platonist Alberti: 'a lengthy argument explaining the travels of Aeneas as an allegory of the soul, forsaking all earthly passions, symbolized by Troy, struggling with the perturbations of the senses and passions, and ultimately arriving in the true heavenly kingdom' (p. 117). Hough thinks the story 'naturally analogous to the story of Israel, captive, wandering and restored' (p. 118). *Ulysses* as detachment finds its way into Ellmann's biography when he says the novel is a 'pacifist version' of epic story (p. 370).

† '[B]y the adequate exploitation of states of mind and by following up all the paths suggested by the impinging of the past, in its multifarious variety, on the present, the nature of potentiality in character can be indicated even without our being shown the occurrences of events that would make these potentialities actual. The most interesting case in point here is the character of Stephen Dedalus in *Ulysses*' (David Daiches, *The Novel and the Modern World*, rev. ed. [Chicago, 1960], pp. 23–4).

Themes like 'detachment', the internal acceptance of external necessity, the conflict of potential and actual, the repetitiveness of life, the preclusion of change or the incessant changefulness which precludes permanence, *stasis versus kinesis*— all concerned with the relationship between the metaphysical and the existential—are thus deeply ingrained in *Ulysses*. Their sources and analogues may be sought, as has been seen, as well within the history of exoteric philosophy and psychology as in the esoteric or occult tradition. Despite Stuart Gilbert's assertion that 'It is impossible to grasp the meaning of *Ulysses*, its symbolism and the significance of its *leitmotifs* without an understanding of the esoteric theories which underlie the work',[36] what he cites as these 'theories' both 'underlie' *Ulysses* only in so far as they relate to thematic elements—the novel does not 'work by magic'—and have eminent analogies within the major western philosophical tradition.

Gilbert's 'authorities' in his exposition of Joyce's supposed occultism, Porphyry, Blavatsky, Traherne, Hermes Trismegistus, Eliphas Lévy,[37] are cited at points where their thought could equally be set into the context of Aristotelian debate: indeed it is to take esoteric (or theosophical) polemic at its own word not to see it in such a context.* Gilbert's discussion of Karma may include such remarks as, 'by our personal *attitude towards* the Karma which we cannot escape, [we may] build up merit for subsequent existences',[38] but when he points to passages in *Ulysses* as illustration of occult theory, his conclusions are usually wholly domesticated:

> To find ourselves we must first lose our way. . . .
> Thus the growth of the soul, the process of self-realization, may be ultimately due to the 'errors' of the individual, his growing-pains.[39]

Joyce used the esoteric to exploit the same paradoxes and tensions he had discovered in the 'garner of slender sentences' from Aristotle.†

* The refusal to acknowledge such contexts, the claim to exclusive, 'secret' wisdom, sets the hermetic philosophers off from the exoteric tradition more than does their actual content.

† The priority and exclusiveness which Gilbert claimed for Joyce's esoterica— quite possibly prompted (he says, 'endorsed') by Joyce [Preface to 1952 edition, p. vi]—has had a deleterious effect. The claim that the 'deeper' meanings of

We have already seen Eliot's broaching of the relationship of possibility and time in 'Burnt Norton'. Emblems of 'solution' there are in that poem—

> Neither from nor towards; at the still point, there the
> dance is,
> But neither arrest nor movement. And do not call it
> fixity,
> Where past and future are gathered. Neither movement
> from nor towards,
> Neither ascent nor decline,[40]

or in 'The detail of the pattern is movement'[41]—but Part V of 'The Dry Salvages' presses the question to a secular 'solution'. There Eliot enumerates the 'usual/Pastimes and drugs' which are the necessarily unsuccessful ways we seek 'the overcoming of a fool's world, liberation from the opposites', ways which are themselves constituents of that fool's world:

> To communicate with Mars, converse with spirits,
> To report the behaviour of the sea monster,
> Describe the horoscope, haruspicate or scry,
> Observe disease in signatures, evoke
> Biography from the wrinkles of the palm
> And tragedy from fingers; release omens
> By sortilege, or tea leaves, riddle the inevitable
> With playing cards, fiddle with pentagrams
> Or barbituric acids, or dissect
> The recurrent image into pre-conscious terrors—
> To explore the womb, or tomb, or dreams.[42]

Taking up the phrasing of 'Burnt Norton', Eliot notes that

> Men's curiosity searches past and future
> And clings to that dimension.[43]

But the time-dimension is history, and merely one sphere of existence. To seek the future in the past (or present) is yet to remain bound in 'history'. Against that dimension Eliot sets 'the timeless'. One does not, however, desert 'time' for 'the timeless', for that would be to jump from one horn of a dilemma

Ulysses were esoteric in nature has led to a praise of Joyce based on dangerously insecure ground—its roots probably lie in the same objection to 'science' that vivified the occult movements—and a derogation by those only too willing to accept the claims of *illuminati*.

163

to the other. Instead one attempts 'to apprehend/The point of intersection of the timeless/With time'.[44] Here, Eliot continues,

> Here the impossible union
> Of spheres of existence is actual
> Here the past and future
> Are conquered, and reconciled,
> Where action were otherwise movement
> Of that which is only moved—
> Driven by daemonic, chthonic
> Powers. And right action is freedom
> From past and future also.
> For most of us, this is the aim
> Never here to be realized.[45]

'Past and future', the world of 'action', time and history are, in their eternal repetition, driven by powers outside themselves. Set against this, as a release from it, in Eliot as in Kierkegaard, is the 'sphere of freedom', a wholly distinct 'sphere of existence', which permits of 'right action'. In this life, the *apprehension* of freedom—'an occupation for the saint—/No occupation either, but something given/And taken'—can occur 'For most of us' only in 'the unattended/Moment',

> and the rest
> Is prayer, observance, discipline, thought and action.[46]

This 'action', which is our daily existence, is to be regarded in terms of process, not of product, as a *kinesis*:

> And do not think of the fruit of action.
> Fare forward.[47]

W. B. Yeats wrote in 1914, when Joyce began serious work on *Ulysses*, that truth was 'the dramatically appropriate utterance of the highest man' and that,

> if I had been asked to define the 'highest man', I would have said perhaps, 'We can find him as Homer found Odysseus when he was looking for a theme'.[48]

Nineteen-twenty-two, the year of *Ulysses'* publication, also saw the fragment of Yeats's autobiography titled *The Trembling of the Veil*, whose very title proclaimed that modern man had arrived at the end of one historical epoch and was now entered into a borderline phase of time—a notion Yeats was soon to systematize in *A Vision*.* Projecting a supreme fiction for that time he saw the necessity of the boundary-situation confrontation of man with his destiny:

> Nations, races, and individual men are unified by an image, or bundle of related images, symbolical or evocative of the state of mind, which is of all states of mind not impossible, the most difficult to that man, race, or nation; because only the greatest obstacle that can be contemplated without despair rouses the will to full intensity.†[49]

Writing from the borderline of time, Yeats extended the human boundary-situation to include not only the 'image' (the work of art), but also the tragic hero and the artist himself, and even the reader, the 'nations, races, and individual men'. Great works and great artists were 'Gates and Gatekeepers, because through their dramatic power they bring our souls to crisis' and they

> have but one purpose, to bring their chosen man to the greatest obstacle he may confront without despair. . . . Such masters— Villon and Dante, let us say—would not, when they speak through their art, change their luck; yet they are mirrored in all the suffering of desire. The two halves of their nature are so completely joined that they seem to labour for their objects, and yet to desire whatever happens, being at the same instant predestinate and free, creation's very self. . . . Had not Dante and Villon understood that their fate wrecked what life could not rebuild, had they lacked Vision of Evil, had they cherished any species of optimism, they could but have found a false beauty, or some momentary instinctive beauty, and suffered no change at all, or but changed as do the wild creatures, or from Devil well to Devil sick and so round the clock.[50]

* The modern age was in Phases 22–3 of the twenty-eight phase historical cycle (*A Vision* [London, 1937], p. 256). Phase 22—June in the annual cycle—is a phase of 'struggle and tragedy', a struggle '[to] lose . . . personality' ('will'): 'After Phase 22 . . . there is a struggle to accept the fate-imposed unity' (pp. 196, 83). In the 1925 edition of *A Vision* (in pages deleted in 1938), Yeats put *Ulysses* along with 'The Waste Land' and Pirandello's *Henry IV* in the 23rd Phase, 'where there is hatred of the abstract, where the intellect turns upon itself'. Yeats continues by discussing the separation of 'myth and fact, united until the exhaustion of the Renaissance' (*A Vision* [London, 1925], pp. 211–12). Phases 22 and 23 are a transition, or borderline between periods dominated by freedom of will and fate.

† See 'the greatest possible ellipse. Consistent with. The ultimate return' (*Ulysses*, 622/494).

To have spurned the 'false beauty' which precludes change on the one hand or involves one in the sickening dull round of cyclic existence on the other, in the service of presenting both himself and his 'chosen men' as 'at the same instant predestinate and free' in a fictional world which is 'creation's very self' is perhaps the fittest tribute which could be applied to the achievement of James Joyce as a literary artist. If *Ulysses* represents his achievement, the play *Exiles* presents the clearest paradigm.

Joyce's notes show that he had much of *Exiles* thought out by November 1913,[51] and the writing of it ran concurrently with the early stages of *Ulysses*. *Exiles* exhibits yet another aspect of 'the tragedy of dedication and betrayal'[52] and is a comprehensive emblem of the problems of human freedom and necessity, heroism and victimage, *stasis* and *kinesis*, aesthetic and ethical behaviour.

James T. Farrell noted the basic aesthetic analogy: Richard Rowan has 'molded' his wife, 'almost in the spirit and manner of a heroine in a novel or play'.[53] This does not mean, however, that Richard intends to secure thereby total control of Bertha. Instead he is attempting to engineer her freedom—'Decide yourself,' he repeats. 'You are free' (78–9). This does not mark an abandonment of the aesthetic analogy, but a redefinition of it: the 'author' is careful not to restrict the freedom of will of his 'creation'.

The condition Richard seeks for himself is one of 'doubt':

> It is not in the darkness of belief that I desire you. But in restless living wounding doubt. (162)

Richard's 'failure' is not his 'wound' (ibid.), but Bertha's refusal to accept his condition, to be 'free'. She wants Richard to be convinced of her fidelity. It would, I think, be an over-simplification to believe that Richard is motivated by a desire for her to be unfaithful, though he himself says so to Robert Hand.* In the play's full logic, Richard goes beyond this, which is, after all, meant for Robert's ears.† Finally, though it may involve such a thing as self-willed cuckoldry, it

---

* '[I]n the very core of my ignoble heart I longed to be betrayed by you and by her' (97).

† 'The play is three cat and mouse acts' (Joyce's note, 172).

is Richard's desire to make Bertha capable of 'now act[ing] on her own, in freedom and in frankness'[54] which has primacy.

That Bertha either does not wish it or cannot so act casts an essential ambiguity over the whole play. Following the aesthetic analogy we may say that the artist cannot endow his creation with complete freedom even if he so desires; there is something recalcitrant, something *given* about it which permits at best an ambivalence. This is not the ambivalence which the artist had at first desired, the 'doubt' into which he would be cast by the assurance of her freedom, but another, in which the creation can attain in the creator's eyes at most a borderline possibility, between the condition of freedom and that of fixity. In *Exiles* it is Bertha's continuing desire to *certify* her behaviour to Richard which represents this fixity.

Francis Fergusson believes that Richard Rowan is an extrapolation of Stephen Dedalus as he appears in the *Portrait*, 'a last look at the soul which Stephen Daedalus [sic] had been impiously constructing'.[55] On the contrary, Richard's behaviour seems to allegorize the aesthetic of *Ulysses*—not the implied aesthetic of Stephen, but the technique whereby the different 'styles', the symbolic texture, the plot-management, all suggest that Joyce was attempting to engineer a similar condition of 'doubt' between himself and his creation.

Richard Rowan's spiritual condition in Act III of *Exiles* is Joyce's penetrating analysis of the human cost of maintaining, with such an untyrannical aesthetic, a dedication to exercise the same responsibility in one's life as towards one's art. In that art Joyce was as careful to preserve his characters' freedom as to attack that freedom, as careful to refrain from final judgement as to construct whole ranges of judgement. This care involved an equal concern to prevent a narrowed basis for his own art, the complementary narrownesses of 'symbolism' and 'realism'. Whether the aesthetic conception molded the human conception, or *vice versa*, one can only speculate, but equally necessary he found them and equally he maintained them, in the face of the greater temptations to aesthetic simplifications which each of his subjects increasingly presented.

NOTES

NOTES TO PREFACE

[1] Charles N. Feidelson, Jr., *Symbolism and American Literature* (Chicago, 1953), p. 69.

NOTES TO CHAPTER I

[1] *Letters*, p. 55.

[2] Herbert Gorman, *James Joyce* (London, 1941), p. 150.

[3] An earlier version of these definitions is recorded in the 'Paris Notebook', dated February 13th, 1903 (*Critical Writings*, pp. 143–5).

[4] Marvin Magalaner, *Time of Apprenticeship, The Fiction of Young James Joyce* (London, 1959), p. 75. Magalaner reprints the *Irish Homestead* version as an appendix (pp. 174–80).

[5] See, James R. Baker, 'Ibsen, Joyce, and the Living-Dead', *A James Joyce Miscellany—Third Series*, ed. Marvin Magalaner (Carbondale, 1962), p. 26; Florence L. Walzl, 'Pattern of Paralysis in Joyce's *Dubliners*', *College English*, Vol. XXII (January 1961), pp. 221–8; and Gerhard Freidrich, 'Joyce's Pattern of Paralysis in *Dubliners*', *College English*, Vol. XXII (April 1961), pp. 519–20.

[6] Henry Miller, *The Cosmological Eye* (Norfolk: New Directions, 1939), pp. 107–34.

[7] Oliver St John Gogarty, *As I Was Going Down Sackville Street* (London, 1954), p. 299.

[8] Ed. O. A. Silverman (Buffalo, N.Y.: University of Buffalo Lockwood Memorial Library, 1956).

[9] Introduction to *Stephen Hero*, p. 23/17.

[10] For a discussion of Joyce's possible reasons for omitting 'epiphany' from *A Portrait of the Artist* see William T. Noon, s.j., *Joyce and Aquinas* (New Haven, 1957), pp. 65ff.

[11] For a cogent argument against regarding Joyce's fiction in terms of 'epiphanic writing' see Noon, pp. 73–4, ending 'the works, with a certain minimum of good will, can be seen to illustrate the theories more successfully than the theories can be used to interpret the works' (p. 74). The use of the works to illustrate the 'theory' continues, however; see Graham Hough, *Image and Experience* (London, 1960), p. 16, '*Portrait of the Artist* is built out of a succession of such instants [epiphanies];' Arnold Kettle, 'The Consistency of James Joyce', *The Modern Age*, ed. Boris Ford (Harmondsworth, 1961), p. 306, 'Nothing is achieved in *Ulysses* but a series of epiphanies.' The most sustained attempt to use the theory to interpret the works is to be found in S. L. Goldberg, *The Classical Temper, A Study of James Joyce's Ulysses* (London, 1961), pp. 44, 89–90, 265, *passim*.

Notes

[12] *Critical Writings*, p. 152.
[13] Sigmund Freud, *A General Introduction to Psychoanalysis*, trans. Joan Riviere (New York, 1960), p. 31.
[14] Ibid., p. 50.
[15] Ibid., p. 101.
[16] This is in fact the interpretation made by Ernest Jones in *The Life and Work of Sigmund Freud*.
[17] Kenner, *Dublin's Joyce* (Indiana University Press: Bloomington, 1956), p. 53. 'Habitual' is gratuitous, meant to imply things like 'habitual drunkard'.
[18] Edmund Wilson, *Axel's Castle* (London, 1961), p. 169.
[19] J. B. Yeats to John Quinn, October 14th, 1920, in *A James Joyce Miscellany*, ed. Marvin Magalaner (New York, 1957), pp. 75–6.
[20] Kenner, p. 53.
[21] Julian B. Kaye, 'The Wings of Daedalus: Two Stories in "Dubliners"', *Modern Fiction Studies*, 4 : 1 (Spring 1958), pp. 31, 32, 33. The relevant pages in Magalaner and R. M. Kain *Joyce: The Man, the Work, the Reputation* (New York, 1956) are 75–9.
[22] See for example Moody E. Prior's discussion of Dryden's *All for Love*, in *The Language of Tragedy* (New York, 1947), p. 194ff.
[23] Eugene Waith, 'The Calling of Stephen Dedalus', *College English*, Vol. XVIII, No. 5 (February 1957), p. 260; see also p. 257.
[24] Magalaner, op. cit., p. 126.

NOTES TO CHAPTER II

[1] Søren Kierkegaard, *Philosophical Fragments*, trans. David F. Swenson (London and New York, 1936), Ch. III, passim.
[2] Reuben Brower, *The Fields of Light: An Experiment in Criticism* (Oxford University Press, 1962 [1951]) is a notable exception.
[3] *The Portable Coleridge*, ed. I. A. Richards (New York, 1950), p. 388.
[4] Graham Hough, *A Preface to the Faerie Queene* (London, 1962), pp. 109–10. Insertions from pp. 105 and 107.
[5] Ibid., pp. 110, 111.
[6] *Letters*, pp. 138–9, 147–8. A. Walton Litz, *The Art of James Joyce* (London, 1961).
[7] Kenner, p. 114.
[8] Ibid., p. 117.
[9] Yves Bonnefoy, 'Shakespeare and the French Poet', *Encounter* 105, Vol. XVIII, No. 6 (June 1962), p. 41.
[10] T. S. Eliot, *Collected Poems 1909–62* (London, 1963), p. 189.
[11] See Kenner, pp. 116–17. The symbolist apotheosis of this particular incident is to be found in Ruth Von Phul's essay 'Joyce and the Strabismal Apologia', *A James Joyce Miscellany, Second Series*, ed. Marvin Magalaner (Carbondale, 1959), pp. 119–32.
[12] Cf. Kathleen Tillotson on Thackeray, *Novels of the 1840's* (Oxford, 1961), p. 239.
[13] Jean Piaget, *The Psychology of Intelligence* (London, 1950), pp. 7–8.
[14] Cf. ibid., under Assimilation and Accommodation; also *Play, Dreams and Imitation in Childhood* (London, 1951), passim.
[15] Grant H. Redford, 'The Role of Structure in Joyce's "Portrait"', *Modern Fiction Studies*, Vol. 4, No. 1 (Spring, 1958), p. 21.
[16] Mark Schorer, 'Technique as Discovery', from James E. Miller, Jr., ed., *Myth and Method* (University of Nebraska Press, 1960), p. 96.

Notes

[17] From *Discorsi del Porma Eroico*, as trans. by E. M. W. Tillyard, in *The English Epic and its Background* (London, 1954), p. 232.

[18] T. S. Eliot, 'Burnt Norton', ll. 6–8, op. cit.

[19] Grover Smith has noted the resemblance of this passage to 'Burnt Norton', *T. S. Eliot's Poetry and Plays* (Chicago, 1956), p. 257.

[20] Kenner, p. 121.

[21] See Robert S. Ryf, *A New Approach to Joyce: The Portrait of the Artist as a Guidebook* (University of California Press: Berkeley and Los Angeles, 1962), pp. 33–5.

[22] Goldberg, p. 46.

[23] Kenneth Clark, *The Nude* (Harmondsworth, 1960 [1956]), p. 6. See also the note on p. 361.

[24] But see Goldberg, Ch. III, who considers it an extension, or development.

[25] Kenner, p. 129.

[26] S. L. Goldberg, *Joyce* (Edinburgh and London, 1962), p. 52.

[27] Kevin Sullivan, *Joyce Among the Jesuits* (New York, 1958), p. 9.

[28] Kenner, p. 119.

[29] Richard Ellmann, 'The Limits of Joyce's Naturalism', *Sewanee Review*, Vol. LXIII (1955), p. 572.

[30] Eugene M. Waith, 'The Calling of Stephen Dedalus', *College English*, Vol. XVIII, No. 5 (February 1957), p. 256. Caroline Gordon, 'Some Readings and Misreadings', *Sewanee Review*, Vol. LXI (Summer 1953), pp. 388–93. Kenner, pp. 109–57 and 'The *Portrait* in Perspective', in *James Joyce: Two Decades of Criticism*, ed. Seon Givens (New York, 1948), pp. 109–33.

[31] Waith, pp. 257, 260.

NOTES TO CHAPTER III

[1] Percy Lubbock, *The Craft of Fiction* (New York, 1957), p. 147.

[2] Kenner, *Dublin's Joyce*, pp. 131–3.

[3] Richard Poirier, *The Comic Sense of Henry James* (London, 1960), p. 190.

[4] Ibid., p. 228.

[5] Ibid., pp. 214, 239.

[6] Ibid., pp. 204–5.

[7] Ibid., pp. 207, 245, 244.

[8] Quoted in Wyndham Lewis, *Time and Western Man* (London, 1927), p. 128.

[9] Geoffrey Wagner, *Wyndham Lewis: A Portrait of the Artist as the Enemy* (London, 1957), p. 177.

[10] Lewis, p. 130.

[11] *Critical Writings*, pp. 73–4.

[12] Lewis, p. 99.

[13] W. B. Yeats, *A Vision* (London, 1937), p. 25.

[14] Wilson, p. 9.

[15] Henry Miller, p. 111.

[16] Lewis, pp. 107, 110.

[17] Schorer, *op. cit.*, p. 99.

[18] Ibid., pp. 99, 100.

[19] Feidelson, p. 135.

[20] Ibid., p. 135.

[21] See W. B. Yeats, *Collected Poems* (London, 1950), pp. 69–70. Subsequently titled 'He Remembers Forgotten Beauty', the poem no longer contains any clue that its subject (in *The Wind Among the Reeds* [1899]) was once Robartes.

[22] 'Ibsen's New Drama' (1900), in *Critical Writings*, pp. 63, 62.

[23] G. Wilson Knight, *Ibsen* (Edinburgh and London, 1962), p. 114.

Notes

²⁴ Ibid., p. 115.
²⁵ Halvdan Koht, *The Life of Ibsen*, trans. R. L. McMahon and H. A. Larsen (London, 1931), I, 169.
²⁶ Ibid.
²⁷ Ibid., I, 272–7.
²⁸ Ellmann, *James Joyce* (New York, 1959), p. 73. Courtney's reply to Joyce, offering to look at a review of Ibsen's newest play, 'When We Dead Awaken', is dated January 19th, 1900. Joyce used a French translation in preparing the review, in which he notes the play had been published in Copenhagen on December 19th, 1899.
²⁹ M. A. Stobart, 'New Lights on Ibsen's "Brand" ', *The Fortnightly Review*, n.s. 66 (August 1st, 1899), p. 239. Stobart prints 'Kirkegaard' throughout. Brandes's monograph on Kierkegaard was published in Danish in 1877 and had been translated into German but not English.
³⁰ M. A. Stobart, 'The "Either-Or" of Soren Kirkegaard', *The Fortnightly Review*, n.s. 71 (January 1st, 1902), pp. 53–60.
³¹ Stobart, 'The "Either-Or" of Soren Kirkegaard', pp. 55 and 56.
³² Koht, II, 27.
³³ Stobart, 'New Lights', pp. 228–32.
³⁴ For recent comment see Brian W. Downs, *Ibsen, The Intellectual Background* (Cambridge, 1946), pp. 83ff; Michael Meyer, in his edition of *Brand*, mentions Brand's reputed analogy to *Either/Or*, but says he finds Kierkegaard's *Fear and Trembling* more illuminating.
³⁵ Downs, pp. 81–2.
³⁶ Ellmann, *James Joyce*, p. 79. The source is Constantine Curran.
³⁷ Downs, pp. 88–9.
³⁸ Ellmann, *James Joyce*, pp. 274–5.
³⁹ Quoted in Koht, II, 27.
⁴⁰ *Critical Writings*, pp. 101, 100.
⁴¹ Ellmann, *James Joyce*, p. 274. (From Stanislaus's diary for September 8th, 1907.)
⁴² Søren Kierkegaard, *Either/Or*, trans. Walter Lowrie (London, 1944), II, 228–9. [my italics]
⁴³ Ibid., Vol. I, trans. David F. Swenson and Lillian Marvin Swenson, I, 33.
⁴⁴ Ibid., I, 29.
⁴⁵ Ibid., I, 78.
⁴⁶ Ibid., I, 33–4. The appositeness to Tennyson's 'The Palace of Art' and 'The Lady of Shalott' is apparent.
⁴⁷ Ibid., I, 20.
⁴⁸ Ibid., I, 22. Cf. Byron's *Manfred*, II, i:
> my days and nights . . .
> Endless, and all alike, as sands on the shore,
> Innumerable atoms; and one desert,
> Barren and cold. . . .

⁴⁹ Stobart, 'The "Either-Or" of Soren Kirkegaard', p. 57.
⁵⁰ Goldberg, *The Classical Temper*, p. 33. But note that 'with experience and growth' assumes Stephen is capable of change and that 'collapse' is ambiguous.
⁵¹ Kierkegaard, *Either/Or*, II, 226.

NOTES TO CHAPTER IV

¹ William Schutte, *Joyce and Shakespeare* (New Haven, 1957), pp. 8–16.
² Søren Kierkegaard, *Fear and Trembling*, trans. Walter Lowrie (New York, n.d.), p. 48 (Copyright Princeton University Press).

Notes

[3] Ibid., pp. 49–51.

[4] Ibid., p. 121.

[5] Noon, pp. 89, 90. Kierkegaard, *Concluding Unscientific Postscript*, trans. David F. Swenson (Princeton, 1944), p. 453.

[6] Kierkegaard, *Concluding Unscientific Postscript*, p. 448; and cf. W. K. Wimsatt and Cleanth Brooks, *Literary Criticism: A Short History* (New York, 1957), p. 379, n. 4.

[7] Noon, p. 90.

[8] Kierkegaard, *Concluding Unscientific Postscipt*, p. 447, footnote.

[9] Brower, p. 198.

[10] Ellmann, *James Joyce*, p. 367.

[11] Cf. 'Eveline', in *Dubliners*, 41/47.

[12] Stuart Gilbert, *James Joyce's Ulysses* (New York, 1956), p. 179.

[13] Goldberg, *The Classical Temper*, p. 35. And cf. 'very specific individuals and a clearly established present', Erich Auerbach, *Mimesis, The Representation of Reality in Western Literature*, trans. Willard Trask (New York, 1957), p. 481.

[14] Lewis, p. 114.

[15] Schutte, pp. 181–2.

[16] R. M. Adams, *Surface and Symbol, The Consistency of James Joyce's Ulysses* (New York, 1962), p. 98. See my review in *Essays in Criticism*, Vol. XIII, No. 3 (July 1963), pp. 288–9.

[17] *Letters*, p. 126.

[18] Ibid., pp. 127, 128.

[19] Ibid., p. 128.

[20] Reproduced facing p. 48 of *A James Joyce Miscellany, Second Series*.

[21] *Letters*, p. 128.

[22] Gilbert, p. 243.

[23] Ibid., pp. 254–5.

[24] *Letters*, p. 129.

[25] Gilbert, p. 257.

[26] Goldberg, *The Classical Temper*, pp. 49, 281. Goldberg consistently undervalues the 'symbolic' dimension of *Ulysses*, believing it merely 'technical experimentation' (p. 313). Underrating the possibilities of conflict between 'Naturalistic "matter"' and a Symbolist "structure"' in the novel (p. 247), he writes from the standpoint of the necessity of 'fusion', and when he has not discovered it, condemns the 'symbolic'. See my review, *Essays in Criticism*, Vol. XII, No. 2 (April 1962), pp. 198–203.

[27] Gilbert, pp. 252–3.

[28] Goldberg, *The Classical Temper*, p. 244.

[29] Ibid., p. 261.

[30] Harry Levin, *James Joyce, A Critical Introduction* (New Directions Books, 1941), p. 109.

[31] Ellmann, *James Joyce*, pp. 560–1.

[32] Levin, *James Joyce*, p. 109.

[33] Goldberg, *The Classical Temper*, p. 185.

[34] Litz, pp. 32, 35.

[35] Adams, p. 186.

[36] Letter of February 1921, *Letters*, p. 160.

[37] Ibid., pp. 142–3.

[38] Ibid., pp. 150–60, *passim*. See also the letter to Harriet Shaw Weaver, August 30th, 1921 (ibid., p. 171): 'I have also added a Messianic scene to *Circe*.'

[39] Ibid., p. 158.

[40] Clive Hart, *Structure and Motif in Finnegans Wake* (London, 1962), p. 65.

Notes

41 Kenner, *Dublin's Joyce*, p. 261.

42 Goldberg, *The Classical Temper*, pp. 188–9.

43 Ibid., pp. 189–90: '*a sensibility* [etc.]', my italics.

44 Ibid., pp. 194, 196. Goldberg's alignment of the mythic and the static, which he considers liberating and potentiating, points to a father paradox when the static is explored as a constriction.

45 Alain Robbe-Grillet, *Jealousy*, trans. Richard Howard (London, 1959), pp. 80–1.

46 W. K. Wimsatt, Jr., 'The Substantive Level', in *The Verbal Icon* (New York, 1958), p. 138.

47 Ibid., p. 144.

48 Cf. Auerbach, pp. 471–6.

49 *Letters*, p. 172.

50 *Ibid.*, p. 160.

51 For Joyce's 'intention' (or interpretation) see ibid., p. 170.

52 Ellmann, *James Joyce*, p. 542.

53 V. S. Pritchett, 'Talented Agrarians', *New Statesman*, Vol. LXVI, No. 1689 (August 2nd, 1963), p. 141.

54 José Ortega y Gasset, *The Dehumanization of Art and Other Writings* (New York, 1956), p. 20.

55 Goldberg, *The Classical Temper*, pp. 291, 315.

56 Ibid., p. 291. As usual, Goldberg's locution skirts the real problem: his 'and yet' relieves him of the difficulty of establishing *how* doing 'the worst' and 'reveal[ing] human validity' are related in the novel.

57 George Bernard Shaw, *Immaturity* (London, 1931), p. xxxiii.

58 Goldberg, *The Classical Temper*, p. 185. 'As well as' obscures the difficulty: if the ideal is absent by which Bloom could be human, how can 'the process point to his essential humanity'?

59 Kenner, *Dublin's Joyce*, p. 242.

60 Cf. Wimsatt and Brooks, pp. 378–80.

61 Kenner, *Dublin's Joyce*, p. 243.

62 Ibid., p. 242.

63 *Don Juan*, Canto II, Stanzas xix–xxi.

64 Ian Watt, *The Rise of the Novel* (Harmondsworth, 1963), p. 308.

65 Ibid., pp. 306, 307, 308, 307.

NOTES TO CHAPTER V

1 Cf. Clive Hart, pp. 94–5.

2 Mircea Éliade, *Cosmos and History, The Myth of the Eternal Return*, trans. Willard R. Trask (New York, 1959), pp. 153, 123.

3 Ibid., p. xi.

4 Ibid., p. 153.

5 Ibid., p. 153.

6 Pp. 134–5.

7 Éliade, p. 66.

8 Ibid., pp. 62, 68.

9 Cf. Ibid., p. 57.

10 Frazer, ed. T. Gaster, *New Golden Bough* (New York, 1959), p. 562.

11 *New Golden Bough*, p. 564.

12 Ellmann, *James Joyce*, p. 258.

13 David Daiches, *The Novel and the Modern World*, rev. ed. (Chicago, 1960), p. 75.

Notes

14 Éliade, p. 68.

15 Ellmann, *James Joyce*, pp. 258-9.

16 Ibid., p. 262.

17 Ibid., p. 262.

18 *Paradise Lost*, XI, 376-7.

19 Being one-armed, Nelson's pose resembles the 'onehandled urn', a chamber-pot? Cf. 'Gas From a Burner', *Critical Writings*, p. 245.

20 Kenner, *Dublin's Joyce*, p. 251. He also notes Bloom's '[Boylan] gets the plums and I the plumstones' (*Ulysses*, 491/370).

21 Gilbert, pp. 300-1.

22 *The Haggadah of Passover* (New York, 1956), p. 63.

23 Ibid., p. 64.

24 Parnell really did lose his hat, which an unknown person handed back (Kitty O'Shea, *Charles Stewart Parnell, His Love Story and Political Life* [London, 1914], II, 180).

25 'Gas From a Burner', *Critical Writings*, p. 243. The lime-throwing incident took place in late December 1890, as Parnell addressed a political meeting in Dublin.

26 'The Shade of Parnell', *Critical Writings*, p. 228.

27 Stanislaus Joyce, *My Brother's Keeper*, ed. Richard Ellmann (London and New York, 1958), p. 168.

28 Ibid., pp. 103-4.

29 *Stephen Hero*, 121-2/116-7. '*Dixit enim Dominus*' is 'corrected in red crayon to read: "*Haec dicit Dominus*" ', and 'Written in the margin in pencil' by 'the sins of the world' 'is the phrase, "the idea of the scapegoat in the Old Testament and of the Lamb of God in the New (Christ's own words)".'

30 *The Daily Missal and Liturgical Manual* (Leeds, 1954), p. 560.

31 Ibid., p. 561.

32 *Critical Writings*, p. 225.

NOTES TO CHAPTER VI

1 W. H. Auden, *The Enchafèd Flood* (London, 1951), p. 60.

2 Henry Adams, *The Education of Henry Adams* (London, 1919), pp. 216-19.

3 Ibid., p. 329.

4 Brower, pp. 195-8.

5 Goldberg, *The Classical Temper*, Ch. II and *passim*.

6 Ibid., pp. 76-7, 74. Doubt may be cast on the extreme rigour with which Goldberg elevates the static at the expense of the kinetic, especially as he writes elsewhere, 'the structure of Joyce's art, far from a static pattern of "symbols" and leitmotifs [etc.]' ('Joyce and the Artist's Fingernails', *A Review of English Literature*, Vol. II, No. 2 [April 1961], p. 68). Cf. 'The Aquinian contemplatio is as much kinetic as it is static and Stephen might have made a better formulation of pity and terror as the essentially tragic emotions had he realized that when the mind is arrested by the artistic vision of conflict and collision it is very much in action and not static at all' (Noon, p. 37).

7 Aristotle, *De Anima*, 431^b-432^a; Goldberg, *The Classical Temper*, p. 73.

8 Aristotle, *Physica*, Book III, I-II (201^{a}10-202^a).

9 Aristotle, *Physica*, in *Works*, ed. W. D. Ross (Oxford, 1930), Vol. II.

10 Werner Jaeger, *Aristotle. Fundamentals of the History of his Development*, Second Edition (Oxford, 1948), p. 296.

11 Ibid., pp. 380-5.

12 Ibid., p. 384.

Notes

¹³ Frank Budgen, *James Joyce and the Making of Ulysses* (Bloomington, Indiana, 1960), p. 129.

¹⁴ Gilbert, p. 224.

¹⁵ W. Empson, 'The Theme of *Ulysses*', *A James Joyce Miscellany, Third Series*, ed. Marvin Magalaner (Carbondale, 1962), pp. 134–5.

¹⁶ R. P. Blackmur, 'The Jew in Search of a Son', *Virginia Quarterly Review*, Vol. 24, No. 1 (Winter 1948), pp. 109, 112.

¹⁷ Goldberg, *The Classical Temper*, pp. 167, 171.

¹⁸ Ibid., p. 167.

¹⁹ On the equivalence of the two states, see W. B. Yeats, quoted below, p. 165.

²⁰ Gilbert, p. 23.

²¹ Aristotle, *The [Nichomachean] Ethics*, Book VI, Ch. 4 ('What is Meant by Art'), trans. J. A. K. Thomson (Harmondsworth, 1953), pp. 175–6. [my italics]

²² Frank Kermode, *Romantic Image* (London, 1957), p. 2.

²³ Ibid., p. 2.

²⁴ Søren Kierkegaard, *Philosophical Fragments*, trans. David F. Swenson (London and New York, 1936), pp. 59–61.

²⁵ Ibid., p. 63.

²⁶ Ibid., p. 65.

²⁷ Ibid., p. 65.

²⁸ Søren Kierkegaard, *Repetition*, trans. Walter Lowrie (London, 1941), pp. xxix–xxx.

²⁹ *Papers*, IV B 120, pp. 308ff.; quoted in *Repetition*, pp. xxx–xxxi.

³⁰ *The Concept of Dread*, quoted in *Repetition*, p. xxxiv.

³¹ Ibid., pp. 6, 34.

³² J. Mitchell Morse, *The Sympathetic Alien* (New York, 1959), pp. 23, 19, 34.

³³ C. J. Jung, *The Development of Personality, Collected Works*, Vol. 17, Bollingen Series XX (New York, 1954), p. 171.

³⁴ C. J. Jung, '*Ulysses* A Monologue', trans. W. S. Dell, *Nimbus*, Vol. 2, No. 1 (June–August, 1953), pp. 7, 9.

³⁵ Ibid., pp. 17–18. Cf. p. 19: 'Who, then, is Ulysses? Doubtless he is the symbol of that which makes up the totality, the oneness, of all the single appearances of *Ulysses* as a whole ... including Mr Joyce'—which, if I understand it, makes Joyce's novel a 'Notes Toward a Supreme Fiction'.

³⁶ Gilbert, pp. 42–3.

³⁷ Ibid., Ch. 2 ('The Seal of Solomon'), pp. 43–7.

³⁸ Gilbert, p. 46.

³⁹ Ibid., p. 49.

⁴⁰ T. S. Eliot, p. 191.

⁴¹ Ibid., p. 195.

⁴² Ibid., p. 213.

⁴³ Ibid., p. 213.

⁴⁴ Ibid., p. 213.

⁴⁵ Ibid., p. 213.

⁴⁶ Ibid., pp. 212–13.

⁴⁷ Ibid., p. 211.

⁴⁸ W. B. Yeats, 'Reveries over Childhood and Youth' (1914), from *Autobiographies* (London, 1956), p. 90.

⁴⁹ *The Trembling of the Veil, Autobiographies*, pp. 194–5.

⁵⁰ Ibid., pp. 272–3.

⁵¹ Ellmann, *James Joyce*, p. 366.

⁵² See above, p. 134.

Notes

53 James T. Farrell, '*Exiles* and Ibsen', in *James Joyce: Two Decades of Criticism*, ed. Seon Givens (New York, 1948), p. 115.

54 Farrell, *loc. cit.* For a view that the two notions of freedom and 'necessary victim[age]' form a conflict in which Richard is 'caught', see Ellmann, p. 366. If the hero's motivation is rendered 'ambiguous' (Ellmann) the two conduce to the same end.

55 Francis Fergusson, 'Joyce's *Exiles*', in *The Human Image in Dramatic Literature* (New York, 1957), p. 72.

INDEX